"The authors effectively show how two compelling and potentially conflicting forces—modern managerial techniques and citizen engagement—can be combined to produce livable communities where things get done and people invest in the future and care about the present. As a local government educator and former mayor, I see in this book a rare combination of practical case examples and intellectual guidance that should appeal to citizens, public officials, and students concerned about community building."

—John Nalbandian, chair and professor,
Department of Public Administration,
University of Kansas

"Read *Results That Matter*. Learn how citizens, governments, and nonprofit organizations can work together and improve their communities."

—Joe Wholey, University of Southern California

"Achieving good governance in public purpose organizations is an uphill battle. Citizens are cynical. Voter turnouts are declining. Trust in institutions is plummeting.

Is there a solution? The authors of this intriguing new book think so. Drawing upon extensive case studies, they explore such questions as what is a citizen? How can we make community governance more focused on results? Why does citizen engagement matter? How do we move from concepts to "getting it done" to practical impacts?

The book argues persuasively that achieving "results that matter" has to start with citizen involvement. Too often, goals are determined by the managers of government and other service organizations, with no assurance that they reflect the priority concerns of community citizens. Citizen-defined goals provide a basis for accountability that is meaningful.

Well-researched and richly footnoted, this book outlines a model of community governance adaptable to different situations. It explores many practical topics, such as how to make use of balanced scorecards in a public sector setting, or when and how to use technology to assist in citizen consultation. Very valuable reading for political leaders, staff, and any others concerned with the performance of public organizations, with the health of our communities, and with the state of democracy today."

—Tim Plumtre, president, Institute On Governance

"What is more important than results? Rock solid examples to emulate."

—Michael Van Milligen, city manager, Dubuque, Iowa,
and International City/County Management
Association 2003 Outstanding Manager of the Year

RESULTS THAT MATTER

RESULTS THAT MATTER

Improving Communities
by Engaging Citizens,
Measuring Performance,
and Getting Things Done

Paul D. Epstein
Paul M. Coates
Lyle D. Wray
with David Swain

JOSSEY-BASS
A Wiley Imprint
www.josseybass.com

Published by Jossey-Bass
A Wiley Imprint
989 Market Street, San Francisco, CA 94103–1741   www.josseybass.com

Jossey-Bass books and products are available through most bookstores. To contact Jossey-Bass directly call our Customer Care Department within the U.S. at 800–956–7739, outside the U.S. at 317–572–3986, or fax 317–572–4002.

Jossey-Bass also publishes its books in a variety of electronic formats. Some content that appears in print may not be available in electronic books.

Many of the case examples in Chapters Three through Nine include graphic figures representing a system or process of a government or nonprofit organization. Unless a source is provided, these figures represent the authors' interpretation of the system or process and not necessarily the interpretation of the government or organization.

Library of Congress Cataloging-in-Publication Data
Results that matter: improving communities by engaging citizens, measuring performance, and getting things done/Paul D. Epstein . . . [et al.]—1st ed.
        p. cm.
Includes bibliographical references and index.
ISBN-13 978-0-7879-6058-2
ISBN-10 0-7879-6058-6 (alk. paper)
1. Citizens' associations—United States. 2. Political participation—United States. 3. Community organization—United States. 4. Neighborhood government—United States. 5. Local government—United States. 6. Government productivity—United States. 7. Public-private sector cooperation—United States. I. Epstein, Paul D.
  JS303.5.R47 2005
  323'.042'0973—dc22
                                                                    2005024314

Printed in the United States of America
FIRST EDITION
HB Printing   10 9 8 7 6 5 4 3 2 1

CONTENTS

PREFACE

At the end of the twentieth century, leaders, professionals, and citizen activists working in our public, nonprofit, and civic sectors had a lot to be proud of. In various ways, many of them brought about important performance-minded reforms focused on getting better results for people and communities. Government organizations and nonprofit service providers across the country have become more proficient at measuring service performance and managing for results for the people and communities they serve. Meanwhile, civic groups across the country have launched projects in which they have engaged citizens to determine what kinds of results to measure and which results should be the focus of their advocacy for improvement. Some of these civic projects measure results of public services. Many others focus broadly on conditions in the community and measure a mix of health, social, environmental, and economic conditions that together paint a picture of quality of life or community well-being as envisioned by engaged citizens.

This book sees these government, nonprofit, and civic reforms as important advances in community governance, describes them in that context, and provides numerous examples that people active in these sectors may learn from to improve their own communities and organizations. This book then builds on these late-twentieth-century reforms by describing a still more advanced state of community governance for the twenty-first century and presents four detailed examples from communities that have already made it there, at least for some of their community improvement processes. These most advanced examples include many collaborations among citizens, governments, and volunteer and nonprofit organizations, such as community development corporations, neighborhood associations, volunteer fire companies, and health and human service providers. The focus of these examples ranges from county government, to city government, to nonprofit community development.

Essentially, this book is about making community governance more effective for the twenty-first century. Not in any abstract sense but in the very real sense of making communities and the organizations that serve them more effective at how they improve themselves over time in ways they can measure, and in ways that matter most to the people of the community. This book is also about how people can become more effective at improving their communities by participating in effective governance practices, whether as leaders or staff of government, nonprofit, or civic organizations or as citizens improving their own communities.

The rest of the Preface raises questions about effective, results-focused community governance that are useful to explore, at least in brief, before diving into models, practices, systems, and detailed examples provided throughout the book. Some questions, such as those that relate mainly to definitions and context, are answered most directly here, to provide a perspective for considering the ideas and examples in the book. Others are questions that the rest of the book attempts to answer. The brief answers to those questions provided here foreshadow what is to come in more depth in the chapters that follow.

- *What is community governance, and who can participate in it?* *Governance* means much more than "government." Governance encompasses the many ways decisions are made and actions taken that affect life in a community, whether by government officials or by other people participating in the community as individuals, organizations, or associations of interests. In addition to government, nonprofit organizations of all types (service providers, civic organizations, grant-making and operating foundations, and others), businesses, groups of citizens or other stakeholders, and individual people can all play important roles in community governance. This broad sense of governance is consistent with international concepts and definitions of governance.[1]

- *What makes community governance effective?* For community governance to be effective, it has to be about more than processes, but also about getting things done in the community. It is only through action that communities improve themselves, especially in a rapidly changing world where not to act often means to fall behind. But just "doing something" is not sufficient. What gets done has to make a difference. That is why measuring results is so important. But what should be done, and what results should be measured and improved? Communities are complex. The most important results vary among communities and among different people or stakeholders within a community. That is why engaging citizens in deciding what to do, or in deciding what results to measure or what goals to measure against, is also vital. The results a community achieves need to matter to the people of the community by addressing their highest-priority concerns. So this book is not just about making governance processes more effective, but about making communities more effective in achieving results that matter to their people.

The heart of this book is the Effective Community Governance Model built on the three critical elements of governance noted above: engaging citizens, measuring results, and getting things done. Using the model involves combining these elements in different ways. The idea is not just to "do" each of these things, but to bring these elements into alignment with each other in a community so they systemically support each other to help achieve results that matter. To help you find ways to make your community more effective at achieving results that matter, this book provides numerous examples of communities and community-serving organizations that have aligned two or all three of these critical elements in various ways to improve their communities.

- *Haven't citizens always participated in community governance?* In the United States, they have in many communities; the tradition of citizens engaged in solving community problems and addressing important community issues goes back hundreds of years. And the Effective Community Governance Model recognizes more traditional citizen engagement in problem solving as an important part of governance, along with the newer, more results-focused advances in governance. However, participative problem solving by itself is missing the critical element of measuring results. The two more recent results-focused advances of community governance noted above have also been missing something, which is why a new advance in community governance is needed for a new century.

- *What was missing from late-twentieth-century reforms?* Leaders, professionals, and volunteers engaged in the civic sector who have initiated citizen-based measurement of community results should be given credit for making an important advance in how citizens are engaged in communities and for calling attention to measurable conditions of great concern to citizens. There has been so much activity of this type in the United States that several movements have emerged, with many of these community civic efforts aligning themselves with larger themes, such as "smart growth," "safe communities," "healthy communities," or "sustainable communities." Taken together, they are sometimes referred to as "community indicators projects" or as part of "community movements."[2] A common element of many of these projects—what makes them citizen based—is that citizens have been engaged either in determining directly what indicators to measure, or in determining priority goals or issues as the basis for selecting indicators to measure. However, something has been missing from most of their initiatives. Their measured results are rarely connected with accountable organizations with resources to dedicate to improving results of greatest concern. Citizens, often with the help of the same civic organizations that helped them measure community conditions, have to advocate to government or other organizations to dedicate resources to improve results.

People in government and nonprofit organizations who have improved service performance management should be given credit for making an important advance in serving people and communities. For example, in the past ten to fifteen years, more and more local governments started measuring service performance, an essential step in managing their services for results,[3] thirty-three states passed broad results management legislation,[4] and the federal government passed and implemented the Government Performance and Results Act and other management reforms.[5] This trend has been echoed in the nonprofit sector, with governments moving to performance-based contracts for nonprofit services and other major funders, such as United Ways, looking for measurable results for the people served by the programs they fund.[6] One of the government and nonprofit service reforms that seems destined to last is a change in mind-set to see public and nonprofit service recipients as valued customers who deserve to be satisfied by high-quality service.

But for all the modernization, satisfaction surveys, and measured performance gains, something has also been missing from most of these initiatives. In most cases, the results measured and improved are determined by the managers of government and other service organizations, with no assurance that they reflect the priority concerns of community citizens. That may be one reason that, by the end of the 1990s, after governments had spent years trying so hard to connect with their customers, those same people were feeling disconnected from their government. In a national public opinion survey, the Center for Excellence in Government found that 60 percent of Americans felt disconnected from government overall. At the local level, people had a greater sense of connection than they did at state and national levels. But still, 46 percent of Americans were feeling disconnected from their local governments,[7] suggesting a lot of room to improve how people relate to the governments of their own communities.

In considering government performance reforms toward the end of the twentieth century, Cheryl King of Evergreen State College cited the Center for Excellence in Government's survey and asked some fundamental questions, including, "Are we focusing attention on the right kinds of performance in government? . . . What would we have to do to make performance or results-oriented government more democratic? On what kinds of performance or results should we focus?"[8] At about the same time, a practitioner-based research team that included two of the authors of this book was essentially examining the same questions when searching for examples of citizens engaged in performance management in their own communities. Like King and her colleagues, our team concluded the most essential questions were not so much questions of government but of *governance*, and a broad range of citizen roles must be considered, not just their role as service customers.[9]

  • *Is there really a problem with focusing on customers of community services?* There is nothing inherently wrong with improving performance from the perspective of customers of government and nonprofit services. It is better that nonprofit service providers really *do* get their customers into jobs, or off drugs, or into affordable homes, than that they just count up the number of people who go through their program. And customers who now apply for government permits or licenses from their homes or offices using the Internet are not likely to prefer to go back to traveling to a city or county office to wait in line for their application. But improving customer service is insufficient by itself for improving our communities. Satisfied customers are not the same as connected citizens. And it is engaged citizens, not satisfied customers, who build communities. Frank Benest, then city manager of Brea, California, recognized this in 1996 when he wrote to his fellow city managers that "the future for local government lies in transforming passive consumers of public services into responsible citizens."[10]

• *How can governments and community-serving organizations reconnect with citizens?* A first step is to recognize that citizens play important roles in their communities besides that of service customer, and they can become engaged in governance in these other roles. Another key step is to support them in these roles to help them become effectively engaged and influence community governance processes to improve their communities. This book explores five major citizen engagement roles, including key variations of several of the roles, and fourteen ways to help citizens be effective in these roles, including examples from communities across the country.

• *Who are a community's citizens?* The word *citizens* is used here in half of the ancient Greek sense, as people who exercise their responsibility to take part in the public life and decisions of their community. This book explicitly does not mean the exclusive half of the Athenian definition that recognized only men of a particular status as citizens. Similarly, this book explicitly does not mean the legal definitions of citizens of modern countries. Both documented and undocumented "aliens" in a country are considered "citizens" in this book, so long as they want to participate in improving their community.

The National Civic League's view that "citizen refers to any community resident who participates in voluntary community enhancing efforts" is consistent with this book's view.[11] But this book goes further: *anyone* who wants to participate in results-based governance of the community they live in, work in, or have a significant interest in (for example, go to school in the community, own a business there, have family there) is considered a citizen, regardless of the person's legal status, or whether he or she has voting rights for that community's elections.

We respect the preference of many community organizations and practitioners to explicitly avoid the term *citizen* and instead use words such as *resident* or *stakeholder* to make it clear that immigrants or others who are not citizens in the legal sense are welcome to participate in community and organizational processes. Many community examples in this book use *resident* and *stakeholder* (often along with *citizen*) if those are prevalent terms used by the organizations involved. In considering citizen roles, however, "resident" is just one type of stakeholder, and "stakeholder" is only one of five major citizen roles. So *citizens* is a better word to use to convey how people participate in their communities in many roles. However, actually improving governance is more important than semantic accuracy. The Effective Community Governance Model still works if "resident and stakeholder engagement" is substituted for "citizen engagement," and practitioners should make that substitution if it will make it easier to use the model in their communities.

• *Is it realistic to make citizen engagement a major part of community governance in an era of complexity and change?* When this book project was started, global terrorism was not on the radar screen in American communities. It now must be considered seriously by hundreds, if not thousands, of them. Two communities featured in this book—Lower Manhattan in New York City and Washington, D.C.—are perhaps the highest-risk communities in the nation. But even before global terrorism was recognized as a threat to American cities, the pace of global, national, and regional change that affects communities had become dizzying. To note just a few patterns, regional economies have been changing rapidly in response to global trade and technological innovation, leaving some people and communities behind while others thrive; new public health problems have been appearing; new approaches to public safety and education have been spreading across the country; and as suburban sprawl continues its advance, interest has been growing in strategies such as "smart growth," "sustainable development," and revitalizing the urban core.

However, effective citizen engagement involves deliberative dialogue, not just quick poll responses. It involves hard work to be sure the people who become engaged in decision processes are representative of the community, without leaving groups out. That takes time. How can communities take the time for proper engagement when faced with rapid change? Also, so many of these issues involve complex problems with serious consequences riding on decisions made by community leaders. How can lay citizens be expected to participate intelligently, when often even professional experts disagree on the answers?

From another point of view, citizen engagement has never been more important. The very consequences of these decisions mean that community leaders need to build the trust of citizens in order to make hard decisions that can be implemented rather than fought and perhaps blocked. The idea that effective engagement takes too long, or that citizens do not have the competence to participate in complex issues, involves too simplistic a view of citizen engagement and sells citizens short on their ability to deal with complexity when given the opportunity to do so deliberatively. Also, citizens usually do not have to deal with the most technical details of a problem to give professionals and leaders valuable guidance on priorities that should be followed and the nature of solutions that will be acceptable or most desired. If citizen engagement is well organized as part of a system of governance, they can be involved in setting strategic priorities, with technical decisions that follow those priorities left to professionals subject to approval by community leaders. Where practical, working groups of citizens can stay involved to ensure the experts and leaders heard citizens correctly and to keep proposed solutions on track with expressed citizen priorities as details are worked out.

Finally, keep in mind that citizens can be engaged in a variety of roles, not just as participants in community decisions, giving them other ways to contribute to governance and community improvement. Citizens can even have an important role in as complex an issue as homeland security as it relates to their community, even if it is not practical or appropriate for them to participate in decisions involving highly sensitive information. For example, after Chapter Two was completed, volunteer citizens from the west side of Lower Manhattan, a community featured in that chapter, began intensive training to become a Community Emergency Response Team that will be prepared to help save lives in their neighborhoods in future disasters.

• *What kinds of communities can benefit from the governance model?* The Effective Community Governance Model is intended to be applicable to any place-based community in a democratic society. Sometimes a "community of interest" sense (for example, "civic community," "business community") is used in this book, but the focus of community governance is always on physical places where people live, work, and carry on public and private activities. The geographic scale of community can vary, as it does from example to example in the book. Sometimes *community* refers to a city, county, or rural village, and sometimes to a broader region that crosses local jurisdictional boundaries. Sometimes the focus of community is narrowed to neighborhoods or multineighborhood districts. Some examples involve both a neighborhood focus and a citywide or regional focus. The specific meaning of *community* should be clear from the context of each example.

• *How do communities with effective governance improve themselves?* In the many community and organizational examples throughout the book that demonstrate aspects of effective governance, four key community improvement themes recur often:

• Robust citizen engagement in multiple roles
• Use of performance feedback in organizational or community decisions
• Linking desired results to resources and accountable people or organizations
• Use of collaborations

Not every example features all four of these themes, as some of these improvement themes are more likely to occur in different stages of effective governance. A community experiencing any of the advanced stages of effective governance is likely to make extensive use of at least three of these community improvement approaches. A community that strongly aligns engaging citizens, measuring results, and getting things done is likely to make extensive use of all four. Briefly in Chapter One, and more extensively in Chapter Six, analyses of parts of the governance model are presented based largely on how these key themes tend to play out in communities experiencing different stages of effective governance.

• *Should every community and community-serving organization strive to align citizen engagement, measuring results, and getting things done?* For communities as a whole, the long-term answer is yes, but the near-term answer is highly situational. Aligning, or systemically combining, all three of these critical elements represents the most advanced stage of effective community governance. It is an ideal to be sought by any community, but it is not always possible to determine, in advance, a direct path for a community to get all the way there from where it is now.

For organizations, the answer to the question depends on their roles in the community and their opportunities to build collaborations with others to help the community achieve more advanced stages of governance. For example, a nonprofit service provider with a relatively narrow mission that serves a clearly defined service population, such as youth at risk of dropping out of school or unemployed adults, may contribute best to the community if it focuses most on managing for improving measurable outcomes of its service population, and limiting engagement to those community stakeholders most clearly affected by its work: their service population and their families, for example, or residents of neighborhoods where they have facilities.

A nonprofit civic organization that has research and community facilitation capabilities may contribute best to the community by helping citizens obtain data on community results, helping them use the data to influence community processes, and facilitating deliberative community conversations about what results are most important and how best to improve results. Assuming the civic organization lacks the resources to provide direct services or make capital investments, if it wants to go further and actually stimulate action to change results, the organization would have to help citizens advocate for change or build collaborations with organizations that have resources to implement change.

However, a general-purpose local government that provides a wide range of services, makes budget decisions on how to use community funds, and makes policies affecting the living and working conditions of many people would ultimately do best to strive for the most advanced stage of governance that combines broad-based citizen engagement, measurement of results, and getting things done. Depending on its current measurement and management capabilities and the openness of its leaders to these approaches, it may not be practical to get there all at once. The local government may have to progress through several stages of improving governance and get there step by step, over a number of years. However, after taking a few modest steps and getting part way there, acceptance of engaging citizens may suddenly increase due to political change, or acceptance of using performance data to inform decisions may increase sooner than expected, so the local government may then be able to take giant steps quickly to get the rest of the way there in a shorter time and by a different route than they at first imagined.

Governments are not the only types of organizations that can take a community to the most advanced level of governance. Other organizations that invest in serving a community or region, such as a community foundation or regional United Way, can do so at least for the range of services it funds. Also, collaborations of investors (which may include nonprofit, business, and government investors) may bring together enough resources to make it practical to take a community to the most advanced stage of governance for important services or functions. This is the case in the detailed example of nonprofit community development presented in Chapter Eight.

Further discussions on appropriate expectations for improving governance, and guidance on setting near-term goals for change, are presented in brief in Chapter One and in some depth in Chapter Nine.

• *Do external forces or contextual situations, such as the regional economy, have more impact on a community's success than community governance?* That depends on how "community success" is defined, which, using the Effective Community Governance Model, should be based on citizens' goals for their community, not externally imposed goals. It is true that the contextual setting a community finds itself in, much of which may be determined by external forces, will have a lot to do with where its governance processes can take the community. A community's leaders should not discourage citizens from having high aspirations, even for aspects of community life, such as the private economy, that are hard for the government and civic sector to influence, let alone control. However, they also should present the facts of current conditions and trends and help citizens understand that specific, measurable objectives and time lines for improvement must be realistic and should be judged against realistic benchmarks.

That said, all in all, in a democratic society, a community should be better off following effective governance practices than not, whatever situational context it faces. The performance feedback attribute of effective governance will help an effectively governed community monitor its local and regional context—both conditions it can strongly influence and those it cannot—and adjust its strategy over time to do the best it can in improving conditions and making progress toward citizens' priority goals.

For example, two of the communities featured in Chapter Seven, Prince William County, Virginia, and Rochester, New York, have faced essentially opposite regional economic conditions for the past ten to twenty years. While any one- or two-year period may have included fluctuations up or down, generally northwestern New York State has faced a long-term economic slowdown that has consistently lagged behind the national economy, while northern Virginia has been a high-growth region that has outpaced national economic growth. That does not mean that northern Virginia communities can make use of effective governance practices and northwestern New York communities cannot. It means they face very different community challenges, so will use effective governance practices in different ways to accomplish different things.

The high-growth regional economy gives Prince William County an advantage over Rochester in raising government revenue to improve services and solve problems.

But that does not mean the county government just throws money at problems. Like Rochester, it uses a performance-based budget and monitors service performance rigorously. Prince William County maintains fiscal discipline and is guided by both performance feedback and a citizen-influenced strategic plan in setting and adjusting its spending priorities to keep overall service growth efficient, so the increase of county spending has not outpaced the growth of the population.

A locally contentious challenge in Prince William County has concerned how—and how much—to control growth and development. Local elections have been fought over growth, and citizens' opinions on the issue can be sharply divided. That has not kept county officials from engaging citizens with different views to help develop strategic economic development goals and measurable objectives, and to help develop land use plans that influence future development. As one citizen explains in Chapter Seven, he thinks growth has become more environmentally sensitive in recent years as a result.

Rochester has faced very different challenges. It has a broad economic development strategy not covered in this book, one that must work against weak domestic regional economic trends (and thus reaches across Lake Ontario to Canada), unlike Prince William, which can work with strong regional trends. Much of Rochester's citizen engagement has focused on neighborhood planning and improvement. With city government revenues severely limited, one of Rochester's challenges is finding resources to achieve citizens' neighborhood improvement goals. So an important part of Rochester's neighborhood planning and improvement strategy is to encourage engaged citizens to reach out to identify community assets, which are usually citizens, businesses, or nonprofit organizations that can bring needed skills or resources to accomplish parts of a neighborhood plan that the local government could not fund on its own. Rochester citizens have had success doing so. A citizen quoted in Chapter Seven talked about having an "asset budget" more than a government budget for implementing neighborhood plans, a budget that takes into account resources from all assets citizens identify, not just from the city budget. A city official quoted in the same part of the chapter said that "government resources only made up 30 percent of contributions" to the plans.

Beyond different economic conditions, many more characteristics of urban Rochester and suburban-rural Prince William County are very different, from their land use and density characteristics, to the age of their infrastructure and housing stock, to the ethnic and racial mix of the population, to the different state laws they operate under. The Rochester and Prince William County stories demonstrate the wide applicability of the Effective Community Governance Model. While the two communities are very different and face very different challenges, they both use effective governance practices in their own ways to accomplish their own community improvement goals. The specifics of their goals, strategies, and processes are different, but both follow the model quite well.

• *Can the Effective Community Governance Model work outside the United States?* All the case examples in this book are from the United States, and almost all of the research that led to developing the model was based on experiences of U.S. communities. However, the late-twentieth-century reforms included in the model—managing for results of public services and citizen-influenced measurement of community or regional conditions—are global phenomena, suggesting that the whole model is likely to be applicable outside the United States.

The better-known examples of public service performance management tend to come from highly developed countries.[12] Indeed, communities and community-serving organizations in developed countries are most likely to have the informational, management, and governance infrastructures for full, systemic implementation of the model. However, some of the civic groups or collaboratives in the United States that have undertaken citizen-based measurement of community conditions consider themselves to be part of worldwide movements, such as "healthy communities" and "sustainable communities," that apply to communities in developing as well as developed countries. Also, a few people with experience working in developing countries and regions who have seen the model have provided positive feedback as to its applicability and potential value in their settings. A former UN official even reports having used an earlier version of the model as an effective conversation starter with public officials in developing countries to help get them to see the value of developing citizen engagement as part of strengthening civil society, and of establishing accountability for improving conditions by measuring results. So while this book demonstrates the Effective Community Governance Model in the United States, practitioners who want to try to use the model wherever democratic conditions prevail are encouraged to do so.

• *Are the best examples of advanced community governance offered in this book, and will they stand the test of time?* Undoubtedly, more good examples of advanced community governance exist that fit the governance model, and some not in this book could be stronger examples than some here. Over the book research period, communities and organizations included here were ones that we found to fit the model and the roles of engaged citizens reasonably well. We were also able to collect enough information about these cases to offer practical examples of the model and the citizen roles and to make useful points for readers.

It is the nature of case study research, and of writing books, that you have to stop somewhere, you never quite get all the perspectives or as much information as you would like, and you would always like to wait a little longer to see how emerging developments will turn out. Given more time and resources, we may have told somewhat different stories about some of the communities in this book. There were also promising developments we heard about in other communities that we did not have the time, resources, or space to follow up for potential inclusion in the book.

By the time you are reading this, it is possible that some communities or organizations in the book no longer do some of the things they are said to practice here. With luck, it is because they have moved on to even more effective governance practices. But there is no guarantee that good practices will survive from one government administration to another, or one nonprofit executive director, board, or funding source to another. We hope this book will lay the groundwork for leaders, professionals, citizen activists, and researchers working in our public, nonprofit, and civic sectors to recognize the value of the advanced governance practices of the Effective Community Governance Model, so they will strive to emulate those practices in their communities, and to reinforce them where they already exist.

• *How can readers learn about new developments in effective community governance, in the communities featured here and others?* Several efforts are underway to develop and update knowledge bases of practices and examples of effective governance and make them available on the Internet. The Web site www.resultsthatmatter.net is keyed to the effective governance model and is intended to focus especially on the advanced governance practices presented here. The Web site of the Community Indicators Consortium (www.communityindicators.net) focuses especially on practices related to the community indicators movement, which includes some of the practices covered in this book.

September 2005

Paul D. Epstein
New York, New York

Paul M. Coates
Ames, Iowa

Lyle D. Wray
Hartford, Connecticut

ACKNOWLEDGMENTS

The Effective Community Governance Model that forms the basis for this book grew out of the work of an earlier research team that included Martha Marshall and Stuart Grifel as well as two of the current authors, Paul Epstein and Lyle Wray. We thank Martha, a Virginia-based consultant, and Stuart, now of the Broward County, Florida, Auditor's Office, for their research and their collaborations on articles, papers, and presentations that helped bring variations of the governance model and other aspects of our research before a wide-ranging audience. We most of all thank them for their creativity and distinct perspectives, which added so much to our team effort and made those early project experiences special. That initial research and many of those articles and presentations were done as projects of the Citizens League of Minnesota when Lyle Wray was executive director, funded by grants from the Alfred P. Sloan Foundation, for which our thanks go to program officer Ted Greenwood.

We thank Jim Perry, consulting editor to Jossey-Bass, for seeing the makings of a book in one of our published papers and the Center for Accountability and Performance of the American Society for Public Administration for commissioning that paper. We also thank Jossey-Bass series editor Dorothy Hearst, who challenged us to expand our scope beyond our initial focus of local governments and their citizens, to recognize the valuable contributions of nonprofit organizations in both serving our communities and improving community governance. We believe our ensuing expansion of the governance model has made it more powerful by providing a way for any community-serving organization, whether from the public, nonprofit, civic, or private sectors, to explore how they can contribute to improving outcomes and improving governance in their communities. Later in our writing process, Jim Perry helped us find some of the most useful insights in the excellent draft manuscript reviews solicited by Jossey-Bass, and Dorothy Hearst provided valuable editorial guidance to help us turn our collection of governance stories into a more focused, goal-directed work. We also thank Dorothy and Jossey-Bass associate editor Alison Brunner for their infinite patience.

When we opened up our model, it was clear we needed a place in it for the rapidly evolving community indicators movement. We are indebted to several people who have been leading practitioners and researchers in the movement for helping us understand it and how it fit within our work. These include Chris Paterson, a Vermont-based consultant; Tyler Norris of Community Initiatives; John Kesler of the Association for Community Health Improvement; Drew O'Connor of Capitol Hill United Neighborhoods in Denver; and our special contributor, David Swain. Not only did David contribute excellent material on Jacksonville, Florida, where, until recently, he was a leader of the Jacksonville Community Council's pioneering community indicators work, his broader insights and clear thinking were invaluable to us in clarifying some of the more complex ideas in this book.

Both opening up our model and expanding our work to book length led to the need for additional research and writing. We were blessed with a string of talented and productive research and editorial assistants over a four-year period. Assisting with primary research were Amy Avant-Kuehl, Zareen Mahmud, Veronica Neville, Eugene Perelson, and Brett Robinson. Assisting with secondary research and editorial support were Dana Barnes, Jennifer Johnson, and Alina Simone. Editorial assistant Kimberly Keaton was invaluable in helping us revise our draft manuscript.

We are indebted to the many people—too many to mention by name—who were generous with their time in the numerous interviews that made up most of our primary research and who also sent us supplementary materials to help us construct many of the case examples from communities and organizations across the country. Of that special group, we particularly thank a few people who not only provided information on their own organization's initiatives, but also helped us obtain information about other organizations doing related work. In some cases, they worked to arrange interviews for us with leaders of other organizations, which helped us make several case examples much richer than they otherwise would be. These included Audrey Jordan of the Annie E. Casey Foundation Making Connections Initiative, David Hunter of the Edna McConnell Clark Foundation, Diane Patrick of the Greater Kansas City Local Initiatives Support Corporation, and Melissa Peacor of Prince William County, Virginia.

Finally, we must always remind ourselves and our readers that the real heroes are the people who play active roles in communities every day, including organizational leaders and staff willing to try new ways to improve their organizations and govern their communities, and especially the people who volunteer their time and effort to participate in governance processes and make their communities better places to live.

P. D. E.

P.M. C.

L.D.W.

THE AUTHORS

PAUL D. EPSTEIN is principal of Epstein and Fass Associates, a New York-based consulting firm. He was inspired to public service by New York mayor John Lindsay, whose office he joined in 1971. He was excited by Lindsay's high-profile attempts to connect people with city government and with each other, from "happenings" in the parks to "little city halls" to the community boards that were later enshrined in the city charter. But Epstein was hired as an MIT engineering graduate, so he was assigned technical projects that led to better, more efficient services, from street repair, to housing, to public health, but involved no contact with citizens. In the late 1970s, for the U.S. Department of Housing and Urban Development, he managed research and demonstrations of performance measurement and improvement of state and local services, which led to his 1984 book, *Using Performance Measurement in Local Government*. He wrote his 2004 book, *Auditor Roles in Government Performance Measurement*, with Stuart Grifel and Stephen Morgan. From 1981 to 1985, he returned to the New York Mayor's Office as manager of citywide productivity and helped integrate productivity improvement with the city budget, leading to over $1 billion in annual savings and revenue. As a consultant, Epstein has assisted organizations across North America, from nonprofits, to state and local governments, to the United Nations. In 2003 he received the Harry Hatry Distinguished Performance Measurement Practice Award from the American Society for Public Administration (ASPA) for his lifetime achievements. An ASPA committee he chaired influenced the development of the Government Performance and Results Act of 1993, as cited by Congress. That year he helped

Vice President Gore's National Performance Review improve federal performance. He has also assisted and coauthored performance measurement research for the Governmental Accounting Standards Board, including a report on what citizens want from public performance reporting. In the late 1990s, Epstein finally started to satisfy his early interest, as citizen engagement in public performance became a central focus of his work, with the help of Alfred P. Sloan Foundation grants that funded the initial research for this book. Recently, when Epstein presented ideas from this book in Russia, he learned that citizens in a neighborhood in Tyumen, Siberia, facing similar issues as citizens in his own Manhattan neighborhood, followed a similar pattern of research and advocacy and achieved the same positive result.

PAUL M. COATES is director of the Office of State and Local Government Programs and associate professor in public policy and administration in the Department of Political Science of Iowa State University. He received his B.A. and M.P.A. from the University of Wyoming and Ph.D. from Iowa State University. Like Paul Epstein, much of Coates's career has been focused on helping state and local officials improve public management, and he recently had the opportunity to make citizen engagement a key focus of his work. Along with Alfred Ho, Coates directed the Sloan Foundation–funded Citizen Initiated Performance Assessment (CIPA) project in nine Iowa cities from 2001 to 2004. CIPA involved citizens in the process of creating performance measures for city government. The office Coates currently heads at Iowa State provides training, applied research, and technical services to state and local government in Iowa. In addition to having spent twenty-five years with Iowa State University, he also has been executive director of the Iowa State Association of Counties, director of extension to communities at Iowa State University, and an associate state planner with the Iowa Governor's Office of Planning and Programming. Coates also has experience providing assistance on performance measures at the national and the international levels through various State Department and USAID projects in eastern Europe.

LYLE D. WRAY is executive director of the Capitol Region Council of Governments based in Hartford, Connecticut. He has a B.A., M.A., and Ph.D. from the University of Manitoba, Canada. Like Paul Epstein and Paul Coates, much of Wray's early career focus was on measuring and improving public services, with citizen engagement later becoming central to his work. Wray started working with mental retardation services in Newfoundland and Labrador in the late 1970s and then on outcome measurement in the Minnesota Department of Human Services. He also worked for Dakota County, Minnesota, first as human services director, then for five years as the county administrator, when he led the county to performance management, with monthly graphic performance reports of key results against budget and performance targets. While Wray was county administrator, public deliberation became part of the budget process through citizen focus groups and broader public meetings. Wray served as executive director of the Citizens League from 1992 to 2003, a more than fifty-year-old civic organization that identifies important state and regional policy issues, and proposes and advocates for solutions developed through citizen research. During this period, he teamed with Paul Epstein and others to co-lead the Sloan Foundation–funded research on citizen engagement and public performance measurement that formed the initial research basis for this book. Wray has also been director of the Ventura County Civic Alliance, a regional civic organization in Ventura County, California. He has served nationally and internationally as a consultant to government and nonprofit organizations, and he teaches graduate courses online and in classrooms in public service outcomes and performance measurement, e-government, Web-based public services, and public service reform.

Contributor

DAVID SWAIN, who made valuable contributions to this book, is a consultant based in Jacksonville, Florida. After education at Oberlin College, he spent the late 1960s doing urban and rural antipoverty work, also becoming involved in street-level advocacy as a citizen activist. Then, as a volunteer and later as staff, he became engaged in the citizen policy study and advocacy process of the Jacksonville (Florida) Community Council Inc. (JCCI). Since 1984, he has been involved in measuring community outcomes, helping JCCI and its citizen volunteers to start and manage the first community quality-of-life indicators program in the country, which has released annual reports since 1985. As JCCI's associate director, Swain shepherded the community indicators through a series of ambitious upgrades and expansions, until he retired in 2002. Since then, he has continued his efforts to keep the Jacksonville project on the cutting edge of community indicators work and to share his experience and perspective with communities across the United States and in many other countries.

RESULTS THAT MATTER

CHAPTER ONE

ENGAGING CITIZENS, MEASURING RESULTS, GETTING THINGS DONE

If you get a community that stays engaged in the process, they begin to trust the system. People realize, "This works," their . . . engagement, and their trust, increase.

PAUL MOESSNER, CITIZEN OF PRINCE WILLIAM COUNTY, VIRGINIA

Prince William County, Virginia, has well-developed processes of engaging citizens. And it also has well-developed processes of measuring and managing the performance of county-funded services. What is especially powerful, for both county officials and engaged citizens, is that all these processes are part of the same system—the system that Paul Moessner and other citizens have come to trust. Because county officials listen to Moessner and others engaged in the process, these citizens have learned that they really do influence the goals and strategies that drive the county's budget and services. Moessner, for example, worked with other citizens to help the county set human service goals that resulted in more public funding of key services to meet the needs of a growing population and do more to address problems such as homelessness and drug abuse, which had been increasing. Because county officials listen to citizens, when they manage the performance of county services to produce measurable results, they get results that matter to the people of the county.

Prince William County is one of many communities, governments, and nonprofit organizations featured in this book that exhibit one or more forms of effective governance to achieve results that matter. Paul Moessner is one of many people in this book who have been empowered by effective governance processes to improve their community.

The purpose of this book is to help people and organizations find ways to become more effective at improving communities. The many people featured here who are effective at improving their communities include volunteer citizens like Moessner, directors and staff of nonprofit organizations, and elected officials and staff of governments. By reading about their experiences, as organized around key governance ideas in this book, you can find ways to:

- Help citizens become more effective at influencing community change.
- Make organizations that serve communities more effective at achieving measurable results and more responsive to the priority concerns of people and communities.
- Help citizens or organizations become more effective at using information to influence decisions and improve results for the community.
- Make investments (for example, by foundations, local funders, governments) in nonprofit service providers or community developers more effective at achieving results.
- Build more effective collaborations or partnerships focused on results that matter for the community.

What you find most useful in this book will depend on your role in your community or your organization's role in communities it serves. It will also depend on the current governance practices and results orientation in your community or organization, including ways results are measured and citizens are engaged, and how citizen engagement and measured results are used to influence community and organizational decisions and actions. To help you think about governance and results in your community and how they can be improved, the Effective Community Governance Model is provided, as well as examples of parts of the model in action in communities and organizations across the United States. Also, to help you explore how citizens can be better engaged in your community, five major roles citizens can play in results-oriented governance are defined and highlighted in many community examples: citizens as stakeholders, advocates, issue framers, evaluators, and collaborators. One gauge of the effectiveness of community governance is how many different roles citizens engage in effectively. "Effective" engagement means citizens are able to exert a reasonable amount of influence on a community decision, action, or process.

The citizen roles and the Effective Community Governance Model take an expansive view of both citizens and governance. In this book, all people who want to participate in the affairs of their community are *citizens,* regardless of their legal status. And *governance* encompasses more than government, to include how many actors in the community—citizens, private organizations, and governments—make decisions and take actions that influence community well-being. See the Preface for more on the expansive views of "citizens" and "governance" used here.

Model of Effective Community Governance

This book tells community and organizational stories from across the country in the context of the Effective Community Governance Model, which involves three critical elements of governance: engaging citizens, measuring results, and getting things done

FIGURE 1.1. EFFECTIVE COMMUNITY GOVERNANCE MODEL

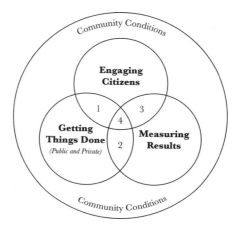

The four Advanced Governance Practices are represented by the overlapping areas in the figure, which represent alignment of "core community skills" as follows:

1. **Community Problem Solving:** Aligns Engaging Citizens and Getting Things Done

2. **Organizations Managing for Results:** Aligns Measuring Results and Getting Things Done

3. **Citizens Reaching for Results:** Aligns Engaging Citizens and Measuring Results

4. **Communities Governing for Results:** Aligns all three core skills

(see Figure 1.1). These elements are core skills a community needs to survive and improve. As community well-being can be affected as much by private actions as by public ones, the model applies to both government and private decisions and actions, as noted by the words *"public and private"* in the lower left circle in Figure 1.1.

Core Community Skills Aligned as "Advanced Governance Practices"

Teams perform best when they combine different skills of their members in effective ways, making the team as a whole more effective than its individual members. When the efforts of people with different skills are all aligned in support of an organization's goals, the organization can perform at a more advanced level than if it applied all those skills separately, with no sense of supporting each other. In the same way, communities perform at a more advanced level if they align individual community skills in support of each other. The real power of using the effective governance model comes in aligning the core skills into one or more of four advanced governance practices shown in Figure 1.1. Every community or organizational story in this book involves alignment of at least two of the three core skills for the benefit of the community. Four of the stories—those of Prince William County, Virginia; Rochester, New York;

Washington, D.C.; and the nonprofit community development corporations in the bistate Kansas City region—involve aligning all three.

The Core Community Skills

This book mostly focuses on the four advanced practices of the governance model. Here are brief descriptions of the three core community skills, with defining characteristics, that are important in ideas and examples explored throughout the book.

Engaging citizens means giving them real opportunities to make a difference, including opportunities to influence decisions and actions that affect the community. That may happen, for example, because decision makers are listening to citizens from the beginning of a community process, or because after citizens have developed their own priorities or solutions, they effectively advocate to decision makers to implement desired community change. While many ways of gathering citizen input can be used in the course of a community process, such as surveys and public comments, deliberative methods involving dialogue among people are most desirable and should tend to be the most decisive methods of a process that uses multiple methods. It is important that all potentially affected interests in an issue be represented in deliberations, which can sometimes be just those most likely affected (for example, people who live near a proposed new building or facility), and other times should be a group that is demographically and geographically representative of the whole community. Citizen engagement can go beyond deliberation and advocacy, to citizens' collaborating in implementing change by volunteering their efforts or other resources to coproduce solutions or services.

Measures of results are measurable indicators of either conditions in the community or the results of services provided to the community as a whole or to targeted groups of people within the community. Indicators of community conditions, often called "community outcomes," can measure health, safety, social, economic, or environmental conditions. They can focus on conditions of people, or on conditions related to place or physical attributes of a community, such as housing, parks, streets, air, water, and sewers. Results can include indicators of citizens' satisfaction with services or perceptions of conditions. Community outcomes may or may not be a result of services or public policies, or they may be affected to different degrees by services and policies and by external forces such as the economy, weather, or actions of private parties such as landlords or businesses. In many examples in the book, terminology of the organizations involved is used, such as "performance measures," "quality-of-life indicators," "community indicators," "targets," or "neighborhood impact indicators." Unless an example separates out results or outcome measures from other measures (such as outputs), all of these types of indicators can, for purposes of this book, be considered "measures of results." Key to the effectiveness of measuring results is how the information is used in the community to improve results. For example, is performance information on measurable results fed back to inform community decisions? Are organizations in the community held accountable for improving measured results, or at least for taking actions that contribute to improving them?

Things get done when plans, decisions, and actions that affect conditions in the community are taken by public or private parties. "Actions" can involve provision of government or nonprofit services, including efforts to improve a service or adjust it to be more responsive to community needs or citizen priorities. They can also involve regulating or subsidizing parts of the economy to enforce or stimulate desired conditions, such as affordable housing, a desired density of residential or commercial development, use of mass transit, or creation of jobs. Actions can be focused on people or on the natural or built environment. Engaged citizens can help implement actions. Plans and decisions can indicate broad policy priorities as a public budget often does or changes in priorities as when funding is shifted to increase emphasis on certain goals or services relative to others. Or plans and decisions can be very specific, such as a plan to gradually replace diesel buses with alternative fuel buses to get cleaner air; a change in a zoning, health, or safety code; a decision on where to locate nonprofit housing or a public facility, or about what gets built on a specific site. A key to effectively getting things done is for organizations in the community to commit resources and to be accountable for implementing policies, plans, and actions as decided. Organizations can get things done on their own or in collaboration with other organizations or citizens. Collaborative efforts can involve multiple parties committing resources and holding themselves accountable, including citizens.

Getting
Things Done
(Public and Private)

Key Themes of Effective Community Governance and Improvement

Each case example in this book describes a community's or organization's own specific approach to effective governance and improving the community. Four key themes that are common to multiple examples are briefly explored here: roles citizens play, use of performance feedback, accountability and resources, and collaborations. Some of these themes are stronger in some practices than others, and some are weak or missing from some practices. The many case examples throughout the book make it clearer how these themes play out differently for each advanced practice of the governance model.

Roles Citizens Play. Citizens can play a variety of different roles when engaged in their community. Generally the more roles citizens have an opportunity to play, the more they will get involved, contributing more energy to community improvement. A community that provides citizens opportunities to play a variety of roles can gain many ways to take advantage of citizens' ideas, talents, skills, and resources. Also, those communities can provide more opportunities for citizens with different interests to engage with each other to find common ground on a solution to a specific problem or, more generally, on priorities for improving the community.

Use of Performance Feedback. The cost and effort to collect and report data on measurable indicators of results is of little value if the information is not used in an effort to improve the community. Communities and organizations increase their ability to improve results when they analyze performance data related to results and feed back what they learn into their planning and decision making. In this way, they can adjust their resource allocation and operations as best they can to get better results in the future. Some organizations and communities have developed cyclical systems of management or governance with built-in performance feedback loops to ensure that performance information is considered in processes such as strategic planning, budgeting, designing programs, and analyzing service delivery practices. When organizations and communities repeatedly use systematic performance feedback, they are repeatedly giving themselves opportunities to find ways to improve results and making themselves more effective at achieving results.

Accountability and Resource Commitments. Community plans to solve a problem or enforce a policy, or goals to improve results, mean little if not backed up by resources for implementation. An organization might commit resources by making a formal budget allocation or assigning specific people, equipment, or funds to implementation. Several collaborating organizations or citizens might also commit resources. Commitments of resources in the community take on greater meaning if the organizations or people involved are willing to be held accountable for following through on a plan or achieving a goal. Measures of results similarly take on greater meaning if organizations in the community can be held accountable for improving results or achieving measurable goals or targets.

Collaborations. Many kinds of partnerships or collaborations can support effective community governance, including collaborative efforts to find compromise solutions to a community problem, reach consensus on community goals, or implement solutions and achieve common goals. Effective collaborations can be formed among organizations, among citizens, and between citizens and organizations. Indeed, the National Civic League sees the need for a broad base of collaborations for communities to be successful today, with businesses, government, and nonprofit organizations working with citizens to meet complex challenges.[1] Often organizations with related missions (say, a public health agency and a private hospital) agree to pursue a common strategy to achieve a goal or coordinate their efforts to solve a community problem, thus forging a partnership that makes more effective use of existing community resources. Some collaborations end up focusing added resources on a community goal, particularly when an effort is made to identify and reach out to citizens or organizations that have not previously been involved but have time, expertise, or other resources useful for achieving that goal. Collaborations can make all four advanced practices of the governance model more effective, and they appear in many of the examples in this book.

The Advanced Governance Practices

The brief descriptions that follow highlight key tendencies of each advanced governance practice to help you begin to understand these practices and the overall governance model.

Advanced Practice 1—Community Problem Solving: Alignment of Engaging Citizens and Getting Things Done

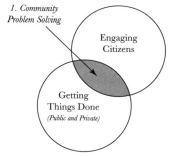

- Robust citizen engagement in all major roles.
- Citizens tend to influence what gets done.
- If solutions are developed collaboratively between citizens and an accountable organization, then accountability is achieved and resource commitments are often made as part of the problem-solving process. In other cases, citizens deliberate among themselves to develop their own solutions, and then must advocate to leaders of community organizations to commit resources and be held accountable for implementing solutions.
- While citizens will generally know whether a solution is implemented, the success of the solution over time with respect to impact on desired community outcomes will probably not be known because results are not systematically measured. Lack of results measurement also means there can be no systematic performance feedback into community decision making.

Advanced Practice 2—Organizations Managing for Results: Alignment of Measuring Results and Getting Things Done

- Engagement is limited. Citizens are primarily engaged as stakeholders, and only occasionally in other roles.
- Regular results measurement provides useful information on community outcomes or the performance of programs and services, or both.

- Performance information is fed back into organizational decision making on a regular basis in systematic managing-for-results cycles, which leads the organization to commit resources and assign clear accountability for achieving measurable results.
- Performance feedback can help identify where collaborations are needed, which tend to be results-focused collaborations among organizations.

2. Organizations Managing for Results

- While this practice can be very effective at achieving measurable results, results achieved do not necessarily reflect citizens' main concerns, because citizens are not involved in framing issues or setting priorities.

Advanced Practice 3—Citizens Reaching for Results: Alignment of Engaging Citizens and Measuring Results

- Citizens can have opportunities to play most or all major engagement roles. Engagement tends to be robust.
- Citizens are engaged in deciding what results get measured, collecting results data, deciding what data to use for advocacy, or using the data themselves. Results measures and data used tend to reflect citizen priorities and concerns.

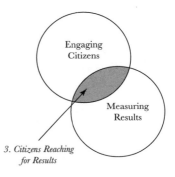

3. Citizens Reaching for Results

- Although citizens act as advocates for change who call results data to the attention of decision makers, there are no built-in performance feedback loops to ensure that measured results are systematically fed back to influence community decisions.
- Measures of results are not systematically connected to resources to achieve desired results or to organizations accountable for achieving results. Citizens must advocate to community organizations or build collaborations with them to get them to commit resources and accept accountability for achieving desired results.

Advanced Practice 4—Communities Governing for Results: Alignment of Engaging Citizens, Measuring Results, and Getting Things Done

- Robust citizen engagement occurs in most or all major roles.
- Citizens tend to influence what gets done. They also tend to influence what gets measured, for example, by developing or influencing priorities, goals, or plans that one or more organizations' performance is measured against, at least in part.

- Regular results measurement provides useful information on community outcomes or the performance of programs and services, or both.
- Performance information is fed back into organizational decision making on a regular basis in systematic managing-for-results cycles, which are also *governing*-for-results cycles because citizen engagement is also a systemic part of the process.
- One or more organizations commit resources and assign clear accountability for achieving measurable results, which tend to reflect citizen priorities.
- Collaborations tend to be results focused and are likely to include both collaborations among organizations and between citizens and organizations.

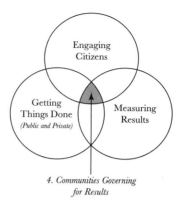

4. Communities Governing for Results

Some Observations About the Four Advanced Governance Practices

Although the concept of the Effective Community Governance Model and its advanced governance practices is new, the combinations of community processes ("core skills") that make up the advanced practices are not. They have precedents that go back to different times, so some advanced practices have become more established and definable, while others are in more of a state of development. The observations about each of the four advanced practices are coupled with brief descriptions of how each is treated in the chapters that follow.

Community problem solving, explored in Chapter Two, is the advanced governance practice that has been with us the longest. Citizens have been actively engaged in getting things done in North American communities since colonial times. Rather than attempt to catalogue or assess the many approaches that have emerged in hundreds of years to engage citizens in community issues, most of Chapter Two uses the lens of community problem solving to examine the five major citizen engagement roles, including ways to support citizens in each role. Examples include citizens engaged in neighborhood groups and district-based boards, self-help coproduction projects, and policy study and advocacy committees.

Organizations managing for results, explored in Chapter Three, has become a well-established organizational practice. A few local governments have practiced some form of managing for results dating back at least to the 1970s,[2] and many more began doing so in the 1990s when the practice also started growing among nonprofit organizations. Performance measurement, which provides much of the required information for managing for results, goes back almost a hundred years for U.S. local government services.[3] Although there are many government and nonprofit organizations that have not yet adopted results management practices, well-defined patterns have emerged. Chapter Three focuses most on the defining cyclical nature of managing for results, including the systematic use of performance feedback to inform organizational planning and decision making. The chapter progresses from simpler to more complex managing-for-results cycles, including examples focusing on a single nonprofit program or government service, examples of enterprisewide managing for results, an example of a foundation investing in results, and examples of governments budgeting for results.

Citizens reaching for results, explored in Chapters Four and Five, is a newer phenomenon that is still rapidly developing. While it has significant precedents in the United States dating at least back to 1985,[4] only recently has it been spreading to a large number of communities. It is emerging in different forms, including very different ways to attempt to empower citizens with measures of results and other critical data about their communities. Different kinds of nonprofit organizations with data management capabilities, and some local governments, have been helping citizens reach for results. Some of these organizations have gone beyond the role of data intermediaries to help citizens advocate for change and help them build collaborations that can lead to results. These projects measure different things, from narrowly defined physical problems citizens find walking their streets and through their parks, to broad indicators of community social, environmental, and economic conditions. Their geographic focus also varies greatly, from neighborhoods within a city, to small and medium-size towns, to larger cities, counties, and regions. Two chapters are devoted to citizens reaching for results to help capture some of this emerging variety.

Chapter Four first presents several key ideas and strategic issues related to citizens reaching for results that have implications for how to increase citizens' influence on improving the community through the use of results data and other community information. The discussion of these ideas and issues is also intended to help you interpret the five community examples in Chapters Four and Five. Chapter Four ends with the first three of these examples, which vary from citizens using handheld computers to record and report on physical problems in their neighborhoods, to citizens working with government staff and elected officials to define performance measures for Iowa municipalities, to a Denver operating foundation that helps put citizens from poor neighborhoods in charge of how to use community information. Chapter Five features two in-depth case examples of regional quality-of-life indicators and how they have been developed and used in different ways by citizens and nonprofit organizations in the Jacksonville region of Florida and the Truckee Meadows region of Nevada.

Communities governing for results, which aligns all three core community skills, is the most complex advanced practice. It is not surprising, then, that it is harder for communities to attain this fourth advanced practice than the first three, and that it is harder to find examples of this practice in the field. Four detailed case examples are presented in Chapters Seven and Eight, but because of their complexity, Chapter Six first provides an analysis of communities governing for results as an overall concept to set the stage for understanding the community examples in the next two chapters.

While the first three advanced governance practices are all beneficial to communities, they also have limitations on their overall effectiveness because they align only two core community skills instead of three. The analysis in Chapter Six looks at the strengths and weaknesses of the first three advanced practices and shows how the three-way alignment of the fourth practice builds on the strengths of the others and resolves governance issues caused by their weaknesses.

For effective governing for results, significant community resources should be systematically guided by citizen priorities and measurement of results. Organizations that normally control significant resources used for community well-being, such as a local government, can be well positioned to help their community govern for results if they are willing to empower citizens and use regular performance feedback. But nongovernmental organizations can also be effective in helping their communities govern for results, particularly if they collaborate to pool or leverage significant resources for citizen-influenced, performance-based use. Chapter Seven presents three case examples of local governments leading governing for results, all in different ways: Prince William County, Virginia; the City of Rochester, New York; and the District of Columbia (Washington, D.C.'s city government). Chapter Eight presents a case example of nonprofit community development being governed for results in the bistate Kansas City metropolitan area. A regional private-public investment collaborative has contributed local funds and leveraged national funds to create a large funding pool to invest in community development corporations (CDCs) that serve low-income neighborhoods across the metropolitan region. The CDCs engage citizens in governing for results at the neighborhood level. Their emphasis on both program results (such as affordable housing) and citizen engagement is reinforced by how they are evaluated and funded at the regional level.

Finding Ways to Improve Governance and Results

This book does not provide a step-by-step map to better governance and results. All communities are different and have to chart their own course. And the course may be very different depending on who is taking the initiative to improve governance and results, what their roles are in the community, and what partners are available and willing to help improve community governance.

Although the Effective Community Governance Model is not a map, it is a template that can be valuable for assessing a community or organization and helping a community find its way to better governance and results over time. Also, the citizen

TABLE 1.1. BRIEF TEMPLATE VIEW OF THE EFFECTIVE COMMUNITY GOVERNANCE MODEL

Advanced Governance Practices	*Aligned Core Community Skills*		
	Engaging Citizens	Measuring Results	Getting Things Done
Community problem solving	X		X
Organizations managing for results		X	X
Citizens reaching for results	X	X	
Communities governing for results	X	X	X

roles and the many examples in this book from across the country can be a source of practical ideas and approaches for local settings. Here are some suggestions for using the model, the roles, and the examples to find ways to improve community governance and results, whether the focus is on an entire community or one organization and the people it engages or serves.

Use the Governance Model as a Template

A useful starting place for finding ways to improve governance or results is to use the Effective Community Governance Model as a template to make an initial assessment of your community's or organization's strengths, weaknesses, and opportunities for constructive change. The graphic in Figure 1.1 and the descriptions of the advanced governance practices express the essence of the model as a template. Table 1.1, which summarizes the four advanced practices based on the core community skills aligned in each, provides a briefer view of the model as a template for an initial assessment.

From your current knowledge of how key community or organization processes work and how citizens are engaged in those processes and what influence they tend to have, you can assess the extent to which your community or organization exhibits any or all of the advanced governance practices. Keep in mind that different community functions or services often exhibit different governance practices. For example, if engaged citizens influence community development decisions, but the results of development are not measured, community development would be assessed at advanced practice 1: community problem solving. Meanwhile, other services may be well managed for measured performance, without citizens involved, so they would be assessed at advanced practice 2: organizations managing for results. Still other functions or services may not exhibit any advanced practices.

If you are assessing an organization with a relatively narrowly defined mission, such as community development, public health, or education, or if you are assessing how your community addresses a narrowly defined set of issues, such as land use or public safety, you may be able to identify a single place on the governance model for your organization or community. If you are considering a broad range of issues in your community or an organization that serves a community in many ways, such as a general-purpose city or county government, you are more likely to find that your community or organization exhibits different governance practices for different things.

It is best to consider this initial assessment of your organization or community as preliminary. For example, you may need to find out more about how key decision processes work and the extent that citizens are really engaged or have influence. Or you may need to learn more about how community conditions or service results are measured, if at all, and how the performance information is used. Also, as you read further in the book, you will develop a fuller understanding of the governance model and the advanced governance practices, which may also cause you to change your assessment of your own organization and community. Be sure to return to the governance model as a template for your own local assessment as you come to understand the model better and learn more relevant information about how things work in your community or organization.

Consider Ways to Strengthen Citizen Effectiveness in Different Roles

As you think about how citizens are engaged in your community, consider whether there are missed opportunities for citizens to play additional roles or opportunities to strengthen their influence by providing them better support in any or all roles. Chapter Two describes fourteen ways to support citizens in five major engagement roles, which may guide you in determining how best to strengthen citizens. Some of the community and organizational examples throughout the book may also offer guidance, especially those that include organizations supporting citizens in particular engagement roles. Another source of guidance may be the section of Chapter Nine on citizen capacity building, which focuses on citizen leadership development programs.

Look for Lessons in the Many Community and Organizational Examples

The community and organizational examples throughout the book provide the richness of detail to bring the Effective Community Governance Model and its advanced governance practices to life. Each example demonstrates at least one part of the governance model. It will then be up to you to determine which examples have the most relevant lessons for your community or organization. To find useful lessons, it makes sense not to focus too much on specific issues or services in an example and whether they match issues or services that most concern you. An example covering different services from those you work with may still describe approaches to general processes (for example, priority setting, planning, budgeting, measuring performance) or citizen roles that are adaptable in beneficial ways to your local setting.

Instead, it is more important to focus on whether any of the community or organizational processes or citizen roles described in an example give you ideas for strengthening processes or roles in your community or organization. For example, is there something you can learn from a community or organization's approach to engaging citizens in setting goals even if your organization sets very different goals? Is there something you can learn from how a community or organization determines what it will measure or feeds back measured results to make operational improvements or inform policy or budget decisions? What ideas do the examples give you for helping your organization or community become stronger at performing any of the advanced practices of the governance model or for attempting a new advanced practice not yet prevalent in your community?

Look for More Ideas for Improving Governance and Results

As numerous and varied as the examples of citizen roles and governance practices are in Chapters Two through Eight, they are not fully comprehensive about how to improve community governance and results. No single book can be. To supplement those governance examples, Chapter Nine takes another look at improvement themes treated throughout the book and presents additional ideas and techniques that can be useful for implementing change, for example, new roles for leaders and professionals in communities that want effective citizen engagement. Chapter Nine also covers additional ideas for effective engagement, including suggestions for ensuring citizen engagement is inclusive, a draft scale for ranking public participation processes from passive to active engagement of citizens, and opportunities and risks of using technology to enhance engagement. Chapter Nine explores as well the use of performance modeling techniques, referred to generally as community performance value chains, to make performance feedback and analysis more effective for improving community or organizational results.

Determine Appropriate Expectations, Near-Term Goals, and a Starting Point

Your assessment of current governance strengths and weaknesses of your community or organization, and the ideas and processes you find in the book that you think can be adapted to your local setting, should help you determine appropriate expectations for change and what your early improvement goals should be. Generally, appropriate near-term goals should depend on your role or your organization's role in your community, how well the community is doing on each governance practice, and what opportunities exist for improvement. Keep in mind that just as the community may exhibit different practices for different issues or services, appropriate near-term improvement goals may vary for different issues or services. Chapter Nine can help guide you in your early planning for improving governance and results.

Work to Attain or Improve Any Advanced Governance Practice

Advanced practice 4 (communities governing for results) aligns all three core community skills and thus has the greatest inherent potential to help a community continually improve its governance and results. However, not all organizations are positioned to move a community to governing for results on their own, and the potential partners they will need in the community may not be ready to help them go all the way there. For example, a nonprofit civic organization may determine that it can help citizens obtain and use data on indicators of community conditions the citizens think are important. However, local government or other organizations that provide services to address those conditions may not have the performance management capability or openness to citizen empowerment to use citizens' indicators in a systematic governing for results process. In this situation, it would be unrealistic for the civic organization to set a near-term goal to implement practice 4. Instead it makes sense to set a goal to attain practice 3 (citizens reaching for results), first by helping citizens obtain data on priority community indicators, and then by helping them use the data to advocate for change or build collaborations to improve desired outcomes.

By developing a measurement capability in the community and building citizens' experience at using data, the civic organization will position the community to move quickly to governing for results should the local government or other major service funders become willing or able to empower citizens and use results measurement in the future. In the meantime, the community may still gain significant improvement benefits from the actions taken as a result of citizen advocacy or new collaborations formed to improve results as measured by the community indicators.

Some community organizations may decide that the best they can do at a given time is to get better at an advanced practice they already perform. For example, a nonprofit service provider with a narrow mission, such as homeless services, may already manage for results. The organization may decide that its opportunities to engage citizens beyond its service population are currently very limited, but it can do a better job of learning from performance data to improve its service program. Therefore, its best near-term goal may be to improve how it manages for results to get better results for the people it serves. That may translate to better results for the community as a whole, as may happen, for example, if better-managed services help more people who have become homeless move expeditiously into transitional or permanent housing.

Community problem solving, managing for results, and citizens reaching for results all can be beneficial to communities. It is worthwhile to attempt to attain or improve any of these advanced governance practices, even if governing for results appears to be currently unattainable. An improvement in a different advanced practice may serve the community well for the near term. Over time, the community may yet find its way to governing for results.

Effective Governance: Communities Keep Learning to Improve Themselves

The Effective Community Governance Model should be viewed as a template for helping communities, and the organizations that serve communities, for the long run, not just once. Active citizens and community leaders can come back to the model from year to year and keep using it to reassess how their community or organization is doing and what their next steps in governance improvement should be.

As the model is based on a community's having core skills, then the advanced governance practices that align those skills are really advanced competencies that the community can collectively learn. Charting a community's progress against the model over time is akin to charting the collective learning by the community to govern itself better and get better results. Community leaders and citizens who stay engaged in this learning process over a period of years may find that they end up charting a winding course to governing for results that they could not have imagined when they started their journey. In the meantime, as the community keeps learning from its experience, it will get better at achieving results that matter for its citizens, even before the community makes it all the way there. In the best case, once a community has demonstrably achieved the three-way alignment of engaging citizens, measuring results, and getting things done, its leaders and citizens will not stop there; they will keep learning from how they govern for results and will keep getting better at it over time.

CHAPTER TWO

CITIZENS' MANY ROLES IN COMMUNITY PROBLEM SOLVING

Tell me, I'll forget; show me, I may remember; but involve me, and I'll understand.

SIGN ON THE WALL AT THE JACKSONVILLE COMMUNITY COUNCIL

The Jacksonville Community Council Inc. is one of a great many nonprofit civic organizations in the United States that give people an opportunity to be involved in public issues and initiatives to improve their communities. Local governments also provide a variety of ways for citizens to become involved, from sitting on an advisory board to mentoring a child at risk of dropping out of school. And there are countless ways that residents of a neighborhood, businesspeople in a community, or citizens from across a region with a common public interest come together in formal nonprofit organizations or less formal unincorporated groups to become involved. Through various groups or acting individually, citizens play a great many roles in community affairs.

This chapter is intended to encourage you to think about multiple roles citizens can play in community affairs, help you think of new roles citizens can constructively play in your community, and help you determine how to strengthen citizens in the roles they already play, so they can be more effective partners in improving the community.[1] The focus is on the five citizen roles that especially relate to effective community governance and how to help citizens become more effective in each role.

The citizen roles are viewed through the lens of community problem solving, which is advanced practice 1 of the Effective Community Governance Model. In performing this practice, members of a community align engaging citizens and getting things done to become more effective in resolving issues or solving problems that affect the community. This practice does not necessarily include measuring results, so there will be less attention to quantifiable outcomes or performance here than in later chapters.

Advanced Governance Practice 1: Community Problem Solving

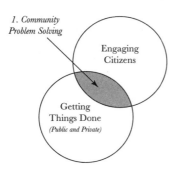

1. Community Problem Solving

Engaging Citizens

Getting Things Done *(Public and Private)*

Advanced practice 1 is not new. Citizens have been engaged in community problem solving in the United States since long before the birth of the republic. Participative community decision-making mechanisms that date back to colonial times, such as the New England town meeting, are still used in some small communities today. Too many different approaches have evolved over the years to catalogue them all here.

Many communities offer citizens multiple ways to become engaged, and the landscape of engagement opportunities in any community can change over time. For example, citizens who become concerned about a particular issue form their own issue-specific groups that may disband after a while, or take on a life of their own and become permanent fixtures in the civic landscape. Rather than analyze many different kinds of citizen engagement mechanisms or organizations, a few are used as examples in the chapter to illustrate citizen roles and how to strengthen them.

To use ideas from this chapter for your own community, it will help to keep in mind your community's existing organizations and processes that engage citizens—whether through government, well-established nonprofit organizations, or less formal grassroots citizen groups. As each role is discussed, consider how citizens get to play the role in your community and how existing organizations and processes either support them in that role or set up obstacles to their succeeding in that role. The examples in this chapter are not meant to present models to be copied, but to suggest ways to strengthen citizens' abilities and influence in these roles. For example, your community or organization may have very different mechanisms for engaging citizens in solving neighborhood problems than those presented here. But the basic lessons found here for making citizen roles more effective may include some you can adapt and implement in different ways in your community. With luck, you will find a few ideas here you can use—or an organization you work with can use—to strengthen citizen engagement roles in your community. It is also possible that you and others in your community may conclude, as citizen leaders in Jacksonville, Florida, did in the 1970s, that new civic processes or organizations are needed, leading them to establish the Jacksonville Community Council Inc. (JCCI) and Leadership Jacksonville in 1975.

Citizen Roles in Achieving Results That Matter

The five major citizen roles are presented here in an order in which a typical citizen or group of citizens might encounter and work through a community problem (Figure 2.1):

1. *A stakeholder,* who is concerned about or directly experiences community conditions, existing or proposed projects or policies, or community service problems.
2. An *advocate* for the community to act on the issue or problem. Actually, one may be an advocate during any or all parts of a problem-solving process, so Figure 2.1 shows advocacy surrounding the entire process.
3. An *issue framer,* who helps get the issue on the community's agenda and defines the problem and possible solutions from a citizen's perspective.
4. An *evaluator* of alternative solutions, or of a service organization's explanation or response to a problem. As shown in Figure 2.1, a citizen may later be an evaluator of whether conditions or services have improved over time.
5. A *collaborator* in agreeing on solutions or implementing improvements.

These roles may be experienced in a cycle, as depicted in Figure 2.1, because once improvements are attempted (or not attempted, after some time), citizens may evaluate how much the situation has improved, and close the loop by considering, back in their stakeholder role, whether the issue is worth trying to bring back to the community agenda for issue framing and further consideration of new or increased action. Figure 2.1 shows a possible additional feedback loop (the lower-right dashed arrow) of information from citizens who evaluate possible solutions and feed back their findings into the issue framing process, which causes citizens to attempt to find a better solution. Along the way through the cycle, citizens' advocacy can feed back to influence their roles in issue framing, evaluating, and collaborating. Simultaneously, citizens'

FIGURE 2.1. POSSIBLE CYCLE OF CITIZEN ENGAGEMENT ROLES

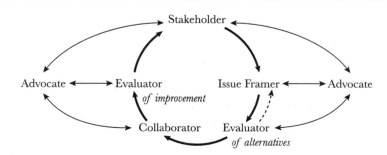

experiences in each of these roles can feed back the other way to influence their advocacy. Many other possible feedback arrows could be shown in Figure 2.1, as citizens may learn things in any given role that influence them in other roles. The idea of a cycle of roles and processes reappears in other chapters.

In any given situation, citizens may play these roles in a different order and in different ways, and most citizens will not play all five roles on a given issue or problem. Also, the roles are not mutually exclusive. As people go about their lives, the roles they play with respect to their community change daily, even hourly. They sometimes play several roles simultaneously, especially as an advocate, while also playing other roles. For example, a citizen may be an advocate for a certain solution or interest while participating in framing the issue. However, not all issue framers come to that role as advocates. By separating out the major roles, one can explore different ways people relate to community governance and influence decisions and results. This can be useful information in determining how to make citizens' engagement more effective.

Citizens play these roles at different levels of intensity from, for example, speaking up at a single meeting, to attending regular working committee meetings or organizing neighbors around an issue. They also play their roles at different levels of focus. Many examples presented here involve citizens' focusing on issues in their own neighborhood, often through government-recognized citizen engagement structures organized by geographic district in Dayton, Ohio; Portland, Oregon; and New York City. These were chosen as good examples of citizens' playing key roles rather than as an endorsement of the particular government-sponsored district engagement systems in these cities.

Some form of recognized neighborhood- or district-based citizen participation structures exists in many cities, some dating back to the 1970s.[2] The need for such structures still arises, as in Los Angeles, which started a system of neighborhood councils as part of a 1999 city charter reform.[3] Citizens also work through other organizations and structures in such cities, such as community development corporations or budget advisory groups. As several examples illustrate, citizens also often focus their engagement beyond their own community or city boundaries. The JCCI citizen study and advocacy processes described later in this chapter engage citizens on citywide and regional issues, and occasionally, JCCI's citizen advocacy extends to state action. Citizen engagement in problem solving is not limited to cities, of course, as illustrated by the example from rural Peapatch, Virginia, with its fifty households.

Strengthening Citizen Engagement in All Five Roles

To ensure that citizen engagement is effective, it is useful to support citizens' efforts in each engagement role, strengthening how they play each role to increase their chances for success. Table 2.1 lists fourteen approaches to support citizens in playing all major engagement roles. The detailed discussions of the major roles that follow include examples from communities relating to each approach listed in the table.

Table 2.1 provides a quick guide to help you take an informed look at your own community by providing a framework for observing how citizens are engaged and supported—or not supported—before embarking on an odyssey toward more effective citizen participation. It can help to think outside the box of Table 2.1, and beyond

TABLE 2.1. QUICK GUIDE TO SUPPORTING CITIZENS IN FIVE ROLES OF CITIZEN ENGAGEMENT

Major Roles	Approaches to Support or Strengthen the Role
Citizens as stakeholders	Help citizens organize and associate with each other close to home.
	Ensure citizens have opportunities to influence things they care about as stakeholders.
Citizens as advocates	Help citizens get technical and political assistance and find their leverage.
	Help citizens learn how things work and learn from each other.
Citizens as issue framers: Foundation builders, agenda setters, problem definers, and solution identifiers	Foster deliberative processes in which people listen to each other and make hard choices.
	Ensure citizens are engaged early to set agendas, define problems, and identify solutions.
	Encourage community-centered, boundary-crossing problem solving.
Citizens as evaluators	Provide support to make citizens' assessments rigorous, credible, and useful.
	Provide citizens with periodic performance reports on issues of concern to them.
Citizens as collaborators: Compromisers, coproducers, and asset leveragers	Help citizens get their voices heard and interests respected.
	Help citizens recognize different stakeholder interests and to think beyond opposition to forge effective compromises.
	Organize opportunities for citizens to contribute to their community as coproducers.
	Help citizens identify and leverage community assets (including themselves) to make limited investments go far.
	Identify "sparkplugs" to energize coproduction projects, and support them in organizing the community.

the examples that follow, to come up with additional or more specific ways to strengthen citizen roles that particularly fit your community. Each community can generate its own ways to get citizens involved. The point is to learn how to make that involvement long-lasting and effective in solving problems that matter to citizens.

Citizens as Stakeholders

As a community stakeholder, a citizen is someone who experiences the community—its environment, its economy, its people. Citizens have a stake in all conditions in a community that can affect their lives and those of their family, friends, and neighbors. You do not have to live in a community to be a stakeholder there and experience at least part of the community. You could own property in a community, work or go to school there, own a business there, or be part of an institution that has a presence there, such as an academic institution, a government, or a nonprofit service provider.

One particular way people are community stakeholders is as customers of community services, including services provided by businesses, governments and nonprofit organizations. Twenty years ago, it was unusual for government officials to think they had "customers." Now, it is not uncommon for a public transit agency's announcements to say, "Attention, customers" rather than "Attention, passengers," or for a public library to address users as "customers" rather than "patrons." Since the late 1980s, public managers across the country and in other countries have been learning that it is important to treat people who use their services as valued customers, listen to them, and focus on meeting the customers' needs, not the bureaucracy's.[4] Some nonprofit managers have also adopted the customer metaphor for the people they serve, including Eric Schwarz, president of Citizen Schools, a Boston-based nonprofit whose results-based management of an after school program is featured in Chapter Three. According to Schwarz, "At Citizen Schools we're trying to change the performance of our customers—children—in vital skill areas: helping make them better writers, better critical thinkers, and more likely to attend college. When is the last time anyone asked Reebok or Nike if its shoes actually make anyone jump higher or run faster?"[5]

The stakeholder role is broader than being a customer of services, because the conditions citizens experience in the community and in their lives are affected by many things other than community services. The quality of air and water, the affordability of housing, and many other conditions that contribute to a stakeholder's sense of well-being in a community are usually affected by many factors besides community services, not the least of which is what other community stakeholders do or do not do (for example, people who use a house on the block for illegal activities, a neighbor or landlord who does not maintain a property well). All stakeholders are potentially affected by the actions of all other stakeholders, including business practices, personal behaviors, investments, or holding back on investment. So having ways to help stakeholders with potentially conflicting interests (say, developers and neighborhood residents) solve problems or resolve disputes is one important aspect of a well-functioning community.

A local government is often an important part of how these problems are solved, for example, through interpretation of zoning ordinances and other laws, enforcement of codes, waiver of rules, or provision of financial or technical assistance to help implement a solution. But it can be difficult for a government bureaucracy, even one with a good customer service ethic, to keep in touch with all the local issues in all parts of a city or county, what problems are developing, and how to provide a responsive solution. And sometimes stakeholders see government as part of the problem, as when the government attempts to site an unwanted public facility, such as a trash transfer station or sewage treatment plant, or, in the name of economic development, helps a developer build a large new building in an area residents want to keep at low scale.

The idea of holding a stake in the community implies "owning" something, which does not have to be tangible property for a citizen's stake to be real. In a democracy, part of a citizen's identity is as an "owner" of the system of governance, which legitimizes all the roles discussed here.[6] While citizens deserve quality customer service, if all they do is passively accept services as a customer, they are limiting the influence their ownership provides them. If they become more active stakeholders and start playing roles such as advocate, issue framer, evaluator, and collaborator, they are choosing to live out their identity as an owner of the democratic system.

Help Citizens Organize and Associate Close to Home.
In communities across the country, citizens have organized themselves to represent their own local stakeholder interests from the grassroots up, through, for example, neighborhood associations, home owners' or tenants' associations, or block clubs. Sometimes a religious group is the locus of organization. Local businesses form local chambers of commerce or boards of trade. In many communities, local governments, nonprofit community development corporations (CDCs), and other community service organizations recognize these groups as ways to engage citizens who are in touch with local needs of a block, neighborhood, or business district. Some of these organizations help citizens organize and strengthen their grassroots groups.

New York City; Dayton, Ohio; and Portland, Oregon, are three of many mid- to large-size local governments across the country that provide formal, geographic-based channels for citizens to engage in community problem solving, by establishing community districts with volunteer advisory boards to engage citizens of the district in a wide range of issues and services. New York's fifty-nine community boards, Dayton's seven priority boards, and Portland's seven district coalitions are all organized differently. District board members are appointed by elected officials in New York and are mostly elected from very small districts in Dayton (with some seats reserved for established local groups such as neighborhood associations and CDCs). Portland's district coalitions are mostly independent nonprofit corporations—with neighborhood association representatives for board members and officers—that contract with the city to coordinate and maintain citizen engagement. The city of Portland's Office of Neighborhood Involvement recognizes almost one hundred neighborhood associations as citizen engagement channels, both directly and through the district coalitions.

Whether through official recognition, as in Portland, or through less formal contacts, grassroots groups often develop their own knowledge about government agency responsibilities and make their own direct contacts. In Portland, Dayton, and New York, which also have larger government-recognized district boards, citizens often get two levels of association and help with problem solving: closest to home with the generally all-volunteer grassroots groups and at the district boards, which are governed by volunteer citizens from a wider district but have staff paid for by city government funds to provide greater support for citizens. Judy Welch, president of the Lents Neighborhood Association in Southeast Portland, notes, "We take our neighbors' concerns directly to the city whenever we can. If there are problems we need extra help with, we may go through the district coalition."

Citizen volunteers on district boards and neighborhood associations also help citizens recognize when their stakeholder interests are affected. In Portland, Welch said, "The neighborhood associations do the door-to-door work organizing people. We have to let them know how an issue really affects them." For example, Welch said that "when they're planning to put a building up, we'll go out and post flyers all over the affected area." Citizens tend to respond to news about building projects and other land use and zoning issues, which often draw high levels of activism.

Ensure Citizens Opportunities for Influence. The district boards in Portland, Dayton, and New York provide ways for citizen stakeholders to influence many issues and services in their districts. For example, they all provide ways to be in touch with district-level government service supervisors, so not every local problem has to go through a bureaucracy at city hall and then back down to the neighborhoods. Longtime Lower Manhattan activist Jim Stratton commented that not every mayoral administration is open to neighborhood concerns at the top, so you need channels to local staff. Stratton called these "people who can say, 'I can get you a stop sign,' or 'we can change the hours the sanitation inspectors come around and ticket' to give businesses a chance to sweep the sidewalk."

District boards in all three cities provide citizen-stakeholders with opportunities to influence the hot-button issue of land use. In Portland, several district coalitions have a standing committee on land use to pull together a consensus opinion from among neighborhood associations to advise the city on the district's view of proposed projects. In Dayton and New York City, every proposed project that must go before the city's planning board or commission for approval must first be reviewed by the priority board or community board. For instance, the government will propose certain actions (say, a zoning change) to enable a project, or a developer will seek a variance from existing zoning to build something larger or for a different use than would be allowed under current zoning. Priority board and community board recommendations are not binding but can carry a lot of weight with public officials. New York community boards have gotten developers to redesign projects to reduce elements citizens find offensive and to add community amenities. District boards also vote to advise on other land use issues, from liquor licenses and sidewalk cafés, to whether the board supports proposed public purpose facilities such as sewage treatment plants, public works garages, and social service operations. Northeast Dayton's Joe Kanak estimated that 90 percent of priority board land use recommendations are accepted by the city plan board.

When citizen-stakeholders are provided channels of influence, decision makers do not have to follow their advice every time, but it is important for them to respect citizens' roles, listen to citizens, and not try to avoid giving citizens their opportunities for influence. The city council of Sunnyvale, California, has shown an interest in ensuring that its citizen boards and commissions have real influence. In 1999, the council adopted a program outcome statement for itself that "the interests of the community are adequately and appropriately reflected in recommendations from boards and commissions on policies and actions as demonstrated through acceptance of recommendations by Council 75% of the time."[7]

Citizens as Advocates

As advocates, citizens actively pursue protecting or advancing specific interests, whether their personal, family, or business interests; interests of a group of neighbors; interests of public service users (such as transit riders); interests of people of similar demographics (say, young or old, a given ethnicity) or with common disadvantages (poor, sick, or disabled); interests of animals; or interests of the environment (which some call interests of future generations). Some citizens become interested in issues that appeal to their social conscience or their personal sense of how the community can be better. Some, like Paul Moessner of Prince William County, Virginia, spend part of their paid career helping people with special needs in the community and then keep advocating for them when they retire. As Moessner says, "When you love helping people, it's hard to stop, even when you stop getting a paycheck."

Other citizens are drawn to advocacy because of an immediate problem or public proposal that will affect their own or their family's life, such as unwanted construction they think will decrease the value of their home, or a districtwide policy change that will affect the quality of their children's education. When citizens become advocates about problems that hit close to home, they sometimes develop relationships with other citizens and learn about broader community issues that cause them to want to stay involved long after their initial issue has been resolved. While advocates often initiate their own actions on behalf of their cause, they also participate in all the other citizen roles described here, often in established community processes.

Jim Stratton discussed a project from over twenty years ago in Lower Manhattan that went through Manhattan Community Board 1's (CB1) open community public review process. A large commercial building was proposed by the investment firm Shearson-Lehman for a vacant urban renewal site. Because nearby residents were concerned with increased congestion the project would cause, CB1 would likely vote to advise against building so large a commercial project on the site. But the project was a high economic development priority of the mayor, so board members were concerned that their advice would go unheeded. Stratton, a CB1 committee chair at the time, and other CB1 members did their homework as advocates and found flaws in the project's environmental impact statement that could make a lawsuit by angry residents credible in court. That helped get the attention of Shearson-Lehman and the lead mayoral agency, the Public Development Corporation, which in this case was willing to negotiate with citizens through CB1.

Help Citizens Find Technical and Political Assistance, and Leverage. Citizens who have been active in shaping their communities for a long time may have connections to political officials from past activism and some basic working knowledge of government. Not all citizens have the resources, contacts, or knowledge to be effective advocates of their own cause. So advocacy organizations—for geographic districts or specific causes—can play important roles in helping citizens become effective advocates by providing legal or other technical assistance and helping them navigate government bureaucracies. Sometimes a CDC plays that role, as Westside Housing Organization, a Kansas City, Missouri, CDC, did to help a neighborhood get rat control funding restored by the city council.

Often, successful advocacy is about finding citizens' leverage in situations, such as the Manhattan CB1 members who found flaws in the Shearson project environmental review. In this case, part of the citizens' leverage was potential for legal action that could stop or delay the project, so parties who wanted to move it ahead had a reason to deal with citizens. Leverage does not have to involve the threat of a lawsuit. For land use, New York City's current community review process goes beyond a community board's voting an advisory opinion, to the opportunity for the city council to vote on proposed land use changes. But sometimes citizen advocates may feel it is important to have legal leverage to back up political leverage and give their interest more power or legitimacy.[8] Political leverage is often found in numbers of citizens, which elected officials see as numbers of votes. Advocacy groups can help citizens develop their numerical leverage through old-fashioned organizing of concerned citizens on a block or in a neighborhood, as Judy Welch's Lents Neighborhood Association does in Portland and as CDCs do in Greater Kansas City (see Chapter Eight).

Help Citizens Learn How Things Work and Learn from Each Other. To become effective advocates, citizens have to learn how to influence the direction of government, and sometimes other community institutions, on a single issue or set of issues. They often learn to become advocates simply by doing it. Through trial and error, they find out which agencies are involved in matters that concern them, how relevant decisions are made, and what they have to do to influence those decisions. If they are lucky, they can find citizens in the community who have gone down that road before and can help them learn the ropes faster—someone like Jim Stratton, who learned the ropes as part of a 1960s battle in New York City to rezone the area now called Soho to allow artists to live in the loft buildings with their studios. That citizen victory led to a movement to save the district's historic cast-iron-front buildings. For the next forty years, he was someone to whom downtown residents turned in neighborhood advocacy battles. By 2004, he had "retired" from his main volunteer leadership positions in the community and was a less active but still highly respected advocate who mentors others who become advocates for their community.

Community organizations can do a lot to ensure that citizens learn how to get things done and even help them learn from each other. Government and nonprofit organizations from several communities featured in this book, including Dayton, Prince William County, Greater Kansas City, and Jacksonville, have formed "leadership institutes" and "citizen academies" that help citizens learn to play advocacy and other roles effectively. Many of them also have "alumni associations" that provide ways for citizens who have been active in the community for years after they went through the program to mentor newer citizen activists. These kinds of programs (described in Chapter Nine) can be a valuable resource to a community by ensuring that a new group of volunteer citizen leaders is always emerging with at least a basic knowledge of how things work in the community and with access to more experienced citizen leaders who can help them make contacts and mentor them through complex community situations. These programs and mentors strengthen citizens not only in their advocacy role but also in all the other roles they play to improve their community.

Citizens as Issue Framers

Issue framer is a large and crucial role for citizens to play. Broadly, there are four stages to issue framing, and a citizen may be involved in one or several stages. Also, not all community issue framing processes include all four stages.

First, citizens may be engaged as *foundation builders* to develop long-term or aspirational ideas as foundation statements to which future community actions can be anchored. For example, foundation builders may develop a community vision, a statement of values or principles, or a set of strategic priorities or goals that citizens can use to guide other stages of issue framing[9] and community leaders can use to guide their plans, decisions, and actions. The broader the representational base of citizens engaged and the more citizens recognize their ideas in the community's foundation statements, the more legitimacy the statements will have as a basis for community action. A foundation should not change often; it should be stable so it can serve as a strong anchor for community decisions. And it takes a great deal of community effort to do foundation building well. It makes sense that it is the least frequent stage of issue framing. But it is not something to do only once. Citizens need opportunities to revisit their vision or goals from time to time to keep the foundation relevant to changing conditions and to changing community values and concerns.

The next stage in issue framing, which has to happen whether or not there is a community vision or other foundation statement, is setting the agenda. It is essential for citizens to be engaged as *agenda setters,* so they can influence which issues get priority attention with respect to determining the level of resources focused on them (such as through public budgeting) and determining which issues make it into the community's civic dialogue for deliberation and resolution. The JCCI citizen policy study process, described later in this chapter, starts out with citizens as agenda setters to influence which policy issues will be studied in depth by citizen committees each year.

The final two stages of issue framing, defining the problem and identifying possible solutions, are important to recognize as two distinct stages to avoid a tendency to jump to solutions before carefully analyzing a problem. How a problem is defined can have a big impact on how it is solved, so citizens who want to engage in resolving issues should first be sure to take the time to be *problem definers* before they become *solution identifiers.* Defining a problem gets to the words and means to communicate the issue—from ideas emphasized to images evoked—and influences how people view the issue. For example, in considering how to improve public education, stating that there are "disparities" between rich and poor school districts may bring a concept of inequity to people's minds. A statement that goes on to define the nature of the disparities (for example, spending per student, teacher salaries, class size, or student achievement levels) can also influence what, if any, solutions will be considered. It is critical to engage citizens in defining a problem before picking solutions, rather than accept issue statements as given by politicians, interest groups, or the media.

Help Citizens Learn to Listen, Deliberate, and Make Choices. Issue framing processes work best when they are deliberative, with time for discussion among people with diverse interests, backgrounds, and perspectives, and structured to encourage them to listen to each other and to learn from and develop respect for each other.[10] In the process of discussion, citizens even learn more about what they themselves value and believe is important. They often come to issue framing with only superficially formed ideas or opinions about issues they will discuss. According to Carolyn Lukensmeyer, president of America*Speaks,* which developed technology-enhanced town meetings used in the Washington, D.C. Citizen Summits described in Chapter Seven, "Many people really don't know what they think about an issue until they hear themselves talk about it." And as what they say picks up influences from what others say, they start developing a deeper understanding of issues from multiple viewpoints and may change their initial point of view or develop a more nuanced position. Even advocates for well-formed policy positions often learn from listening to others with different perspectives. They may learn to accommodate others' interests with their own to build a stronger, more broadly supported policy. To get an indication of how engagement in discussions affects individual participants, America*Speaks* regularly seeks feedback on what percentage of participants felt they changed their mind or significantly shifted their position on at least one issue discussed.

Some of the most important agenda-setting processes in communities are the annual or biennial budget processes of local governments, in that a public budget sets the agenda for what a community will try to do with its collective resources. But most opportunities for citizen input comes in public hearings after detailed budget proposals have been prepared by public officials for approval, leaving room for change mainly at the margins. Also, public hearings provide only one-way communication from citizens testifying to decision makers, with little or no dialogue between citizens and officials or among citizens with different viewpoints. Budget hearings often boil down to a few citizens' advocating for more money for particular services or for less spending to cut taxes. Real deliberation is missing, leaving no opportunity for people with diverse views and experiences to learn from each other and develop creative solutions.

It is not uncommon for a county or municipality to have a citizens' budget advisory committee whose members get an opportunity for deliberation among each other and with public officials. With luck, these citizens will be selected by public officials not only for their expertise or political allegiance, but also for their independent thinking, and their diversity of geographic, demographic, and other interests. Or, as in Dayton, such a committee may have a level of independence and geographic diversity because a majority of its members were appointed by the citizen priority boards.

Deliberative processes help people work through their different viewpoints to make trade-offs among competing priorities. But the people involved still have to be willing to make those hard choices. It is easier for a budget advisory committee's members to simply support each other's desired funding increases, but that is less likely to influence elected officials, who will see a community wish list to choose from rather than a set of priorities with some balancing of interests or strategic reasoning behind it. Jim Lindsey, who served on a citizens' budget advisory committee in Dayton for ten years, described how "from the beginning, all of our committee budget recommendations were based on a zero sum approach. In other words, if we wanted more funding in a certain area or for a specific line item, we always identified where we thought the money should be taken from, in other budget items." Lindsey felt the zero-sum approach "forced the citizens to recognize that nothing is without cost." He added, "I believe very strongly that this approach significantly increased the credibility of our recommendations to the administration and to the mayor and city commissioners."

Ensure Citizens Are Engaged Early in the Process. While committee meetings can be more deliberative than public hearings, budget advisory committees' influence can still be marginalized if they enter the budget process late in the game. Jim Lindsey observed that while the citizens' committee was effective from the start, in its first five years, it met only after city staff had internally negotiated a complete draft budget, leaving limited flexibility to influence change. He said that "the members of the committee recognized that the further upstream they can get involved in budget development, the more leverage they can exert in forming the final budget." They then started meeting earlier each year and more often, until they were meeting monthly, with opportunities all year long to learn about and comment on budget alternatives. It also provided more opportunities for committee members to bring budget issues back to priority boards for broader review by citizens in each district and feedback to the committee. From September to December, the committee met more frequently as draft department budgets were being readied for the city manager, and then for the mayor and city commission (Dayton's city council). Engaging citizens early in open, deliberative dialogue among each other and with decision makers is important not just for budgeting but for any other decision process in which citizen stakeholders have an interest.

Because citizens were engaged early in the 1980s Shearson-Lehman project on the west side of Lower Manhattan, broader thinking emerged in defining the problem and identifying solutions. Rather than use legal leverage to stop the project and leave a site undeveloped, CB1 members redefined the problem to go beyond economic development versus resident concerns about congestion. Instead, they defined the problem as how to use the government's desire for economic development—a citywide concern—to also address a top-priority local problem of downtown's growing residential population: no neighborhood public schools. As its proposed solution, CB1 asked that the size of the Shearson office building be reduced and the site also be used for a public school. Shearson had no interest in a school on its office site but agreed to a modest reduction in building size. CB1 members then identified another school site a few blocks away, and part of the proceeds of the city's sale of the site to Shearson was used to build a school. CB1 and the city approved the arrangement, and in a few years downtown children were going to P.S. 234, a new elementary school.

Encourage Community-Centered, Boundary-Crossing Problem Solving. New York City development officials tend to view a problem from the perspective of their mission and focus on the solution from that narrow perspective: create conditions for development and "do the deal." They are not likely to focus on community issues normally addressed by other agencies. But bureaucratic boundaries mean little to citizens. In the Shearson project, by expanding the problem to include a community perspective, CB1 members came up with a solution that crossed government agency boundaries to include both development and education. At the time, the city was open to a boundary-crossing solution and learned from it. The project set an important precedent, as several later downtown projects were developed to include schools, and a growing community with no local public schools got several brand-new ones in later years, at least on its far west side, where there was developable land.

Twenty years later, with the help of the downtown city council member's negotiations with a deputy mayor, CB1 found a land use solution that crossed another boundary: Broadway, the unofficial dividing line between the west side and east side of CB1's district. By then, P.S. 234 and newer schools in the district no longer had enough room to accommodate all the families who had moved downtown. Also, the center of population growth was shifting to the east side of the district, which had no schools and no suitable projects submitted for public review by the mayor that gave CB1 leverage to negotiate for community amenities. In 2004, when two west side land parcels adjacent to P.S. 234, known as parcels 5B-5C from an urban renewal designation, were offered for development, the project required public review because they involved the disposition of city land, and many stakeholders participated in the review. Then CB1, with the help of downtown's city council member, secured an agreement with the city administration and developers to put height limits and setback requirements on new buildings at 5B-5C so P.S. 234 would not end up in perpetual shadow, to build new community facilities on the site including an early childhood center and a public pool, and to build a new pre-K through eighth-grade school.

The difference between this solution and earlier ones, such as the Shearson-Lehman solution, was that the city agreed to build the new school east of Broadway, not on or very near the development site, so families on the east side of the district would finally get their first neighborhood school. West side families would get other amenities, and would also be part of the catchment area for the new school, as P.S. 234 was already overcrowded. The solution crossed both bureaucratic and geographic boundaries.

District boards can run the risk of people focusing so inwardly on their own community that they ignore larger citywide or regional interests. Perhaps because CB1, more than most other New York community boards, has a mix of residential and business interests among its members, they have been more open to considering developments that address citywide economic concerns, so long as community interests are served as well.

Sometimes when neighborhoods within districts are well defined, as in Dayton, it can be a challenge to get citizens to take a boundary-crossing view of issues. Jim Lindsey, referring to when he was chair of the Fair River Oaks Council (FROC) Priority Board, complained of "interneighborhood squabbling over development money." But the FROC board also could generate cooperation across neighborhood boundaries, as when it got five neighborhood associations to cooperate on a plan to improve the Main Street corridor they all border. Lindsey said, "Each neighborhood had a different issue: too many businesses, not enough businesses, too much traffic, and so on. The priority board put together a planning group of the five associations, who shared ideas and realized there were problems common to them all. A common decision on improvement by the five neighborhoods helped the city focus its Main Street reform plans." Another boundary-crossing mechanism Dayton uses is the Priority Board Chairpersons Council, which Lindsey chaired in the late 1990s. The council helps all seven boards set citywide priorities during the city budget process and helps achieve consensus among boards on issues that affect more than one of them.

In Dayton, the Northeast Priority Board crossed a political boundary to fix Kitridge Road, which had an inadequate bridge and dipped in one spot to create a dangerously obstructed view. While many northeast Dayton residents used the road daily, the problems they encountered were outside Dayton in neighboring Huber Heights, so the city of Dayton would not fund the improvements. According to the Northeast Priority Board vice chair at the time, Joe Kanak, "the priority board organized a meeting between the Dayton and Huber Heights city managers. They agreed to jointly ask for funding from Montgomery County to do the necessary repairs. The priority board also allocated some of its funds to the project. The residents of northeast Dayton and Huber Heights were very happy to see the road improved."

In Dayton and New York, both city governments offer a boundary-crossing mechanism to help district boards solve public service problems. In both cities, government departments designate staff with service responsibilities in each district to work with the district boards. Dayton calls these staff a priority board's "administrative council." In New York, they are called a community board's "district service cabinet," chaired by the community board's lead staff, the "district manager." Paul Goldstein, district manager of Manhattan CB1, does not convene his entire cabinet. He said he "has little use for meetings of people from twenty city agencies. But I will call together a police captain, sanitation foreman, someone from the health department, housing, or environmental protection—whoever is needed to solve a particular problem. Those smaller meetings of a few agencies focused on one problem at a time are what gets us better services." By focusing on the community problem, not bureaucratic structures, district boards cross organizational boundaries to improve their communities.

Citizens as Evaluators

Acting as "customers," citizens may fill in a reply card, answer a survey, or join a focus group to rate a public service. A citizen who becomes more actively involved in policy or service assessment takes on the role of *evaluator*. Citizens cross over from customer to evaluator when they do not just answer questions asked by others but start asking questions, as in shaping research questions for a policy study or conducting a resident survey. Citizen evaluators may also be out in the community, systematically collecting data on physical conditions.

Citizen evaluators cannot be expected to always be unbiased, as "professional" evaluators are supposed to be. Citizens bring their interests to their evaluation role and play their advocate role at the same time by trying to influence what evaluation questions are asked, to be sure issues that concern them will be addressed. But they become more evaluators than advocates when they let information drive the solutions they seek rather than staying fixed on a solution that sounds good to start out, but is not supported by data, and thus may not provide the desired community improvement.

Citizens may evaluate alternative solutions considered for service problems or policy issues, or, as is often the case, they evaluate a "solution" brought to them—or already implemented—by a service provider, to help determine better alternatives. A recent example in Manhattan Community Board 1 was when the public transit agency removed the stop of a heavily used bus from in front of a housing development with many elderly residents. A roar went up in the community, as residents complained of having to cross a dangerous, visually obscured intersection to get to the next stop. At least one resident injury was reported, and some said their frail elderly friends and relatives were staying home and missing social activities and doctors' appointments. The transit agency explained to CB1 that a combination of putting extra-long, articulated buses on the route, and the closure of streets around nearby police headquarters for antiterrorist security concerns, forced them to eliminate the bus stop so the articulated buses would not have to make left turns across two lanes, which the agency called too dangerous. That sent citizen evaluators out to observe the buses at that intersection, who counted, in a few hours, over fifty articulated buses (mostly running on less used bus routes) still making the supposedly dangerous turn. The transit agency representative then said they knew they could not eliminate those turns entirely, but wanted to reduce them as much as possible. That left room for negotiation of alternative solutions. One solution CB1 members recommended was to bring the bus stop back about twenty feet down the block, which they thought would give the buses more time to swing into the left lane before making the turn, and cut down on multilane turns, though not eliminate them. The transit agency studied this option and then agreed to it, which left both the agency and the community satisfied.

Provide Citizens Support for Rigorous, Credible, and Useful Assessments. JCCI provides staff research assistance to help Jacksonville citizens play policy evaluator roles. In several examples in Chapters Four and Five, nonprofit organizations provide technology and staff support to help citizens obtain, manage, and use community data. Those are good examples of helping citizen evaluators assess community conditions, evaluate alternatives, and recommend solutions.

Provide Periodic Performance Reports on Issues of Concern to Citizens. In some communities and regions, nonprofit organizations issue regular reports on community indicators (for example, of the local or regional environment and of people's health and economic and social well-being) to help citizens play an evaluator role by giving them information to assess the community's quality of life. To ensure their community indicators reports are of interest to citizens, many of these organizations have engaged citizens in determining what data would be collected and reported.

Some local governments provide regular reports to citizens on the performance of their services. New York City's twice-a-year *Mayor's Management Report* (MMR) gives citizens, in printed reports, citywide performance data related to major service objectives.[11] The MMR on the city's Web site also gives citizens ways to examine service performance, issues, and conditions in community districts in greater detail, including comparisons of results across districts.[12] Portland's annual *Service Efforts and Accomplishments Report* includes both citywide performance data and maps for selected performance indicators that show comparative performance across geographic districts.[13]

The Governmental Accounting Standards Board (GASB) recently issued "Suggested Criteria for Effective Communication" of state and local government performance information.[14] The goal is to encourage more governments to report periodically on their performance, and in ways that will interest citizens and help them assess service results and government accountability.

Few service institutions interest parents more than their children's schools. Citizens participating in several discussion groups on performance reporting held by the GASB in 2000 and 2001 particularly cited reports that compare student achievement in schools and school districts as being popular and useful.[15] One participant's experience showed why: "I used to get infuriated over the very small amount of writing that my son was doing. With the school report cards getting out, it showed one of the weaknesses in my district was writing—the English arts exam. They started doing more writing. Well, thank God for these school report cards."[16] That is an example of a public performance report working well because school officials could see that citizens were interested—they were taking their evaluator's role seriously.

Citizens as Collaborators

This book is full of collaborations among citizens, among organizations, and between citizens and organizations to improve communities. Success in all four advanced governance practices depends on collaboration, because individual government or private organizations cannot solve all community problems on their own. Three ways citizens play collaborator roles are as *compromisers* willing to accept solutions that are not everything they want in order to satisfy others and make progress; as *coproducers* who contribute their own time, expertise, or resources to help implement solutions and enhance community services; and as *asset leveragers* who identify organizations and individuals who are "community assets" and bring them into collaborative solutions and make limited resources go further to get things done.

Help Citizens Get Their Voices Heard and Their Interests Respected.   Being willing to compromise does not mean giving up one's advocacy or completely avoiding conflict. Sometimes citizens must loudly oppose proposals to get attention, so decision

makers will be willing to compromise with them. In Portland, neighborhood leader Jere Retzer described how a land use task force of neighborhood associations "grew out of a contentious relationship between the city and the associations over a zoning change the city wanted. The associations were fighting a measure to turn part of Southwest Portland into a series of row houses" that neighbors opposed. "The neighborhood association chairs got together, organized rallies against the proposal, and won the right to propose their own neighborhood zoning map." As a result, said Retzer, a "task force was created and formed a set of compromise policies, more in line with what neighbors wanted than the original proposal, but in line enough with what the city wanted to get passed." Retzer estimates the task force achieved "95 percent agreement with the City Bureau of Planning and Zoning" when a new zoning map was approved.

In this case, citizens' advocacy created the conditions for compromise, by getting the city of Portland to recognize neighborhood residents' interests. In taking on the compromiser role, these citizens did not give up their advocacy but found a different, more collaborative way to advocate for their interests: a compromise that built on common interests of neighborhood residents and the city government. In being effective compromisers, these citizens made it easier for citizens from all neighborhoods to be effective advocates for desired neighborhood zoning in the future, as the Southwest task force set a key precedent. According to Retzer, "The task force has enabled any neighborhoods to advocate for their own neighborhood zoning map."

In New York, Community Board 1 district manager Paul Goldstein sees citizen opposition as holding the potential for beneficial compromise. He said, "Anytime there's a development the community hates, it creates an opportunity to extract something for the community," as in the Shearson and 5B-5C projects.

Help Citizens Recognize Different Interests to Forge Effective Compromises. Just as it is not a good idea to jump to solutions without first identifying the problem, it is also a mistake to design a compromise based on people's different "positions"—what they say they want, without first understanding each others' "interests"—what they are really trying to achieve or protect, and the costs or benefits to them of different aspects of a solution.[17] Splitting the difference between what different stakeholders want, meeting halfway, or making an equal number of concessions can produce tremendously uneven results for each stakeholder or totally unviable solutions. For example, if a development project such as Shearson or 5B-5C in downtown New York is looked at purely as positions of no growth versus high growth, splitting the difference—making a project half the planned size—probably will not work and may satisfy no one in the long run. In the Shearson case, for example, such a project would not be large enough to meet a city economic development interest of providing a company enough office space for a modern headquarters so jobs will be added or retained in the city.

When broader community interests are considered—the need for schools and recreation facilities, for example, or concerns for allowing existing residential buildings or an existing school adequate air and light—then more creative solutions can be reached, such as using some of a project's economic benefit to provide community amenities, or putting design restrictions on a project without reducing the project size so much that economic interests cannot be met. Identifying different stakeholder interests is essential not only for effective compromise and collaboration; it also is important for issue framing: knowing different interests helps people redefine problems with respect to those interests and determine what boundaries need to be crossed to solve the problem.

As in neighborhood zoning in Portland, opposition-based advocacy may be a necessary place for citizens to start when they approach some projects. But if citizens cannot get beyond opposition, problems will fester and retard a community's progress. If a NIMBY ("Not In My Back Yard") attitude is all that prevails, communities may block undesirable projects but never make the compromises among themselves or with local authorities needed to enable positive development. In New York as elsewhere, some citizen groups have gained a NIMBY reputation, but that has not characterized Manhattan Community Board 1. Of course, it takes more than one party to compromise, and CB1 has at times maintained an opposition stance on an issue or project for many years when no partner has emerged with a willingness to collaborate to find a reasonable compromise. But as Jim Stratton observed, "Community Board 1 took on a 'let's solve this problem attitude' in the early 1980s," a few years after its inception. That attitude, apparent in the Shearson project, was still there twenty years later when the 5B-5C problem was solved.

Paul Goldstein was CB1's district manager during both the Shearson and 5B-5C negotiations and has helped solve many other problems in between. It helps when some solutions, such as the one for the Shearson project, can set a pattern for the future. Nevertheless, every problem involves its own set of interests to be balanced. Goldstein understands that: "You have to be flexible, be willing to compromise. You have to play out each issue differently. It's a balancing act."

Dayton's Jim Lindsey came to recognize that some disagreements are inevitable, but citizens can participate effectively when they are willing to compromise: "It would be naive for anyone to expect that individual priority boards always agree on the key issues across our city." From his budget review experience, he learned that "truly effective citizen participation requires compromise because resources are always limited and everyone's 'need' must be taken in the context of all other 'needs' across the city."

Organize Opportunities for Citizens to Contribute as Coproducers. Citizens play many volunteer roles as coproducers that enhance community services, such as helping to plant a public garden, clean up a park, mentor a child, or coach a team.[18] Coproduction works best not as a substitute for public services, but as a citizen complement to make limited public and nonprofit resources go further. For example, in Jacksonville, citizens once a year clean up small swamps and creeks that feed the St. John's River, while other volunteers go out in their canoes and motor boats to clean up the river itself and its navigable tributaries. They pick stuff out of the water and take it to designated locations, where city crews come and cart it away. While hundreds of citizens provide volunteer coproduction efforts in the annual river cleanup, it all works because of the complementary paid effort by the Jacksonville city government, which mobilizes crews and trucks and pays the crews extra to work on Saturday, so the cleanup can be held on a day when lots of volunteers are available. A good organizing and logistics effort is needed to make it all work and get the job done with a combination of volunteer and paid effort.

Portland district coalitions work with neighborhood associations to organize area cleanups and other activities in which citizen volunteers take on coproducer roles to improve their neighborhoods beyond what the city can do with limited tax dollars. For example, all Portland district coalitions help organize citizens for crime prevention. In Dayton, priority boards and neighborhood coalitions have also organized neighborhoods to increase security. The associations work with Dayton police to set up neighborhood watch groups and train citizens to carry out volunteer security functions. Citizen coproduction in public safety is quite common across the country.

Volunteer effort is not the only means of coproduction. Citizens, businesses, and other organizations also sponsor targeted efforts or services produced by others, as in "adopt a highway" programs; provide in-kind support, as when a business pays employees for their hours assisting community projects; lend equipment; or donate materials. For example, a local florist might donate flowers for a public garden, or, as in Rochester, New York (see Chapter Seven), a business may provide a small grant for citizens to buy a VCR and television monitor to show public safety videos to senior citizens.

Help Citizens Identify and Leverage Community Assets, Including Themselves.

Closely related to collaboration and coproduction is the idea of identifying and building on community assets, rather than depending on service organizations, such as local governments and nonprofit social service providers, to satisfy all the needs of the community and solve all its problems. These service organizations themselves can be seen as assets, as can local schools, libraries, businesses, houses of worship, neighborhood associations, informal associations among people, and citizens themselves who have individual talents they can bring to improving communities. Once organizations and individuals are identified as *assets*, they can be *leveraged*—turned into partners or coproducers working together on collaborative projects.

In the 1980s in Lower Manhattan, CB1 members not only leveraged Shearson-Lehman's desire for an office building to get a school, they also leveraged other assets for a better solution. At the time, the city board of education had a reputation of taking twenty years to build a school and allowed little design flexibility. So

Jim Stratton and other CB1 members pointed out that the Public Development Corporation (PDC) that had championed the Shearson project had construction powers, and they asked that the PDC build the school, with the involvement of parents—including professional designers and architects who lived downtown. The city agreed to this unusual arrangement. In this case, CB1 members identified and leveraged the assets of a private corporation's money, a public agency's construction powers, and citizen coproducers' interest and design skills. P.S. 234 was built in record time and within budget, and it quickly became the most desired elementary school among downtown families.

Many small communities, especially whose citizens are poor, do not locally have the resources needed to solve big problems, such as failing or inadequate water or sewer systems, or other capital infrastructure problems. Although state or federal funding may be available, it often requires a local matching contribution that poor communities cannot provide in cash. And when many communities in an area are relatively poor, government funds are often far short of what is needed to fully pay for all the serious environmental and infrastructure problems faced by the whole region.

Peapatch, Virginia, is a rural community of fifty homes in southwest Virginia. In Peapatch and the region around it, water has disappeared for years as coal mining has created cracks in the earth that drain off families' well water. As wells and springs have gone dry, families have had to make hauling water a regular ritual and take exceeding care to conserve water every time they do the laundry, take a shower, and use a sink or toilet—if they are lucky enough to have enough water to flush their toilet. The poor local tax base cannot support the investments needed to bring in the engineers and contractors to build typical water projects.

In 2001, the citizens turned to the most essential asset they had in the community—themselves—and a dozen local volunteers became coproducers who laid nine miles of four-inch water pipe up an elevation of 2,970 feet to Peapatch, to leverage a relatively small capital investment from the state of Virginia to provide fresh water to their homes and those of their neighbors. Peapatch was one of several communities throughout the southwest Virginia coal region where water projects were completed at a fraction of the typical cost, bringing water to 520 homes at a cost of $3.1 million, or less than $6,000 per home. State officials are more willing to channel state and federal funds to communities that can organize a large share of self-help—who can identify their own community assets and get them to work for the greater good. State officials said that the work would have cost three times as much if done completely with construction contractors.[19] With funding limitations, either many fewer families would have been reached, or the work would not have been done at all.

Proponents of an *asset focus,* such as John McKnight of Northwestern University, argue that focusing on *needs* or *problems* can stifle improvement by making residents feel stuck in a community full of deficiencies and fragmenting resources by splitting them up among services aimed at specific needs rather than focusing resources on whole solutions aimed at desired community outcomes. McKnight and others argue for identifying the assets or strengths in a community and developing improvement approaches that build on those strengths.[20] Government and nonprofit service providers can be assets or resources that contribute to improving the community, but should not act as outside experts that disadvantaged residents must depend on to tell them what they need and to fix things for them. Rochester, New York, drew on McKnight's work, including the widely used manual on asset-based development he wrote with John Kretzmann, *Building Communities from the Inside Out*,[21] when it made asset mapping a key part of its Neighbors Building Neighborhoods program (see Chapter Seven). As a result, their citizen-planned neighborhood improvements go much further than they could if they depended only on government.

From this perspective, whether it is finding friends and neighbors to haul pipe in Peapatch or identifying the construction powers of the PDC in New York and asking it to do something it never did before—build a school—citizens who forge collaborations leverage a community's assets to get big things done.

Identify and Support "Sparkplugs" Who Energize and Organize the Community.
The self-help approach to building community capital projects used in Virginia and sixteen other states was developed by the Rensselaerville Institute, a nonprofit organization based in Rensselaerville, New York. The tasks that citizen volunteers take on vary from project to project, depending on the skills, experience, and labor available in the local community. Virtually any part of a project—from engineering and design, to project management, to skilled crafts, to basic labor, to work site supervision—can be done by volunteers, paid government staff, or paid contractors. The common denominator in all these projects is the energy of local "sparkplugs," who organize and energize many other citizens to keep community momentum alive for however long it takes, from developing initial plans to turning on the taps and tasting the fresh, flowing water. In Peapatch, a key sparkplug was a former coal miner, Thurmon Hackworth Jr. Hackworth was disabled, so he could not haul the pipe uphill himself, but his efforts to organize his friends and neighbors were critical to making the improvement possible.[22] The Rensselaerville Institute has a benchmark goal that a community should be able to organize itself to reduce project costs by 40 percent from typical fully contracted capital projects. Most projects meet or exceed that benchmark. Some projects, as those in the Virginia coal country, are completed at far greater savings.

Public Policy Shaped by Citizens

Many private organizations conduct research on public issues and use their results to advocate for particular policies. Whether they are well-known national think tanks or focus on their own states, regions, and communities, they often focus their agenda and studies to support specific interests or narrow public policy perspectives. They include, for example, taxpayer groups seeking to cut taxes and public spending, or "economy leagues" focused on efficiency and "value for tax dollars." They may be research arms of advocacy organizations such as chambers of commerce and other business groups; environmental groups; or social welfare advocacy groups for children, poor, or at-risk families and neighborhoods, people with disabilities, and the elderly.

In several communities, civic organizations have emerged that do not approach policy research from a preset agenda. Instead, they engage citizens as issue framers in setting the research agenda and shaping policy studies, then as policy evaluators in conducting the research and determining recommendations. It is only after studies are completed that the organization knows the policies and community actions it will advocate for, and engages citizens as advocates to help get the policies implemented.

Citizen-Driven Policy Research and Advocacy in Jacksonville

The Jacksonville Community Council Inc. (JCCI) has engaged citizens in a policy study process since its founding in 1975. JCCI was one of two organizations founded that year by Jacksonville community leaders who sought a civic reform to match the government reform—including city-county consolidation—implemented in 1968 to end corruption and promote efficiency. As Fred Schultz, a prominent business and reform-movement leader, put it, "We had the government we needed, but we lacked the civic involvement to make it responsible and accountable." Their answer was to form Leadership Jacksonville (discussed in Chapter Nine) to build a growing network of citizens capable of and interested in engagement, and JCCI, to engage citizens in public policy.

JCCI adapted its citizen policy study process from one that was pioneered and is still used by the Citizens League in Minnesota and has also been adapted for use by civic groups in Cleveland and St. Louis. JCCI, like the Citizens League, often follows the policy study process with what it calls an "implementation process," in which citizens advocate for the policy choices recommended in the study. According to JCCI executive director Lois Chepenik, "Our ongoing use of the study process for nearly thirty years has proven its validity, as well as its strength and resilience. We keep tweaking the process to make it more user friendly, but we remain committed to the basic model."

While the basic process has endured, JCCI made a major change early on concerning who participates. In the late 1970s, it shifted from its founders' leadership-focused concept to invite any and all interested citizens to participate on its study committees. This change attracted a different mix of interested citizens and representatives of public and private stakeholder organizations for particular topics. Eventually JCCI moved beyond relating exclusively to individual citizens by developing working partnerships with the Jacksonville Chamber of Commerce, the Northeast Florida United Way, and the consolidated city of Jacksonville government. The combination of openness to all citizens and partnership with important community institutions is especially empowering. Angie Vanatter, a neighborhood activist, calls herself "an ordinary citizen" and says, "I have benefited personally and as a neighborhood leader from my JCCI involvement because it gives me a way to be a conduit or bridge between my neighbors and JCCI, the city, and the community. JCCI gives me a place to take all the concerns my constituents bring to me, a place where I can expect that these concerns will be given some attention."

The JCCI policy study process takes citizens through most of the issue framer role—including agenda setting, defining problems, and identifying solutions—as well as the evaluator role. Citizens play an advocate role in the JCCI implementation process. These processes involve the use of three successive types of JCCI citizen committees.

Citizens on a Program Committee Set the Agenda. Each year, about twelve to fifteen people serve on the program committee, usually chaired by JCCI's president-elect, to play an agenda-setting role of picking policy issues to recommend to the JCCI board. People are invited to serve on the committee based on their demographic diversity and mix of interests and expertise. JCCI usually starts only two new citizen studies a year, but solicits widely for study topic ideas, including personal outreach efforts by program committee members, resulting in several hundred study suggestions submitted to JCCI by the public. John Cobb, 2003–2004 president and former program committee chair, says, "The selection process needs to be done well, with a broad cross-section of input and involvement to ensure that the important decisions about JCCI's study issues will be made effectively."

With JCCI staff support, program committee members work through a two-stage process based on standard criteria, first to determine a short list of about ten issues. Then they divide the issues among members to explore and to prepare "advocacy presentations" they make to each other on why each issue should be studied. The committee selects four issues to recommend to the JCCI board, which makes the final selection. Program committee members perform a preliminary problem identification role when they shape the issues for each of the final four topics to assist the board in its deliberation, and to guide the citizen committee that may study the issue in detail.

Citizen Policy Study Committees Find Facts, Define Problems, and Identify Solutions. Once topics are chosen, JCCI solicits volunteers and develops large, diverse citizen policy study committees, which meet weekly for several months. The committee has citizen volunteer leadership: a volunteer chair and a volunteer management team, appointed by the chair. In the first study phase, between committee members' own community sources, JCCI staff research, and presentations by resource people—issue experts and stakeholders with key interests in the issue—the committee establishes its findings of fact for the issue, which gives them the information they need to define the problem they are addressing in more depth than the program committee had in its proposal to the board. As they decide which facts are most relevant and interpret their findings, they may significantly change how the problem is defined. The citizen study committee is empowered to restate the issue or problem from what was originally presented to them by the JCCI board, so long as they support their new problem definition with the facts they have obtained. The study committee's problem definition helps drive the potential solutions they identify and consider.

Citizens Evaluate Alternatives and Make Recommendations. Citizens on the policy study committees next play an evaluator role when they assess alternative solutions and decide on a course of action to recommend. Their recommendations include which entities should take responsibility for decisions and actions needed to improve the current situation in the community. The committees prepare reports, which are released at a public venue to gain wide media and community attention.

Implementation: Citizens Advocate for Change. Most policy study committees finish their work in about a year. Then, the JCCI board president appoints a volunteer implementation chair, and a citizen implementation task force is formed to raise public awareness of the study and play an advocate role for each recommendation. The task force develops its own timetable and strategy for each recommendation, which can involve advocacy aimed directly at decision makers or at building public support for change. Task forces monitor progress as they work and conclude, generally after two years, with a report on the extent of community action implemented.

JAXPORT: A Citizen Study That Made a Difference

In 1994–1995, after the Jacksonville Port Authority (JPA) announced a need to expand and improve publicly owned seaport facilities called JAXPORT, the JCCI Program Committee proposed a port study and the JCCI board selected it. The JPA welcomed JCCI's decision because they hoped a JCCI policy study would confirm the benefits of expansion, giving the JPA's proposed sales tax increase a chance to win voter approval. In their findings of fact, the citizens on JCCI's policy study committee identified potential benefits to support port expansion and improvement, essentially agreeing with the premise of the problem. As they went further in their issue framer role, they did not limit themselves to the JPA's proposals, but identified and considered other possible solutions. In their evaluator role, they concluded that the JPA's financing plan was flawed, and its public marketing had been insufficient and misguided. The citizen recommendations called for phased expansion, using existing JPA bond capacity rather than new tax authority, and for an overhaul of JPA public relations to better inform the public of the benefits of JAXPORT and its proposed expansion.

The JPA responded quickly by withdrawing the sales tax proposal. It also began a new planning process that led to a phased expansion plan, tied to its bond financing capacity. The JPA took major steps toward reinventing its public relations image and strategies.

In this case, JCCI's study implementation and advocacy effort turned out to be relatively easy. That does not always happen, as in JCCI's long history of advocating for education reform, described in Chapter Five as an example of how quality-of-life indicators, citizen policy studies, and advocacy fit together.

Results That Matter from Citizen Studies and Advocacy

The JAXPORT study is only one of many JCCI citizen policy studies that have made a difference. Past JCCI president Shep Bryan, who has been on study committees, believes that "the citizen study process has been JCCI's greatest contribution to the community. Over the years, JCCI has produced many well-researched studies that have been the catalyst for numerous improvements in our public institutions and the policies they pursue." The list of community actions—sometimes involving state legislation—that JCCI's citizen studies and advocacy have stimulated is long and impressive, for example:

Education, Health, and Social Issues

- Jacksonville elementary schools achieved accreditation.
- A major after-school program was expanded.
- A dropout prevention program was started.
- A racial tolerance curriculum was developed by the school board.
- The local Literacy Coalition was created.
- The Older Adults Services Council was started.
- Six new health clinics were opened for the poor.

Land Use, Housing, and the Environment

- A new city planning department was created.
- Housing and zoning codes were strengthened.
- A city ordinance was passed to pay for replacing failing septic tanks in areas with health risks.
- City recycling was expanded and composting was started.
- Water consumption monitoring was started.

Economic Opportunities

- The chamber of commerce started Adopt-a-Business to support minority businesses.
- The Partnership for Workforce Preparation was started
- City contracts to minority-owned companies were increased.

Government Reform and Civic Development

- City pension fund solvency was assured by city council action and state-legislated standards.
- Civil service was restructured.
- Growth was excluded from a local tax cap by voters for long-term city financial health.
- JCCI started new in-person, televised, and online citizen dialogues.[23]

The Importance of Open, Representative Participation

Community stakeholders' interests often diverge. So excluding anyone with a potential interest from involvement, or not having a stakeholder group represented, can undermine an entire problem-solving process, cause decisions to lose legitimacy or be challenged in court, and leave community problems to fester as conditions get worse.

The Challenge of Keeping Working Groups Representative

Most of the problem-solving groups described in this chapter involve people who make long-term volunteer commitments to play roles such as issue framer, evaluator, or collaborator in the community, from the community boards of New York, to the policy study committees in Jacksonville, to the neighborhood associations and district coalitions in Portland. Whether members of such a group are elected, as in Dayton, or selected in other ways, it is always a challenge to maintain a working membership that reasonably reflects the demographic mix and full range of interests of the community—or part of the community—that the group is supposed to represent. And even if a board or committee looks representative on paper, its effective working membership may not be, if, as inevitably happens, some volunteer members cannot participate as much as they had hoped. It is useful for these groups (and, if they are appointed, the people who appoint them) to take a hard look at themselves from time to time to see how representative their working membership really is. Then, when there are opportunities to add or replace members, to reach out to underrepresented groups to diversify the interests represented, always trying to make their working membership better reflect the actual diversity of their community.

For Each Issue, Engage All Potentially Interested Stakeholders

In reality, the representativeness of communities' standing boards and committees is never perfect, and those who are able to put in the most time often end up with the most influence. Perhaps more important than the representativeness of a standing committee's or community group's membership are its efforts to keep their whole community or district informed of the problems and issues coming before it, keep their processes open, and reach out to be sure all potentially affected interests in an issue are engaged in a deliberative process. People who cannot make the long-term commitment to be a regular group member will often take the time to come to key meetings when they learn that a major land use change near their home is being deliberated or other issues they care a lot about are up for consideration.

Members of community groups, like Judy Welch of the Lents Neighborhood Association in Portland, do their community or neighborhood a great service by spreading the word widely when issues affecting the neighborhood, such as proposed building projects, are being considered. In Jacksonville, as hard as JCCI works at making its study committees representative of community diversity, it also works hard to be sure all key interests in the policy issue being considered get to make their case to the committee. They not only bring experts to inform the committee's deliberations, they also include other stakeholders with interests in the issue among the resource people who make presentations to the study committee.

Seek the Broadest Possible Representation for Foundation Building and Agenda Setting

When focusing on specific community problems or proposed projects, it is often possible to identify a limited set of people or groups who are likely to be especially affected and target outreach to bring them into the problem-solving process. But when undertaking broad foundation-building or agenda-setting processes, such as setting priorities for planning or budgeting, it is especially important that participation be broadly representative of the entire community. For example, as discussed in Chapter Seven, Prince William County held thirty-one strategic planning focus groups, not just two or three, to attain representativeness, and the District of Columbia government conducts extensive outreach to ensure the thousands who attend its agenda-setting "Citizen Summits" are representative of the whole city.

However, many communities find it difficult to get some groups to participate, leaving those groups unrepresented in key community decision processes. Special efforts to reach underrepresented groups are important. Chapter Nine provides suggestions for achieving broad representativeness in community processes, including suggestions for overcoming barriers to participation by underrepresented groups.

Dangers of a Closed, Unrepresentative Process

Not all public leaders seek open, representative citizen engagement on important decisions and projects. They may tolerate it when they are required to but try to avoid it whenever possible. As a result, decision making becomes a closed process. Some stakeholders who feel especially affected and can raise resources (for example, to pay attorneys) or use political contacts may force their way into the process, but others are not represented, and problem solving by lawsuit may be the end result.

In Lower Manhattan, at the same time as 5B-5C deliberations went on in the open, with opportunities for all stakeholders to participate from the start, a different process unfolded around a proposed development on the east side of the district. Exploiting a legal gray area concerning the site—a hospital parking lot—the mayor and his development officials claimed they were taking "business actions," not "land use actions," so public community review was not required to lift restrictions on sale and use of the lot. Using this legal interpretation, the mayor enabled what the city calls an "as-of-right" project, and deprived Community Board 1 (CB1) of its formal leverage to influence the project through community review. Soon, newspapers reported a proposed fifty- to fifty-five-story building with about 1 million square feet of space and land uses previously not allowed. Nearby citizens were angered. Residents of two buildings next to the lot were frightened: unrestricted development enabled by the mayor could potentially result in many of the 162 families in these buildings losing windows and much of the value of their homes.

CB1, anticipating the project, had already voiced serious concerns and passed resolutions calling for "mitigations," including siting the new building away from the two adjacent buildings and inclusion of a major community amenity such as a school or recreation center in the project. But the mayor and his development staff were not listening; they used their claim of "as-of-right" to ignore the pleas of community residents.

The developer refused CB1's invitations to open public meetings, but came to smaller, invitation-only meetings first convened by State Assembly member Deborah Glick and later by other downtown elected representatives, such as City Council member Alan Gerson, in response to requests from CB1 and community stakeholders. Only a few community interests and CB1 members could be present at a time in these meetings. Eventually the developer presented designs for an ample plaza between the planned building and the adjacent buildings. To some people involved, the developer seemed to be responding to the one group that had hired an attorney and was prepared to sue: home owners in the adjacent buildings calling themselves "Concerned Neighbors."[24] Soon press reports of a building that would now be seventy-five stories tall (though slimmer, due to the plaza) caused other stakeholders to complain to elected representatives and seek compensating property improvements. Some CB1 members lamented that as separate groups pressed their own claims and tried to negotiate, the community would be divided and lose opportunities to gain amenities for the use of the whole community.

Before long, several of the Concerned Neighbors sued the mayor, the hospital, and the developer because a legal commitment to the plaza was not reached before the statute of limitations would expire on the mayor's action. Meanwhile, downtown's only hospital warned it could become financially insolvent and have to sharply curtail community health services if it did not close its sale of the lot soon, which the lawsuit blocked. Through eight months of mostly closed processes, nothing was assured.

Whatever the outcome of the project, the disadvantages of engagement through closed processes instead of open, representative ones are clear. Without open meetings in which all stakeholders could deliberate with decision makers, community interests were fragmented as different parties came into the process at different times, and responses to interests were based on power, not deliberative problem solving.

Just before this book was sent to the publisher, the project was resolved favorably for the community. It helped that part of Lower Manhattan is represented by the Speaker of the State Assembly, one of the most powerful politicians in the state, who began convening stakeholder meetings in the last few months of the ad hoc process. The Concerned Neighbors lawsuit also helped: it slowed the project, so it could not quickly roll through to approval unchanged. But perhaps the two biggest reasons for a favorable resolution were luck and the terms of the 5B-5C compromise settlement whose open process had concluded while the east side closed process was proceeding.

The luck involved a university dropping out of the project, leaving no tenant for the lower stories of the building. The same day, community leaders, led by the speaker, began to press the developer to include a school in the building in part of the newly vacant space—the school the mayor promised for the east side of downtown in the 5B-5C compromise. City Council member Gerson and CB1 chair Madelyn Wils had retained political leverage for the community by putting off approval of a major part of proposed 5B-5C developments until an east side school was sited and funded. Most of the funding had been put in the school construction budget, but finding a site for the school had proven difficult. The community's leverage from the 5B-5C compromise, and the suddenly open space in the hospital lot project, made the mayor's development officials suddenly interested in helping the community they had earlier shunned on this project.

While negotiations on reconfiguring the project with a school proceeded, the developer and the Concerned Neighbors reached an agreement on conditions for a plaza between the new building and the neighbors' homes. This allowed the hospital to sell the land to improve its financial security and the lawsuit to be settled. About two months later, the mayor and the speaker jointly announced that a kindergarten through eighth-grade school for six hundred children would be built into the project.[25]

Does the apparent happy ending make this a good process? No. An open, representative process would have been better and may have led to a solution as good as or better for the community without a lawsuit or luck. In part, community citizens and leaders got as much as they did because they knew some of the lessons noted earlier in this chapter, especially about finding their leverage, learning the way things work, helping citizens voice opposition, and recognizing different stakeholder interests. These lessons of advocacy and compromise are useful no matter what situations citizens face. But a good resolution of this closed process was also made possible by the success of the open 5B-5C process. One must also consider, what would have happened to citizens who felt threatened, as the Concerned Neighbors did, but could not afford costly legal fees? And what would have happened to a community that did not have powerful political representation?

How to Leverage the Power of Citizens Even More

From the Peapatches of the country, with fifty households, to New York City, with 8 million people, citizens have been organizing themselves and engaging in community affairs to get things done. They may build water projects in rural Virginia, conduct policy studies in Jacksonville, create neighborhood zoning maps in Portland, improve the Main Street corridor in Dayton, trade an office building for a school in New York, or seize opportunities, wherever they live, to improve their community. Engaged citizens extend their influence and generate community energy to get things done. After each problem is solved, the community can move its energy to new issues. But the stories of citizens and communities in this chapter are missing one ingredient that can leverage the power of citizen engagement even more: measurement of results. If systematic measurement and feedback of results is not part of community governance, success is likely to be episodic, with the community lurching from issue to issue without a sense of whether long-term progress is being made toward a stronger community.

In later chapters, the uses and benefits of results measurement are explored from different perspectives. The next chapter demonstrates how results measurement helps government and nonprofit organizations systematically manage for results. Chapters Four and Five show how citizens increase their influence by becoming engaged in measuring results. Finally, Chapters Six through Eight demonstrate that when measurement of results is aligned with citizen engagement and with systematic processes for improving how things get done, citizens and communities can gain a continual sense of progress on all their important goals, not just on specific projects they tackle at a given time.

CHAPTER THREE

ORGANIZATIONS MANAGING FOR RESULTS

You mean we clean only clean sewers?

WAYNE TANDA, FORMER DIRECTOR OF STREETS AND TRAFFIC, CITY OF SAN JOSE

In the mid-1990s in San Jose, Wayne Tanda, then director of streets and traffic, was surprised to learn that his sewer cleaning crews focused all scheduled operations on cleaning sewers that were already clean. Cleaning dirty sewers would slow productivity and cut down the miles of sewers they cleaned. Crew chiefs told him they were rated on how many miles of sewers they cleaned, and they were very proud of the high mileage they cleaned each year. But the purpose of cleaning sewers was to keep sewage from backing up into people's homes and businesses, not to rack up cleaning mileage. And it is the dirty sewers that clog and back up. Tanda told the sewer cleaning manager, "This is absolutely wrong. I could care less about how many miles of sewers you clean. What I care about is how many get clogged."

By questioning how his crews measured success, Tanda took the first step toward managing for results. This chapter focuses on how government and nonprofit organizations align measuring results with getting things done to perform the Effective Community Governance Model's advanced practice 2: organizations managing for results. This practice does not necessarily involve citizen engagement, so citizen roles are not especially stressed here. With a few exceptions, citizens in this chapter mostly play stakeholder roles, generally as service customers. But as the rest of the San Jose story makes clear, it can still be useful to help citizens move beyond their passive customer role to play active roles in improving results.

Advanced Governance Practice 2: Organizations Managing for Results

2. Organizations Managing for Results

This chapter is intended to help you consider how to improve results management in community organizations. If you or your organization is new to managing for results or your focus is on specific services, the examples focusing on individual services (San Jose, Citizen Schools) may be a starting point for you to consider how to improve results management. If you work on a policy or enterprise management level of a multiservice or multiprogram organization, public or private, or if you are involved in funding decisions, you may find that one or more of the examples that focus on entire local governments or on results-based investment by a foundation will give you ideas you can relate to your own setting. If you have a general interest in building organizations' measurement and improvement capacity, any or all of the examples may be useful.

If your passion is engaging citizens to improve communities, managing for results, as presented here, should still be useful to you. The cause of community improvement is well served when organizations dedicated to the well-being of a community or its people master the art of managing for results. And it is easier to see a clear picture of managing for results without the complexities of how citizens become engaged in it. So while citizen engagement is not a main focus here, this chapter can help you understand key managing for results concepts and start you thinking about how you might apply them. Examples in Chapters Seven and Eight bring citizen engagement and results management together.

Managing for Specific Results or Outcomes

Articulate and Measure the Results That Best Meet Your Purpose

The most basic requirement of managing for results is to measure results that are most important to accomplish. Put another way, be sure your measures meet your purpose. Infrastructure managers need to know the output of work done by maintenance crews, such as the miles of sewers cleaned. But if the measurement focus is too narrow—only on output, for example, and not on desired outcomes or results—the wrong things can be done to maximize that output at the expense of more important results, as happened in San Jose until Wayne Tanda questioned this approach. Then, instead of focusing only on miles of sewers cleaned, they began to measure success differently. Said Tanda, "We would measure how many sewers are clear and not clogged. The bigger the percentage, the better job you are doing. . . . So with that, the miles of sewers actually cleaned using mechanical techniques stayed about the same or decreased. What increased was the use of enzymes to eat grease. What increased was education in the neighborhoods that would typically use a lot of grease in their cooking. What we saw was a better condition, a better outcome." The sewer cleaning strategy in San Jose switched from a goal of racking up a large output of work, to a goal of achieving discernible results—fewer clogged sewers—for the community. Because they articulated and measured their result, they could manage for it, and they changed their strategy to achieve better results for the community.

Managing for Results as a Performance Feedback Cycle

The essence of managing for results is to feed back measured performance information into decision making so operations can be adjusted or policies, priorities, or program designs can be changed to improve future measured results.[1] That feedback means that any managing for results process is really a cycle of measurement and assessment of results, planning and decision making, and implementation. The examples in this chapter progress from simple to more complex results management cycles.

San Jose's improved sewer cleaning approach follows the simple cycle in Figure 3.1. Once they articulated and measured what was most important, they could assess results by analyzing where sewers were clear and where they were clogged with grease. Then they planned a variety of actions to respond differently to varying conditions in different sewers and neighborhoods, unlike their previous one-size-fits-all approach. San Jose's sewer cleaning responses primarily varied geographically, but as noted in Figure 3.1, for other services an organization's responses to measured results may also vary based on other dimensions, such as different needs or outcomes of different demographic groups or different types or ages of facilities maintained.[2]

They complete the cycle by implementing their planned actions and measuring results again to determine progress and how to respond in the future to changes—or the lack of changes—in conditions in sewers across the city. In other words, they keep checking how results change, keep feeding that information back into their operational plans, and keep adjusting their services to improve results further in the future.

Accountability for Outcomes

Too often, public and nonprofit managers complain that they do not control the things that most affect outcomes, defined here as conditions in the community or conditions of people. They do not control how much grease people pour down their drains, how much trash people drop on the street, whether people maintain healthy lifestyles, or millions of other factors that service providers often consider external to their work that affect people's health and welfare or the physical condition of the community and

FIGURE 3.1. A SIMPLE MANAGING FOR RESULTS CYCLE

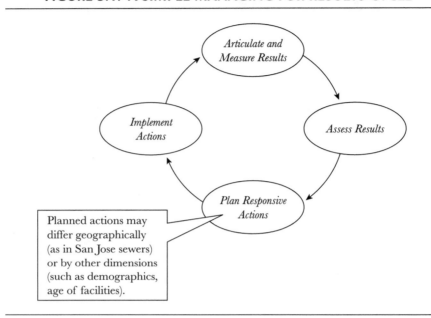

its living environment. Should service managers be held accountable for things they cannot control? Or can they influence and improve outcomes more than they think they can?

Outcomes Can Be Improved, When Viewed as Results to Be Accomplished. Many public and nonprofit managers would rather have their performance measured based on the efforts they exert on activities to affect community conditions, the resources or "inputs" they dedicate to a problem, or how much of a service they provide ("outputs"), not on relevant outcomes—the actual conditions of people or the community their service is supposed to maintain or improve. But as Wayne Tanda proved with his sewer cleaning team, when you shift the focus to desired outcomes, people can get out of their standard service production mode and find a way to accomplish results. In San Jose, they not only applied their technical knowledge by using enzymes on greasy sewers, they showed extra creativity by doing something that public works operators are not especially known for: becoming engaged with people in targeted neighborhoods to educate them in proper ways to dispose of grease in order to reduce the size of the problem. In this case, San Jose staff engaged citizens in these neighborhoods as stakeholders and helped them become more than passive service customers to play a role as collaborators in improving their own neighborhood conditions:

they helped them become coproducers in solving sewer backup problems. Often when service providers focus on desired outcomes, not just service activities or production, they find ways they can affect—if not totally control—some of those external factors and have a bigger impact on outcomes than they at first imagined.

Appropriate Levels of Outcome Accountability. In fairness to service providers, there are some external factors—severe weather including natural disasters, a major downturn in the regional economy, a new drug of choice flooding the street narcotics market, for example—that in the short run can overwhelm the positive impact local public or nonprofit service providers can have on certain human or community outcomes. In the long run, some decision makers in a community—particularly those at higher policy levels—should be accountable for anticipating some of these uncontrollable events or external factors, and adjusting to all of them, so performance results can move in the direction of desired outcomes.

If a service provider has a narrow scope of services and few flexible resources, the people who run that organization may be limited in what they can accomplish. But they should still do their best to change how they serve the community to reflect changing conditions, even if they can do only so much. It would not be appropriate to hold them accountable for improving outcomes communitywide, but it would be appropriate for them to show incremental gains in outcomes of just their immediate service customers or in just the neighborhoods—or even just the blocks or buildings— where they operate.

However, public officials who budget for services at all levels of government (including those beyond the local community, such as relevant state and federal officials) and private foundations that invest in community services should be accountable for learning whether the current mix of services they fund does not solve the problems they are intended to address and for adjusting their investment strategy to better achieve desired outcomes, whether that means providing more funds to services that work well but are overwhelmed, or finding more cost-effective—perhaps very different—approaches to solving problems and achieving outcomes. As is clear in the next example, Mayor Martin O'Malley believed in taking accountability for improving conditions in Baltimore and made sure his service managers were also held accountable as part of Baltimore's managing-for-results strategy.

Relentless Management for Results: City of Baltimore

When William Donald Schaefer was mayor of Baltimore from 1971 to 1987, he was famous for personally demanding that city agencies immediately fix service problems he encountered in daily travels around the city. He even spent parts of his weekends traveling through streets and alleys around town to make his own inspections for problems that city workers should know about and fix.[3] Service departments got the message that Mayor Schaefer had better not see that same derelict vehicle on the corner or a noticed pothole unrepaired the next time he passed that way, and they would respond quickly to the problems he reported. While the energetic mayor seemed as if he was everywhere, he really could not see everything in the city in a systematic way all the time and still do his job as chief executive. So service departments' responses to problems he reported did not, by themselves, represent a systematic approach to all major city service issues and were not necessarily representative of their responses to all Baltimore neighborhoods all the time.

Twelve years after Schaefer's last term as mayor, enter Mayor Martin O'Malley, who could take advantage of advances in geographic information systems (GIS) and advice from former New York City deputy police commissioner Jack Maple, to make city agencies' responsiveness to problems both relentless and systematic. Maple was an innovator behind the New York Police Department's much-heralded and much-copied Compstat program, the centerpiece of department strategies that led to rapid, sustained crime reduction. Compstat involved computer mapping of crime levels and patterns by location and time, and frequent review at police headquarters with precinct captains and district commanders who were held accountable for changes in results and for developing credible strategies for improvement. Compstat also involved wide sharing and use of timely, accurate data, and stimulated creative problem solving to enable the police department to manage for impressive results in reducing crime.[4]

In 1999, Jack Maple, by then a consultant to police departments across the country, gave Baltimore mayoral candidate O'Malley the idea that a Compstat approach could work for any city service agency.[5] O'Malley, acting on the idea, launched Citi-Stat on June 29, 2000, and over the next twelve months, all of the city of Baltimore's major operating departments became participants in the CitiStat program.[6]

High-Frequency Feedback of Mapped Results Drives Accountability and Performance. Baltimore's CitiStat uses the same four precepts as the New York's Compstat: "Accurate and timely intelligence; rapid deployment; effective tactics; and relentless follow-up and assessment."[7] Managers of regularly participating agencies attend biweekly meetings that drive home their accountability for results. The meetings are held in a specially designed room in which up-to-date data on key agency service and cost issues are displayed on screens, and agency managers are questioned by members of the mayor's cabinet, with Mayor O'Malley often in attendance.[8] CitiStat operations and technical teams check and analyze the data, compare performance with previous periods, prepare briefing books, and code data for "computer pin maps."[9] Wherever a problem appears on a map, the mayor wants to know his agencies have a strategy to solve it. As Mayor O'Malley said, "The nice thing about maps is that the map doesn't know whether a neighborhood is black or white, rich or poor, Democrat or Republican. And a map doesn't know whether a judge lives there or a congressman lives there or a senator lives there. The map tells us where problems are; then we relentlessly attack those problems, and we abate those problems and the tide rises for everybody."[10] Baltimore finally had a mayor who really was "everywhere," at least virtually, because of the high-frequency, systematic, geographic-based performance data at his disposal.

The CitiStat story involves Baltimore's using performance information well to achieve financial gains by the city government, measurably more responsive services to citizens as service customers, and outcome improvements for the community as a whole. The city government credited CitiStat with leading to over $13 million in savings and revenue across agencies in its first year of operation.[11] Baltimore's relentless management for results, enabled by CitiStat, has also led to improved service performance. A common priority for many services has been speeding response to service requests, better meeting service frequency standards such as annual restaurant inspections, and reducing service backlogs. Response time standards, including a "forty-eight-hour pothole guarantee" (largely met, except after severe winter storms), were established for many kinds of service requests and tracked to determine overdue responses. Other significant timeliness and backlog reduction improvements reported have been in animal control, repair debris removal, cleaning clogged storm drains, food establishment inspection, design and construction of city projects, and street light repairs.[12] A key part of Baltimore's strategy to improve customer responsiveness was creation of a 3–1–1 call center for all non-public-safety-emergency service requests, which opened March 28, 2002.[13] Significant public health and safety outcomes have also been achieved, including steady reductions in violent crime[14] and in the number of cases of syphilis.[15]

Figure 3.2 depicts a managing-for-results cycle as driven by CitiStat, featuring high-frequency review and accountability, and geographic, strategic responses.

Frequent Review of Mapped Results Can Clarify Where Strategic Partnerships Are Needed. CitiStat has also stimulated improved cooperation to solve problems that cross city agency lines or require efforts by the city government and other entities, as noted by the references to strategic partnerships and collaborative responses in Figure 3.2. For example, the street light repair improvements came in cooperation with a private utility. When long-standing problems are exposed on maps and charts in CitiStat meetings, it quickly becomes clear when the reporting agency cannot solve the problem alone. In response, interagency (and sometimes intergovernmental) efforts have been initiated to focus on, for example, arson, lead poisoning ("LeadStat"), drug abuse ("DrugStat"), and coordination of inspection and enforcement functions.[16] Some of these collaborative efforts have led to impressive improvements in public outcomes. For example, in January 2003, Mayor O'Malley reported that Baltimore had the largest two-year drop in drug-related hospital emergency department visits in the nation (18 percent decrease overall, 36 percent for heroin cases).[17] In June 2003, the mayor reported that his initiative on lead poisoning prevention led to 675 homes being made lead safe through a combination of

FIGURE 3.2. A MANAGING FOR RESULTS CYCLE BASED ON HIGH-FREQUENCY REVIEW AND GEOGRAPHIC AND STRATEGIC RESPONSE

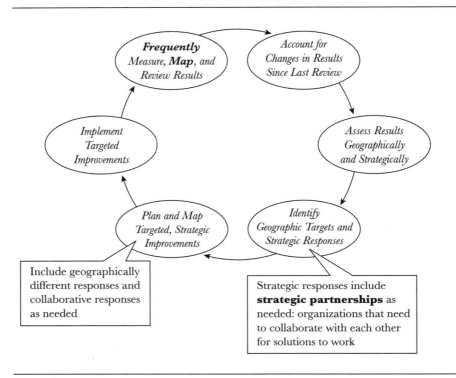

grants for repairs and the first legal actions taken against property owners in a decade. Perhaps most impressive, child testing revealed a 50 percent reduction in children ages up to age three with lead poisoning from 1999 to 2002.[18]

Managing for Results by Design: Citizen Schools, Boston

CitiStat is part of Mayor O'Malley's design to achieve responsive improvements and better results for the many different services provided by the City of Baltimore. In San Jose, minimizing the number of clogged sewers is a small part of a big design by the city government to align the measured performance of operational services, in several strategic stages, with the mayor and city council's vision for the desired quality of life, part of a system San Jose calls "Investing in Results."[19] Public and nonprofit organizations with a narrower focus than a multipurpose local government can also develop specific designs to achieve their desired outcomes.

In Boston, Citizen Schools, a nonprofit organization, has designed ways to help children in fourth through eighth grades achieve results by making effective use of their out-of-school time. These middle school years have been seen as problematic in the United States as a whole (for example, student math and science performance, relative to other countries, has been dramatically lower for U.S. eighth graders than for fourth graders)[20] and Boston in particular, and most traditional after-school programs have not engaged this age group. By the late 1990s, only 10 percent of after-school participants in the United States were age ten or older, yet about half of middle school-age children were "latchkey kids."[21] To Citizen Schools, that represented a huge untapped potential in an era when working parents have little time to be involved with children at home and school.

Design Programs for Results Based on Assumptions on How to Achieve Desired Outcomes. The Citizen Schools program design grew from a prototype experience in a school in Boston's Dorchester community in the summer of 1994. Eric Schwarz, a Boston-area reporter, and Ned Rimer, a former emergency medical squad leader, conducted apprenticeships in journalism and first aid for twenty fifth graders and were excited by how much the children loved it and how much they seemed to learn. In 1995, Schwarz and Rimer cofounded Citizen Schools, using apprenticeships of small groups of students as the core of their design. Their desired outcomes were for middle school children to make progress in developing new basic skills to succeed in the twenty-first-century economy, including data analysis, writing, oral communication, use of technology, and teamwork.[22]

Their program design was based on several underlying assumptions in how those outcomes can be attained. Perhaps the most basic assumption is similar to that of any other after-school enrichment program: regular school classes are not the only opportunity for children to learn; one can take advantage of some of the 80 percent of children's waking hours not spent in school to achieve skill building and youth development results. Citizen Schools' underlying belief that, like adults, middle school and older students learn better by doing things than by being told about them, led to other design assumptions represented by a learning triangle concerning how well children of this age retain knowledge based on different types of learning, as depicted in Figure 3.3.[23] (The Citizen Schools learning triangle remarkably parallels the Jacksonville Community Council slogan about adult citizen volunteers at the start of Chapter Two.) Following these assumptions, Eric Schwarz says Citizen Schools provides "cognitive apprenticeships. It's all about learning through producing."

Citizen Schools apprenticeships are specifically designed to attract and engage older children by giving them the chance to work with talented professionals and produce high-quality products and performances that address real community needs. The professionals are volunteers, serving as "citizen teachers" (and, more generally, as co-producers of community services). Schwarz says the "Citizen Teacher's role is not quite

FIGURE 3.3. CITIZEN SCHOOLS LEARNING TRIANGLE

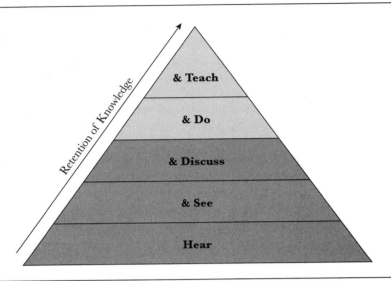

Source: Citizen Schools.

mentoring and not quite tutoring," but developing the skills of student apprentices through four key phases by playing four different roles. Schwarz explains that the Citizen Teacher "first models the skills as an expert, then provides scaffolding for the apprentices, then provides coaching, and finally fades into the background," essentially taking apprentices up the learning triangle until they can practice their new skills by doing them without help. Apprentices' team projects are designed to build all the skills involved in the desired outcomes. To build students' pride in their accomplishments and help ensure students retain the skills and knowledge they gain, each apprenticeship culminates in what Citizen Schools calls a "WOW" presentation,[24] which takes students to the top of the learning triangle ("teach"). The Citizen School design also involves other assumptions about what students need to succeed, including time and support for homework, access to community resources and technology (which Citizen Teachers, apprenticeship projects, and other activities provide), and good support networks, which Citizen Schools strengthen through communication with teachers and parents.

A Managing for Results Cycle to Improve Both Delivery and Design. Citizen Schools not only designs for results; it measures results. Schwarz says, "We're very committed to measuring results. For two reasons: to be a learning organization—get better at what we do, and to prove to policymakers and funders that our approach works." When a program such as Citizen Schools has an explicit design based on assumptions about how to achieve outcomes, measured results can be fed back to provide two kinds of opportunities for improvement: to improve program delivery and to improve program design, shown in Figure 3.4 as a dual cycle of managing for results. Generally the more frequently used feedback loop will be to assess results to learn where operational adjustments are needed to improve program delivery (for example, for students of a particular school, spend more time on homework or on writing skills or advise a Citizen Teacher how to get more students to take initiative in their work sessions). But it can also be extremely valuable, from time to time, to ask some hard questions about what results are saying about the program design. For example, if some expected results are not achieved, are the underlying assumptions incorrect, or are parts of the program design not robust enough to act on those assumptions?

Citizen Schools did not achieve its current design all at once, but has regularly enhanced it over the years to improve performance. For example, it learned that training and support for Citizen Teachers was important to improve the likelihood of learning and progress by student apprentices. Over the years, they went from having

FIGURE 3.4. MANAGING PROGRAM RESULTS BY DESIGN: DUAL CYCLE

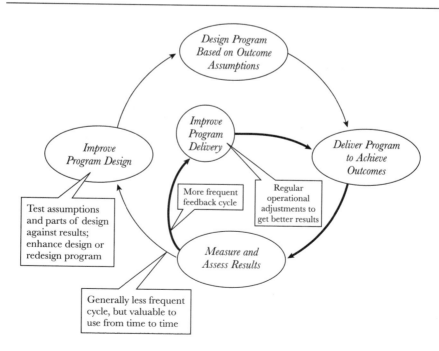

only limited preparation requirements and support for Citizen Teachers, to providing them with two preparatory training sessions and materials on good practices, and holding Citizen Teachers to high standards for being prepared to work with students, including the use of lesson plans. Citizen Schools staff also now regularly provides feedback and support to Citizen Teachers between sessions with students, reviewing how the last session went and making suggestions for improvement. This last design enhancement has the effect of strengthening the inner performance feedback loop in Figure 3.4, as the feedback to Citizen Teachers serves to keep improving the learning experience for students throughout their apprenticeships.

Citizen Schools' outcomes have been measured by improvements in student writing and data analysis (for each of these two skill sets, over two-thirds of students did significantly better in pre- and postassessments in the 2001–2002 school year), parent and teacher satisfaction (over 90 percent of each group rated the program "good to excellent" in 2002), and student perceptions of their improvement (in 2002, 69 percent felt more comfortable speaking in front of groups, 77 percent felt more confident about schoolwork, 72 percent said they were more likely to finish their homework, and 74 percent said they got along better with other students).[25] The Edna McConnell Clark Foundation was impressed enough in Citizen Schools' design to invest in building its capacity to scale up the use of the model across the country. By 2002–2003, Citizen Schools had grown to serving 1,340 children at twelve Boston campuses and at affiliate campuses in other cities across Massachusetts, in New Brunswick, New Jersey; Houston, Texas; Tucson, Arizona; and farther west—all the way to San Jose, California.

Investing in Results

Often one of the strongest representations of a public or nonprofit organization's policies is seen in how the organization spends money, whether or not decision makers consciously relate spending decisions to policy. Governments, foundations, and service providers that want their spending decisions not only to reflect policies, but to reflect successful policies that achieve results, have become more strategic in deciding what to fund and in considering the performance of services they support in their budgeting, grant making, or other resource allocation decisions. A shift from simply distributing money based on policy, to strategically targeting resources to achieve results, reflects a shift in mind-set from that of a "funder" to that of an "investor."[26] When a funding organization becomes a true "investor" in results, it does not simply make stock market-like bets in successful organizations, expecting their success to grow. As in the examples here, performance-informed investment can be more complex. When some results are lagging, a service provider may be underresourced and need an investment in more service capacity. Other useful capacity-building investments can be made in improving the productivity of service providers[27] or, as the Edna McConnell Clark Foundation does, improving the level of performance evaluation.

Measurement and Evaluation as a Key Focus of Investment: Edna McConnell Clark Foundation

The Edna McConnell Clark Foundation (EMCF) takes a performance-based approach to youth development by seeking out and investing in high-performing organizations that are focused on achieving specific results for young people in any of four types of outcomes: (1) improved educational skills, achievement, and attainment; (2) preparation for the world of work and successful transition to employment and self-sustainability; (3) rewarding civic engagement; and (4) avoiding high-risk behavior. EMCF makes large grants to help these organizations build their organizational capacity so they can grow stronger and better able to help young people develop the skills they need to make a successful transition to independent adulthood. Often this includes building their capacity to serve more youth either locally, or, as with Citizen Schools, expanding to serve more communities. The strength of the information an organization can provide to assess its effectiveness at achieving youth outcomes plays into EMCF's funding decision. Then, improving effectiveness evaluation is an important element in building a funded organization's capacity.

Considering Performance Measurement Practices in Selecting Grantees Helps a Funder Manage Investment Risk. After EMCF identifies an organization for potential investment, a foundation staff team conducts an extensive due diligence assessment covering six areas: compelling product, leadership and management, financial health, operational viability, performance tracking and outcome measurement, and finally a sense of the fit between the potential grantee and the foundation.[28] Due diligence assessments often take as much as two hundred staff-hours in site visits.

In considering "compelling product," foundation staff look for evidence that an organization's programs and services are effective in that they are likely to produce youth outcomes as intended. In doing this part of the assessment, staff rely on a tool the evaluation unit designed that identifies a hierarchy of three levels of knowledge about program effectiveness at which staff will consider funding a program:

- *Apparent effectiveness:* Through the more or less systematic collection of various kinds of information about program participants and youth outcomes—ranging from impressionistic and anecdotal to highly systematic—the assumption that one can reach an initial assessment of a program's likely effectiveness is deemed justifiable.
- *Demonstrated effectiveness:* Through participant outcome tracking and use of comparisons (such as comparison groups and population benchmarks), likely program

effects on service recipients have been identified, but with no way to calculate how much the program contributed to outcomes.

- *Proven quality (or impact):* Through the use of a random assignment experimental research design, the impact of a program on service recipients has been verified in a statistically significant manner.[29]

Each of these levels of rigor is further defined to have low-end and high-end levels within it, ranging from less to more systematic and from less to more rigorous. For example, the high end of apparent effectiveness includes collection of preprogram and postprogram participant outcome data, but without using external comparisons to the program participants. External comparisons used at the low end of demonstrated effectiveness can be based, for example, on general population benchmarks. For the high end of demonstrated effectiveness, a rigorously matched comparison group must be used. For proven effectiveness in achieving impacts, an experimental research design is needed, with a control group and some form of random assignment. The difference in outcomes between program participants and control group members needs to be confirmed statistically at a 90 percent degree of certainty at the low end and 95 percent degree of certainty at the high end.[30]

Before deciding to support an organization, EMCF determines where it ranks in this hierarchy and whether it meets the foundation's investment criteria. For instance, for an organization that serves youth in a single community to be considered for investment it must, at a minimum, collect performance information systematically enough for EMCF to rate it near the high end of apparent effectiveness. However, EMCF sets the bar higher for national organizations, such as Boys and Girls Club of America and Big Brothers Big Sisters of America. According to David Hunter, EMCF director of evaluation and knowledge development, the foundation "will only invest in a national youth serving organization if it is at least at the 'demonstrated effectiveness' level because the stakes are higher, as national organizations work with their local chapters or affiliates to implement programs and serve many thousands of young people across the country." Using this approach, EMCF essentially considers the existing performance measurement practices of an organization as an important element in deciding if it is a good investment risk.

When EMCF considered funding the local Big Sister Association of Greater Boston (BSAGB), it helped that BSGAB was already using a systematic balanced scorecard approach to measure performance and manage for results. BSAGB executive director Jerry Martinson said the balanced scorecard helps "us articulate what we're trying to accomplish, what we expect we can measure. If we can't measure it, it is not an outcome."

Business Plans Based on a "Theory of Change" to Achieve Outcomes. When an organization has passed through EMCF's due diligence assessment, the foundation will work with it to develop a business plan. As part of business planning, the foundation will make an unrestricted grant—usually for $250,000—to help the organization defray some of the expenses in dedicating staff to this effort. A starting point for business planning is for the grantee to articulate, with the help of EMCF evaluation staff, a *theory of change* behind the programs to be funded. As in designing a program for results, a theory of change requires understanding the assumptions behind how the program is intended to achieve desired outcomes.

To EMCF, a theory of change must fully identify all the steps needed to get to an outcome, and the outcomes sought must be measurable. According to Hunter, in doing theory-of-change work, foundation staff engage the organization in a rigorous discussion that "starts by clarifying the groups of young people the organization wants to serve and the outcomes it expects them to achieve, then works backwards to identify all the program elements and services that, in the organization's view, it takes to get to those outcomes." The theory of change describes how the organization's programs, resources, and efforts are intended to lead to expected outcomes.[31] "Business planning essentially involves designing the means through which the theory of change will be delivered to program participants, and in this way makes the theory of change real," according to Hunter, "by detailing what hard decisions have to be made, what the organization must accomplish—with specific milestones, what the resource costs will be to achieve its outcomes, and what the organization's likely revenue streams will be."

Jerry Martinson of Big Sister Association of Greater Boston appreciated EMCF's "helping with our whole theory of change," which, she said, is based on the assumption that "a caring adult in the life of a girl at risk can make a significant difference." A measurable business plan based on a theory of change meshed with BSAGB's existing measurement approach. Martinson said, "Clark's emphasis on the theory of change helped reinforce our use of the balanced scorecard in setting goals that were measurable."

Using Business Plans to Manage for Results.

EMCF's capacity-building grants run for several years and are structured against the grantees' business plans. They are also conditional, with funds paid annually based on grantee performance. Each business plan has a series of annual milestones to be accomplished to keep the organization on track for success. The milestones can include financial targets, management capacity objectives, and steps in infrastructure development. Annual reviews include identifying milestones reached or missed and, in the case of the latter, how the organization plans to adjust activities to hit its targets in the future or revise them in the light of the year's experiences or changed circumstances. Before renewing its investments for another year, EMCF will review these adjustments and business plan revisions to be sure the organizations it is funding are still managing toward a realistic plan for producing desired outcomes for youth.

Building Evaluation Capacity as a Key Part of a Managing for Results Cycle.
EMCF considers grantees' internal evaluation capability to be critical to their ability
to monitor and manage program quality and assure program effectiveness. Thus, every
business plan includes development and implementation of a rigorous, ongoing internal evaluation system as part of the expected cost of doing business. EMCF goes
well beyond more typical funders' requirements that a grantee have an evaluation plan
to evaluate the effect of a program for the grant period. Instead, EMCF's intent, according to Hunter, is to "help grantees build evaluation into the fabric of their operations, so they're always measuring and assessing outcomes and other performance
metrics, and learning from the data to improve their results."

Figure 3.5 shows the resulting managing for results cycle in which EMCF builds
both program and evaluation capacity. There are really several cycles in one, including two performance feedback loops. The outer feedback loop, in the upper left of Figure 3.5, gives EMCF and the grantee measured results to compare with performance
milestones in the business plan to help make decisions about funding levels and revisions in milestones for the next year. The inner feedback loop gives the grantee performance information throughout the year for more frequent program adjustments to
improve results. Because EMCF keeps investing in improving evaluation capacity, the

FIGURE 3.5. EMCF INVESTING IN RESULTS CYCLE: BUILDING BOTH PROGRAM AND EVALUATION CAPACITY

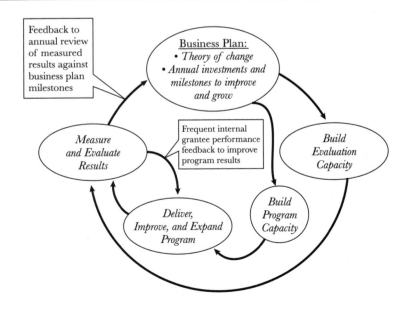

quality of performance information available to both the foundation and the grantee improves each year.

How an organization builds its evaluation capacity depends on its capability when it becomes an EMCF grantee. If a grantee starts out only tracking performance on paper, for example, its business plan will include a strategy to implement electronic data management, including both systems and staff development costs. A grantee may start out meeting EMCF's minimum requirement of measuring what happens to the young people it serves, but it may need to build a better system to track the basic demographics (for example, age, gender, family background, socioeconomic status) of those it is serving so they know whether they are reaching the groups they are targeting. The evaluation system is typically built in successive stages. Next may come measuring participation patterns (the number who attend program activities) of targeted groups to determine whether participation is adequate, given the grantee's theory of change, for enough targeted youth to achieve their outcome objectives. A later stage may involve improving how the grantee defines and captures outcome data.

Investing in Improving the Rigor of Measured Results. Once grantees have well-functioning evaluation systems, EMCF does not expect them to keep their measurement approaches static through the rest of the life of their business plans. For example, the apparent effectiveness evaluation level is only a minimum standard for possible funding. That is not where the foundation expects grantees to remain. According to Hunter, EMCF's local grantees "all intend to use their grant support, among other things, to move to the level of demonstrated effectiveness over time."

EMCF also helps grantees expand evaluation to new programs and outcomes that have been unmeasured for existing programs. For example, Jerry Martinson explained that Big Sister Association of Greater Boston defines outcomes for girls they serve under categories of "confidence, competence, and caring" and uses survey instruments tested by the Big Brothers Big Sisters of America to help measure them. But EMCF has helped her Greater Boston organization go further. Martinson said, "They helped us go beyond instinct and anecdote on some of our newer mentoring programs. Clark put us in touch with local people who are good at designing measurement tools." EMCF also helped Citizen Schools go beyond its perception surveys of customers and stakeholders. According to Citizen Schools president Eric Schwarz, "They helped us develop rubrics to determine improvements kids are making in leadership, writing, and data analysis."

EMCF also encourages grantees with programs at the demonstrated level to determine when it might be appropriate to invest in an impact study that uses an experimental research design[32] to prove their program's effectiveness. Starting in 2001, with EMCF funding, Citizen Schools embarked on a longitudinal evaluation, using an external evaluation firm, to follow students for at least four years, including at least two beyond the time in their program. They are being compared with demographically matched control groups. Schwarz says Citizen Schools will find out "how well we're really doing at kids staying in school, getting into better high schools, getting onto a college track and staying on track." Schwarz added that EMCF helped Citizen Schools "understand the difference between shorter-term and longer-term outcomes and appreciate the value of external evaluation." As EMCF grantees increase the level of evaluation rigor, the foundation can become more confident that it will know how much of a difference its investments are making in helping youth develop and succeed.

Long-Term Strategic Investing in Results

A challenge for funders of community services, whether governments or foundations, is ensuring that investments make a difference for the long term. For a foundation, that can mean seeing its grants yield increasing measurable outcomes over time. For a local government, that can mean both improving service results and being able to afford to produce results most needed by the community for many years. To meet this challenge, funders must be strategic about their investments, which can sometimes mean not investing in even good programs if they do not meet a determined need or strategic focus or if funding cannot be sustained for the long term. It can also mean making hard decisions about whether a service that is not producing needed results should have its funding reduced or eliminated or should get extra investment in hopes of catching up with the need. The following examples explore these challenges.

Narrowly Focusing Investment to Make a Difference. The Edna McConnell Clark Foundation's results-based grant management approach is relatively new. While committed to helping low-income people and communities for over thirty years, until well into the 1990s the foundation did so by spreading its investments across a wide range of social issues and grantees. Soon after he became president of EMCF in 1996, Michael Bailin concluded that the foundation's reach had exceeded its grasp, and it was time to try another approach. As Bailin recalled, "The problem, in a nutshell, was this: In all of those programs . . . we were trying to reform huge, complex, entrenched, multi-billion dollar public systems with a staff of 25 people and around $25 million a year in grants. . . . We were proceeding as if we had some independent leverage over social systems that had been many decades in the making. . . . How could we ever imagine that we could accomplish anything so significant in our lifetimes? And how would we even know if we did?"[33]

Bailin led EMCF through several years of introspection and experimentation, culminating in the foundation's trustees' voting in May 2000 to change EMCF's approach to grant making. The foundation decided to focus approximately $25 to $30 million in annual grants in one field: youth development. Rather than design programs and complex initiatives around intended youth outcomes and then make grants to organizations to execute them, EMCF decided to stake its success on finding, selecting, and strengthening high-performing youth development organizations already addressing desired outcomes. EMCF's grants would help these organizations build their organizational capacity so they could grow stronger and better able to help young people develop the skills they need to make a successful transition to independent adulthood. Among other things, this meant drastically reducing the number of grants made each year from some two hundred to thirty or so, significantly increasing the size of each grant, and, usually, staying with each grantee for a period of years.

To achieve these long-term goals, EMCF reorganized its operations. Foundation vice president Nancy Roob, who had been leading experimentation with new methods (and who would succeed Bailin as president in 2005), took responsibility for getting the new approach up and running. Today, the foundation grant-making approach comprises the comprehensive, multistage process described earlier in this chapter, with a strong emphasis on building organizations and programs according to business plans and measuring and evaluating results over time.

By narrowing its focus to a single field and making fewer but larger grants to organizations it helps develop and become more sustainable over time, EMCF is trying to be more strategic with its investments to make it more likely they will yield measurable results for years to come. However, despite the foundation's transformation to a new way of working, no one at EMCF is willing to say yet whether this new approach to grant making will succeed. Only time will tell if the foundation's approach will lead to improved life prospects for young people from low-income backgrounds. However, as foundation officials also note, over time the results of this new approach to grant making will be measurable and clear—and the foundation will share what it learns publicly on an ongoing basis. In this way, the foundation will hold itself accountable to its trustees, its grantees, and to the field of youth development.

Budgeting for Strategic Results. General-purpose local governments are often mandated to provide a wide range of public services, so they cannot focus their investments as narrowly as the Clark Foundation does. Instead of narrowing funding to one or two fields, the challenge for multipurpose governments is to determine how to make shifts in allocating available funds from year to year to keep pace with strategic trends in the community (for example, regional economic trends, population changes, aging infrastructure) and achieve outcomes people feel are important, while still meeting basic community needs with quality services. This is really two challenges: knowing what is strategic to the community and budgeting for results.[34] Prince William County, Virginia, meets these challenges by using both a multiyear strategic plan and measured results of service performance as key drivers of its annual budget process. Chapter Seven describes how citizens are engaged in major updates of the strategic plan every four years before it is approved by a newly elected board of county supervisors, giving the plan a high degree of credibility as a source for what is most important or strategic to emphasize in funding from year to year. Prince William County has used its strategic plans to make multimillion-dollar budget shifts to increase investment in the county's priority goals.[35] These investment choices, as well as an overall emphasis on performance measurement and improvement, have helped the county earn consistently high ratings in citizen satisfaction surveys.[36]

County executive Craig Gerhart has used the chart in Figure 3.6 to describe the county's approach to considering both strategic priorities and performance results in making budget decisions. According to Gerhart, while it is not a universal rule of county budgeting, programs with low strategic importance and poor performance results become targets for budget cuts, while programs with high strategic importance and poor performance results become targets for increased funding. In one 1990s example, the county police's clearance rates (percentage of crimes resolved or cases closed) were reported low compared with other local governments Prince William uses to benchmark its performance. That represented a measure of low performance related to a high-priority goal in the county strategic plan of improving public safety. Other comparative measures revealed that the Prince William County Police appeared underresourced compared with the benchmark jurisdictions, with Prince William having fewer officers per capita. A police department staffing plan was approved that increased the number of officers in order to improve results, as measured by increased clearance rates.[37]

FIGURE 3.6. USE OF STRATEGIC GOALS AND PERFORMANCE RESULTS IN PRINCE WILLIAM COUNTY BUDGET DECISIONS

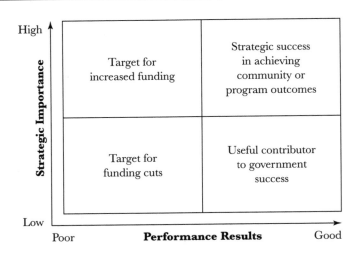

Budgeting for Performance and Long-Term Fiscal Impact. Across the country from Prince William County, and just northwest of San Jose, is the City of Sunnyvale, California, which has over twenty years' experience using performance measures in its city budget process to influence resource allocation decisions. Sunnyvale has achieved impressive results, broadly realized as high levels of citizen satisfaction with public services, as measured by sample population surveys, and increased government efficiency, as measured by reduced unit costs of services.[38] These results are achieved not only through the budget, but because performance-influenced budgeting is one part of an integrated managing-for-results process described later in this chapter.

As an example of using results data in budgeting, a Sunnyvale City Council member described citing long-term reductions in crime rates to resist calls for adding police officers, despite population growth. In other cases, Sunnyvale has used unit cost and demand data to determine whether a program's inability to meet customer demand is a result of inefficiency or of being underresourced. Where low unit costs indicated high efficiency but demand was higher than expected, funding was increased.[39]

In addition to using performance measures in budgeting, Sunnyvale relates its budget decisions to long-range plans. It examines how proposed new or expanded services will affect municipal finances over a twenty-year period as part of the city's long-range financial plan. The city council does not just consider whether the city government can afford the service in the coming fiscal year but what the long-term fiscal impact will be. It may cause the council to scale back a proposed service expansion, look for other programs to reduce, or new future revenue sources, to ensure their desired service increase will be fiscally sustainable. As a recent council member described it, "Make certain assumptions and plug them into the spreadsheet and you can identify a problem really quick. Revenue and expense lines go upside down. It allows you to do something today rather than wait until year nine or fifteen and say, 'Oops! We have a major problem on our hands right now!' Not only measuring things well, but also taking a long-term view."[40] This fiscal discipline has helped Sunnyvale avoid some of the fiscal volatility experienced by other California local governments, which have tended to add services in fat years only to suffer severe cutbacks in lean years,[41] and it has also influenced Sunnyvale's long-term emphasis on efficiency improvement as a way to improve services. So when services have been expanded to serve a growing population, they have often expanded at reduced unit costs, keeping the overall cost of city government affordable to Sunnyvale citizens.

Integrated Enterprisewide Results Management Systems

When Baltimore's Mayor O'Malley took an approach pioneered in New York's Police Department and applied it to all major services as Baltimore's CitiStat, he made it an enterprisewide managing-for-results tool. Some governments and more complex nonprofit institutions have taken a systems approach to enterprisewide management by integrating long-range and short-range planning and decision processes, including budgeting, that affect all programs and services—at least all that are locally funded. These become enterprisewide managing-for-results systems when performance measurement and reporting is used as a key informational and accountability tool tying these processes together.[42] Sunnyvale's integrated system is described here. Integrated systems that include extensive citizen engagement are described in Chapter Seven (Prince William County) and Chapter Eight (nonprofit community development in Greater Kansas City).

The results-based budgeting approach of the City of Sunnyvale, California, was described above as being influenced by longer-range financial planning. Sunnyvale's success has depended not only on its planning and budgeting processes, but on how the city government has linked these and other processes in an enterprisewide, integrated system of managing for results, which Sunnyvale calls its Planning and Management System (PAMS). Like all true managing for results processes, PAMS is cyclical in nature. As illustrated in Figure 3.7, Sunnyvale's long-range financial plan and its state-mandated general plan influence shorter-range budgeting and performance planning. Performance targets included in the budget and service plans influence service delivery and figure prominently in managers' performance plans. As Figure 3.7 also shows, multiple results management cycles are completed when measured results are fed back to inform (1) how managers improve service delivery on a day-to-day basis; (2) future short-term action planning including budgeting, and evaluation

FIGURE 3.7. MANAGING FOR RESULTS CYCLES OF SUNNYVALE'S PLANNING AND MANAGEMENT SYSTEM

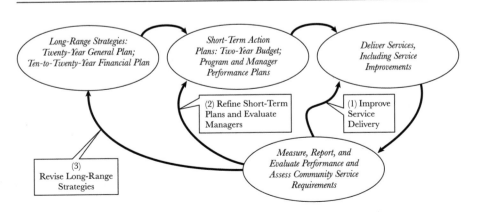

of managers against their performance plans; and (3) revisions of long-range goals and strategies.

As noted in the lower right of Figure 3.7, the service requirements of the community (for example, based on how the population and its needs change, the infrastructure ages, parts of the community are developed or redeveloped) are also fed back and considered in making long-range strategic plans and short-range action plans. Also, not only are services delivered to the community, but performance is reported back to the community as an additional level of accountability.[43]

While it is easy to draw conceptual pictures of systems like Sunnyvale's PAMS, the hard part is getting people in the organization to understand the system and use it. Sunnyvale has succeeded at that. The systemic connections in PAMS are apparent to city managers, as one remarked: "It is a very integrated system. Looking at it, you can see that the performance management piece ties very much into the budgeting piece, ties very much into the reporting and accountability pieces."[44]

The ties the manager was referring to represent the strong alignment of the parts of the integrated managing for results system. To help achieve alignment, Sunnyvale does not structure its budget by department, but by the twenty-six elements and subelements of its twenty-year general plan. California requires local governments to have general plans, mainly for land use purposes. However, Sunnyvale broadened the concept of a general plan to serve as a broader long-term strategic plan to drive service performance as well as land use policy. The seven main elements of Sunnyvale's General Plan are Land Use and Transportation, Community Development, Environmental Management, Public Safety, Socio-Economic, Cultural, and Planning and Management. Performance measures are developed for programs and service delivery plans within the elements and subelements, and targeted based on amounts budgeted. The measures used for program performance evaluation can then be tracked back to priorities in the general plan. All Sunnyvale managerial employees are on performance-based pay plans: their individual performance evaluations and pay levels are based in part on measured performance versus budget and service plan targets for the programs and services they manage, taking alignment down to a level of personal responsibility and accountability.[45]

On a personal level, alignment helps people working throughout the enterprise understand their contribution to the system. For elected officials and executive management, strong alignment means understanding the implications that broad community outcome goals have for narrower service accomplishments agency programs must achieve, so they can set service-level targets and budget for them appropriately. For line employees, alignment means understanding how their day-to-day work not only produces service outputs (say, miles of sewers cleaned) but also contributes to high-level priority community goals (say, an environmentally safe, healthy community).

Learning and Improving How to Manage for Results over Time

An important lesson from organizations that succeed at managing for results over many years is that they tend to change how they do it over time. Often the changes are minor adjustments that may go unnoticed to people outside the organization, but that keep performance measurement and improvement approaches relevant to managers and employees. But successful organizations do not shrink from making dramatic changes when needed, as when the Edna McConnell Clark Foundation adopted a new investment focus and new approach to grant making.

Governments That Have Changed Successful Results Management Systems

The city of Charlotte, North Carolina began using performance measurement to manage for results in 1971, using performance feedback as part of a Management by Objectives system that tied measurable performance objectives to the budget process. The city government made gradual, evolutionary changes to its performance management approach over the years, such as adding performance auditing and contract evaluation, to ensure measurement leads to improvement.[46] In the 1990s, Charlotte was not afraid to make a major systemic change when it became the first general-purpose government to adopt the balanced scorecard approach to performance management on an enterprisewide basis (see Chapter Nine).

The city of Sunnyvale has systematically used performance measures to manage for results for over twenty years, strongly integrated and aligned through the Planning and Management System (PAMS) since the early 1980s. Starting in 1996, following recommendations of the interdepartmental Committee on the Future of the Organization, the city began phasing in a major shift in its program structure and performance measures to outcomes, with an outcome management approach integrated into PAMS, especially in performance budgeting and management appraisal. The new approach emphasizes fewer, more results-based performance measures.

Recently, as an extension of its new outcome focus, Sunnyvale added another level of performance measurement and reporting to its system: the Quality of Life Index, developed based on the work of two city council–appointed citizen task forces and a citizen participation process. The Quality of Life Index, intended to be more citizen friendly than Sunnyvale's detailed service plan and budget-related measures, covers a limited number of measures for eight strategic priorities similar to the seven main elements of the general plan, but formulated more to address priority citizen concerns directly. Each strategic priority has associated performance measures, some of which are existing measures in the program budget (an example is "community perception of safety") and some new measures (for example, "percent of houses and apartments that are affordable for households with median income"). By design, some goals and measures go beyond municipal services, reflecting citizen concerns that go beyond what the city government directly provides. For example, while a separate school district provides public education, "education" is one of the city's eight strategic priorities.[47] The Quality of Life Index will provide a new alignment challenge to Sunnyvale. The real challenge may not be for the city government to internally align this new measurement tool with its exquisitely aligned PAMS results-based management system, but to get other organizations, such as the school district and private housing developers, to collaborate in aligning their performance goals with the priorities in the Quality of Life Index. Sunnyvale completed its second Quality of Life Index Report in late 2003.[48]

Learning, Changing, and Improving as an Organizational Value

The city of Phoenix, Arizona, was a leader in performance measurement and improvement in the early 1970s, with its aggressive use of industrial engineering approaches, including stopwatch analysis and employee work standards; labor-saving mechanization, such as single-staff trash collection trucks; detailed program and policy analyses; and its own version of a planning, program budgeting system. While the city documented tens of millions of dollars in savings from these approaches (by the 1980s, cumulative trash collection savings alone was over $25 million), it has not hesitated to try new approaches to performance management, and change or drop older ones that no longer seemed worth the investment needed to keep them going. A second wave of improvement approaches began in 1977, with a shift from industrial engineering to organization development approaches (for example, quality control circles and surveying and improving employee satisfaction), managerial performance-based pay, and less complex performance reporting. In 1979, Phoenix started a public-private competitive proposal process to reduce costs of selected services. By the 1980s, articles were being written emphasizing "evolution and change" as Phoenix's performance management theme.[49]

Through the 1980s, Phoenix kept adding and adjusting measurement and improvement approaches, especially emphasizing quality customer service and citizen satisfaction, and it has conducted community attitude surveys every two years since 1985. Into the 1990s, Phoenix kept reinvigorating its results management approaches, including, among other initiatives, a citywide strategic planning process, efforts in 1991 and again in the late 1990s to involve citizens in developing measures of results that were more relevant to citizen concerns and priorities, and a "seamless service" mission. Also, every two years the city auditor department has surveyed all city departments to assess their continued focus on results and provided the city manager with a comprehensive inventory of the organization's use of results data. It is not surprising, then, that when Phoenix managers and employees developed a "Vision and

Values" statement in 1995, one of the core values was—and still is—"We learn, change, and improve."[50]

Phoenix did not invent most of the performance management approaches it has used over the years. Through several administrations, the city established a pattern of finding best practices in other organizations and adapting them to work in Phoenix, showing a remarkable openness to ideas from outside the organization. The current city manager, Frank Fairbanks, has said, "We'll steal a practice from anyone if it will help us improve."

Perhaps the most extraordinary thing about Phoenix's history of frequently trying new performance management approaches is that the city seems to have avoided falling victim to the "fad of the month" syndrome, in which staff get jaded and show no enthusiasm for new approaches because they do not think they will last. That is probably because despite all the changes through the years, many results management approaches have lasted quite a while, at least in part. Phoenix has had a knack for keeping and improving those parts of older approaches that continue to add value—such as public-private competition, started in 1979, and the quality customer service emphasis, started in the 1980s, both still in use—while it keeps adapting new results management approaches for use by the organization.

Always Learning to Get Better Results, But What Makes Them Results That Matter?

Learning over many years by large organizations such as the city governments of Phoenix and Sunnyvale is impressive. But at any time scale—years, or just weeks at a time using high-frequency feedback—managing for results is about learning to get better results. Whether focusing on a single program or a large enterprise that manages many services, each step along the way of any managing-for-results cycle should be part of a learning process. As in the more complex cycles in this chapter, the learning is most effective when it takes place on several levels, including learning to:

- Improve results of current services, whether by targeting services better, tinkering with existing work practices, or significantly redesigning a program
- Determine what programs to invest in, how much to invest in each, and what performance and improvement targets should be met as a result of that investment, as with the Edna McConnell Clark Foundation, Prince William County, and Sunnyvale
- Find better ways to articulate and measure results, for example, change the emphasis from outputs such as miles of sewers cleaned to outcomes such as percentage of sewers clear and not clogged
- Improve how to manage for results over time, as Charlotte, Sunnyvale, and Phoenix have

If learning through performance feedback is incorporated into regular management practice, organizations not only become better at improving results, they become better at holding themselves accountable for community outcomes. If they are always learning to better articulate, measure, and understand results, they will also better understand the broader community environment in which they perform and become better at adjusting to changes in that environment.

Of course, managing for results, while important, is not everything. The key ingredient missing from most of this chapter is regular, sustained citizen engagement. If citizen engagement is added in ways that influence goals and decisions, managing for results becomes much more powerful and relevant to achieving the outcomes the community deems important, so the results achieved are results that matter. Chapters Six to Eight focus on communities where citizen engagement comes together with systematic results-based management, transforming managing for results to *governing for results*. But first, it should be useful to explore Chapters Four and Five, with examples of citizens getting directly involved in the measurement process itself, whether by helping to determine what should be measured in a community, collecting the data, or using the information to try to influence community decisions and actions.

CHAPTER FOUR

CITIZENS REACHING FOR RESULTS I

Key Ideas, Strategic Issues, and the First Three Case Examples

Even though the items we identify are small, the little things that are improved are improving the appearance of the whole community. I feel good about being involved.

PRISCILLA, HARTFORD, CONNECTICUT

Priscilla spoke as a fifteen-year-old high school student who had been walking the streets of a Hartford neighborhood with a team of her classmates, identifying many kinds of visible problems, from broken sidewalks and streetlights to graffiti on walls and entering the data into handheld computers for transmittal to responsible government agencies. She was one of many citizens reaching for results as part of digital neighborhood survey projects that have emerged around the country. Whether the conditions they identify are dangerous, requiring urgent action, or merely unpleasant or unsightly, they detract from the livability of a neighborhood. Getting them fixed can go a long way to increasing citizens' sense of well-being in their community.

This chapter and the next focus on *citizens reaching for results,* advanced practice 3 of the Effective Community Governance Model, in which engaging citizens and measuring results are aligned, as suggested in the graphic below. In reaching for results, citizens may focus on specific neighborhoods, as Priscilla was, or on whole cities and regions, as they do in other examples in this chapter and the next. And they may focus on different kinds of conditions from one community to another. What citizens who reach for results have in common is an effort to use objective data on community conditions or public services to influence community improvement.

Advanced Governance Practice 3: Citizens Reaching for Results

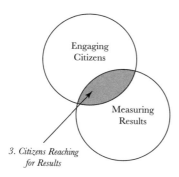

3. Citizens Reaching for Results

Advances in information technology have brought the cost of community information projects down over the years, making them possible in more and more communities. Nevertheless, collecting, compiling, reporting, and using community data on a regular basis still requires a level of technical rigor and steady attention to detail that makes these projects difficult to start or sustain on a purely volunteer basis. So organizations that act as *data intermediaries* are essential to help citizens play active roles in using data to reach for results. A data intermediary can be a nonprofit organization, as in most examples in this chapter and the next, or a university, a government agency, or any other organization—or group of organizations working in collaboration—that can combine applied research and data management capabilities with the trust of a broad range of citizen stakeholders in the community. Also, as with the Piton Foundation in Denver in this chapter, and the Jacksonville Community Council Inc. (JCCI) and Truckee Meadows Tomorrow (TMT) in the next chapter, some community organizations go beyond being a data intermediary helping citizens measure results, to helping citizens become advocates and collaborators of community change to improve results that matter.

This chapter and the next are both intended to help you find ways to increase citizens' influence in improving measurable results in your community by helping them collect, report, or use community information. You may find ways your organization—or a community organization you work with and can influence—can become a data intermediary to help citizens influence results. If your organization already serves as a data intermediary, you may find ways to become more effective in that role or take on a more active role in helping citizens reach for results.

Three community examples are presented at the end of this chapter, and two are in the next chapter. First, key ideas and strategic issues related to the advanced practice of citizens reaching for results are discussed, with illustrative references to the examples in both this chapter and the next. The ideas and issues are meant to guide your interpretation of the examples in both chapters, to help you learn things from those communities that can enable you to make citizens more effective at using data to influence improvement in your community.

Citizens and Data

Citizens who do not analyze data for a living usually do not relate to data in the same way that professional data analysts do. Key ideas about how citizens relate to data, and what they really want when they become involved with data, have important implications for when and how to engage citizens in measurement projects and how decisions are made concerning what data to collect, report, and use.

Citizens Want Results, Not Data. With the exception of a few policy wonks or data geeks, citizens who get involved in community measurement are not primarily interested in data. They are interested in improving conditions they care about in their community—in getting results that matter. They participate because they expect—or hope—that they can use data on community conditions or service performance to influence change. To them, information is a means to an end, not an end in itself. That is why advanced practice 3 of the Effective Community Governance Model is called "citizens *reaching for* results," *not* citizens "measuring" results. When used well, the data can extend citizens' reach in their efforts to improve results in their communities.

Citizens' Priorities Should Drive Choices in Data Collection, Reporting, and Use. Because citizens are interested in results, not just data, it is important to help them be selective in finding and using data that relate to the specific results they most want to see improved. The information should speak to issues representing their highest-priority concerns at a given time. So in all five examples in this chapter and the next, citizens have played important roles in determining what information on community conditions or public services would be collected, reported, or used. In the first example, on digital neighborhood surveys in several communities, citizens decide on the specific physical problems in their neighborhoods that they will collect data on, to be reported to government agencies responsible for fixing those problems. In three of the four other examples—the Citizen Initiated Performance Assessment (CIPA) project in several Iowa cities (this chapter) and in the quality-of-life reporting projects of JCCI in Florida and of TMT in Nevada (in Chapter Five)—citizens have played important roles in determining what data are reported to the community.

In the remaining example (the last in this chapter), the Piton Foundation maintains a data warehouse with a great mass of information potentially useful to residents of poor Denver neighborhoods. The residents themselves, members of the Denver Community Learning Network (CLN), determine what issues they will address and thus what data they use at a given time. For example, Piton researcher Matt Hamilton recalls giving Sun Valley resident Phillip Kasper a computer printout with detailed school data: "If I had given him that data five years ago, it would have been meaningless to him. But now he has a deep concern for the school in Sun Valley, where he lives. So he delved into that data because it was relevant to an issue he cared about deeply."[1] At times, CLN residents have collected data themselves when Piton's data warehouse does not yet have information to address a particular concern, such as unreported crime. The Denver CLN example is presented in the context of the National Neighborhood Indicators Partnership, of which Piton is a partner, and the Annie E. Casey Foundation's Making Connections initiative, which funds the CLN.

Engage and Support Citizens in Multiple Roles

The major roles for citizen engagement in effective governance all come into play in advanced practice 3, leading to ideas and implications for supporting citizens in key roles to make them effective in reaching for results.

Support Citizens as Issue Framers and Evaluators. When citizens are engaged in selecting what data will be collected, reported, or used, they are engaged as issue framers in a powerful way, as they are influencing what kinds of information will be available to frame the terms of debate about public issues or services. Citizens play issue framer roles in all five examples in this chapter and the next. In most of the examples, they also play evaluator roles, whether by collecting data, as in the digital neighborhood surveys, or assessing results and using that assessment to recommend change, as Jacksonville citizens have done in their studies of public education and teen pregnancy.

All of the intermediaries in these two chapters support citizens as issue framers, evaluators, or both by, for example, providing group facilitation to reach consensus on key issues or services to measure, conducting research to provide citizens choices of performance indicators, finding sources of data for indicators and obtaining the data for citizens, or, in some cases providing technology and methods for citizens to collect data themselves. Intermediaries can also produce maps, charts, or other forms of data analysis to help citizens interpret results, decide priorities for improvement to emphasize in a public report and press conference, and determine how to use the data to influence change. Intermediaries can also build citizens' skills in issue framing and evaluation, based on citizen priorities for what they need to learn, what Denver CLN residents call *taking charge of their learning agenda.*

Use Measurement to Engage and Support Citizens as Advocates and Collaborators. Community measurement not only helps citizens frame and evaluate issues, it can also support them in advocating for change and building collaborations for improvement. JCCI's quality-of-life indicators have supported citizen advocacy, by, for example, providing data to fuel Jacksonville citizens' repeated attempts to improve public education. In Nevada, TMT has been creative in engaging citizens as collaborators by getting them to "adopt an indicator"—to commit to specific things they will do related to any TMT quality-of-life indicator to make their own small contributions as coproducers in improving their region. TMT members include citizens who have also forged large-scale collaborations, called quality-of-life compacts.

Strategic Issues in Helping Citizens Reach for Results

Community measurement efforts need boundaries to be manageable and a clear focus for citizens to become engaged in them. A key strategic issue is setting the geographic and measurement boundaries to match the purpose of the endeavor. Other strategic issues involve building partnerships, linking measurement with accountability for results, and developing the relationships and credibility for measurement efforts to take root and make a difference in the community.

Set Geographic Boundaries and Measurement Focus. Any community measurement effort needs a sense of focus. Ultimately data that are collected and used should be driven by citizen priorities. But citizens should come into a project knowing its boundaries—both for what gets measured and where—so they will have reasonable expectations of what their data can be used for. The geographic and measurement focus chosen by project organizers should fit what they want to help citizens achieve.

The digital neighborhood surveys and the Iowa CIPA projects both attempt to influence local government decisions or service actions, so both focus data collection on information related to local government services. The digital surveys' geographic focus is necessarily limited to the specific neighborhoods surveyed by citizens, putting these projects in the lower left quadrant of Figure 4.1, which maps the focus of the examples in this chapter and the next. The CIPA projects hope to influence decisions at the municipal level, including budgeting, so they focus on community-wide measurement, putting them in the upper left of Figure 4.1. As reflected in Figure 4.1, each of the other three examples has a measurement focus that includes some things addressed by local public services, such as educational achievement, but also is much broader, to include many aspects of the quality of life whether or not those conditions are directly addressed by public services. In Truckee Meadows (Chapter Five), for example, this is in keeping with the original intent of determining whether regional growth controls are needed, as growth affects many economic, social, and environmental conditions whether or not they are addressed by local services. Also, the TMT geographic focus is necessarily regional, putting it in the upper right of Figure 4.1.

The Piton Foundation and the Denver Community Learning Network measure a broad range of conditions to support residents in poor neighborhoods trying to lift themselves, their families, and their neighbors out of poverty. As their main geographic focus is four CLN neighborhoods, this project is in the lower right of Figure 4.1. But they use data from a much broader geographic base, because a focus on social and economic conditions in targeted neighborhoods requires benchmark data from beyond those boundaries. That can allow income levels, home ownership rates, crime rates,

FIGURE 4.1. GEOGRAPHIC AND MEASUREMENT FOCUS OF EXAMPLES IN CHAPTERS FOUR AND FIVE

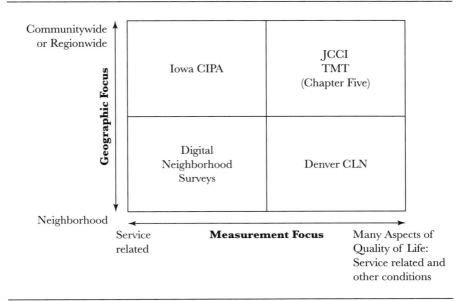

or other conditions in the target neighborhoods to be compared with regional averages for the same conditions, or with those conditions in other neighborhoods. Also, Des Moines, a CIPA city that uses digital neighborhood surveys, demonstrates that service-related measurement efforts can vary in geographic focus in the same community.

Start from Generic Scales to Set Measurement Boundaries. The scales of Figure 4.1 are specifically defined to explain the focus of the five community examples of this chapter and the next. However, those scales are too narrowly defined to cover all possible community measurement projects, such as a project that is not service related but focuses on only one or two quality-of-life issues, or a project for a rural district that is smaller than a region, but for which the term *neighborhood* may not be relevant.

Figure 4.2 provides a grid for mapping the focus of any community measurement effort. The more generic scales in Figure 4.2 may help any group organizing a community measurement project define and communicate their scope with respect to their geographic focus and measurement focus. Each scale should be considered a continuum, so a particular project may not fall neatly in one corner or another of Figure 4.2 but may appear anywhere on the chart. Although the dashed grid lines outline four broad quadrants, they are provided more as reference lines to help a group map the focus of its project rather than to define specific points on each scale.

FIGURE 4.2. GENERIC GEOGRAPHIC AND MEASUREMENT SCALES FOR DEFINING THE FOCUS OF A COMMUNITY MEASUREMENT EFFORT

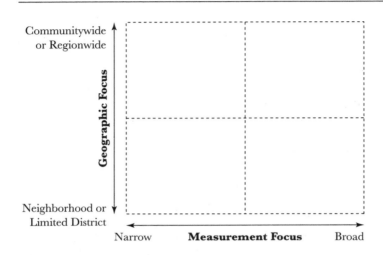

Key to End Points on Scales:

Geographic Focus:
Communitywide or Regionwide: An entire town, city, county, state, province, or multijurisdiction region.
Neighborhood or limited district: A neighborhood or other defined small urban or suburban district, or a defined rural district that is considered part of a larger region.
Measurement Focus:
Narrow: Specific community services or a limited number of closely related narrowly defined quality-of-life issues or community conditions.
Broad: A broad spectrum of community conditions related to community well-being or quality of life, some of which may be service related and others not.

Build Partnerships That Focus Resources on Desired Results. Organizations that have achieved managing for results and communities that have achieved governing for results explicitly or implicitly have a systematic cycle in place, with feedback of measured results driving how organizations or communities use their resources better over time to improve desired results. When citizens are reaching for results, they have measurement tools that provide data about results, but that performance information is not built into a systematic feedback cycle that focuses resources on action. Without such systematic feedback, special efforts by citizens and their community organizations are needed to close the loop and focus community resources on improving desired results. Citizen advocacy is an important way to build public support for actions to improve results, as citizens working with JCCI have done in advocating for education reform. An important complement to advocacy is partnership building, to get public and private organizations to agree to collaborate by focusing significant resources on desired outcomes.

Truckee Meadows Tomorrow calls itself an "advocate," but also says its "mission is to improve the community's quality of life through collaboration and partnership."[2] TMT depends on many partners for a great deal of what it gets done in the community, including publishing and distributing its annual quality-of-life indicators reports. To move from measuring the quality of life to improving it, TMT has developed quality-of-life compacts, an innovative type of partnership. TMT has influenced major public and private organizations in the region to put their resources behind results by signing compacts in which they commit to substantial measurable actions to help move quality-of-life indicators in the desired direction, such as upgrading their fleet with alternative fuel vehicles to reduce pollution.

An important JCCI partnership with the United Way of Northeast Florida has helped focus nonprofit resources on improving results of health and human services as measured by a subset of JCCI's community indicators originally developed for health and human services planning. Once these indicators came to be used in the process of allocating $16 million in annual United Way contributions, service providers seeking funds started using the indicators in their own strategic planning and have been citing how they contribute to desired results to justify their funding requests. Also, a larger partnership of major human services funders in Northeast Florida has started to become much more focused on outcomes as measured by indicators.

The entire CIPA project was conceived around partnerships among citizens, elected officials, and municipal staff of participating Iowa cities, with citizens forming the majority of performance teams that determine what to measure. The assumption behind CIPA is that such a partnership will produce performance measures that citizens will feel are important, that staff will be willing and able to provide data for, and that elected officials will be likely to use for policy decisions such as budget allocations. In a few years, if some of the CIPA cities progress from anecdotally reported uses of project data to regular, systematic use of citizen-driven performance measures for allocating resources and improving results as part of a systematic performance management cycle, those cities will progress from advanced practice 3 (citizens reaching for results) to advanced practice 4 (communities governing for results).

Connect Measurement with Accountability. Managing for results and governing for results processes not only systematically focus resources on results, they also create built-in accountability of organizations and their leaders for achieving results. When citizens are reaching for results, accountability is not assured; citizens and their supporting organizations have to work to achieve it. Advocacy and partnership building are among a variety of ways to draw organizations into accepting accountability for improvement. The different ways accountability has been developed in different communities can be instructive.

Where the information collected is focused on specific problems that specific organizations such as government agencies are supposed to respond to, as in the neighborhood digital survey projects, reports of the data provide a level of accountability by making it clear where responsible organizations have corrected a problem and where they have not. In Des Moines, that accountability is stronger and more direct because citizen-identified physical problems are entered into the city government's automated complaint system, which enables citizens to use the Internet to track city progress in resolving the problem. On a communitywide scale, in all Iowa CIPA cities, the intention is to build accountability for action by having public officials personally involved with citizens in selecting performance measures.

In its additional role as a convener of community deliberation, JCCI pulls together decision makers and stakeholders to move community improvement processes along, which can lead to agreements for action that then serve as an accountability tool. Also, JCCI's partnership with, and advocacy to, the Jacksonville city government has led to the city's adopting selected JCCI indicators into its own outcome measurement, creating accountability for those indicators.

In Truckee Meadows, citizens were disappointed when public officials did not build TMT's indicators into regional plans, which would have made the top officials of local governments in the region accountable for adjusting and enforcing plans to improve the indicators. TMT's response was to become a catalyst for bottom-up action, with the Adopt an Indicator program and especially the quality-of-life compacts, through which organizations have voluntarily accepted accountability to make substantial, measurable commitments to improve the quality of life in the region.

Build on Existing Credibility and Relationships, or Build Them New. The variety of different kinds of organizations helping citizens reach for results in the examples that follow suggests that there is no single formula for an organization to succeed in this role. One thing they all have in common is that they all already had, or worked to build, strong credibility in the communities they serve. That credibility comes not only from having the technical capability needed, but also, perhaps more important, from being perceived as impartial in the community, in a way that goes beyond formal nonpartisanship but is not the same as neutrality. For example, JCCI is not neutral on many issues: it supports policy recommendations that emerge from citizen studies. But JCCI is seen as impartial because it does not come to issues with any a priori positions based on narrow interests. Instead, it has a reputation of fostering open deliberation among many stakeholders with different, often competing, interests and not advocating for policy positions until citizens hear different viewpoints and make their own evaluation. Credibility as open and impartial is especially important if the organization is to go beyond the role of data intermediary to helping to get citizen-driven indicators or other community information used for community improvement.

The organizations supporting citizens in the examples also built on relationships they already had to gain acceptance of community information projects by both citizens and decision makers, and they worked at establishing new relationships where needed. The Fund for the City of New York could build on its past history of working with New York City agencies to get agencies to accept digital neighborhood survey data collected by citizens. In Iowa, two universities' and the Iowa League of Cities' relationships with municipal officials throughout the state helped them build CIPA partnerships in nine cities. In Des Moines, the partnership between the city of Des Moines and Des Moines Neighbors, an umbrella group of neighborhood associations, provided ready relationships with both city agencies and citizens active in neighborhoods across the city. The Connecticut Policy and Economic Council (CPEC) worked to build relationships in communities with citizens and municipalities, which sometimes came easily, and sometimes not—as in Hartford. But CPEC kept trying. Eventually a new city administration took office, which cooperated with CPEC's digital surveys in Hartford. In Denver, the Piton Foundation worked hard at listening to residents of poor neighborhoods to build positive, trusting relationships with them.

Finally, Truckee Meadows Tomorrow demonstrates that citizens do not necessarily need an existing organization to help them reach for results. They can build their own. After Truckee Meadows' quality-of-life indicators emerged from a regional planning process, interested citizens came together to form TMT to support the indicators and build community support for improving the quality of life. It was a good strategic choice to establish TMT as a membership organization with both individual and organizational members, which provided a ready base of people and groups for building relationships and forming partnerships. The broad range of interests among TMT's members, and TMT's efforts to solicit an even broader range of interests in refining its indicators, helped the new organization establish credibility in the region.

The three examples of citizens reaching for results that follow, and the two in the next chapter, demonstrate the key ideas and strategic issues discussed above, and they go further to provide the context for real community practice and lessons learned in each community setting.

Digital Neighborhood Surveys

Citizens intimately know the problems in their own neighborhoods because they pass by them every day. They observe many details and know why they are important. For example, William, a senior at Bronx Regional High School, entered data in the fall of 2003 with other students on broken streetlights, clogged catch basins, potholes, graffiti, broken or missing signs, broken sidewalks, and many other street-level problems into a handheld computer for mapping and reporting back to city agencies responsible for fixing those problems. William observed an exposed wiring box and knew exactly how it could be abused: "People can steal electricity from it. Little kids can get electrocuted. And drugs get stashed in there."[3] And students familiar with the neighborhood in the Bronx could track results. When William examined a map from a previous class, he could tell that ten broken streetlights near his school had been reported to the New York City Department of Transportation. William's class found that six of them had been fixed. The Bronx students were a few of the hundreds of citizens, most of them adult volunteers, who had surveyed over 130 miles of streets in fifteen New York City neighborhoods—almost seventeen hundred blocks[4]—in the first five years of the Computerized Neighborhood Environmental Tracking (ComNET) project of the Fund for the City of New York (FCNY), a private operating foundation. Digital neighborhood surveys such as ComNET help citizens use their street-level awareness to systematically identify and communicate street-level problems to government.

Putting Digital Power into the Hands of Citizens

There is nothing new about citizens walking their streets and surveying conditions to try to get public officials to take heed. But FCNY's ComNET, and similar projects it has inspired in other communities, literally puts more power in citizens' hands when they are reaching for results. The handheld computers volunteer citizens use, programmed with the street grid and a long list of observable physical problems, enable faster, more systematic, and accurate reporting of problems to public agencies, delivered in the compact form of computer files, not on reams of paper. The ComNET device includes a digital camera citizens use to document out-of-the-ordinary or severe problems that do not fit a standard description, so an agency can see if an urgent or special response is needed. The digital power of ComNET data also enables fast, low-cost mapping of problems and charting comparative results when a neighborhood is resurveyed.

Citizens using the technology literally become extra sets of eyes for their community, identifying many detailed problems that need to be fixed. Local governments cannot afford to put all the extra paid inspectors out on the streets to find what citizen surveyors find. Even if public agencies could pay more inspectors, citizens can be more efficient surveyors because they know no bureaucratic boundaries and can find and report the many types of problem they care about. Meanwhile, especially in a large local government, it might take an inspector from one agency to find street defects, another inspector from a second agency to look for trash problems, another for sewer problems, and so on. In New York, one citizen surveyor can find neighborhood problems handled by as many as fifteen different city agencies responsible for different street-level problems. And the digital format of the surveys enables automated sorting of problems recorded so it is easy to transmit the right problems to the right agency.

Making Technology Transfer Easy

ComNET's off-the-shelf, inexpensive technology makes it easy to transfer. Some organizational capacity is needed to adapt the technology for use in a different community and to organize and run the project. The Alfred P. Sloan Foundation, which funded FCNY to develop and implement ComNET in New York, has also funded adaptations of ComNET in Worcester, Massachusetts; San Francisco; Des Moines, Iowa; and Seattle. In several Connecticut communities, also funded by a Sloan grant, the nonprofit Connecticut Policy and Economic Council (CPEC) decided to develop its own variation on the ComNET technology and programmed a different off-the-shelf palm-top computer, also equipped with a digital camera, for citizens to use to conduct digital surveys in projects they call City Scan. There are now at least two versions of handheld digital technology that organizations can readily adapt for citizens in their communities to use. Both FCNY and CPEC have provided technical assistance to organizations in other communities to adapt and use their technology. In some communities, the handheld technology has been adapted to survey and report on physical conditions of parks as well as streetscapes.

Harnessing the Power of Citizens Playing Multiple Roles

While the technology involved in digital surveys is nifty, it is merely an enabler. These projects work because citizens are empowered in several roles to help improve their communities. In particular, digital survey projects can enable citizens to act in a powerful way as issue framers and evaluators. Although details vary by community, citizens are often engaged up front as issue framers to determine what kinds of physical problems to cover in their surveys. Then they become evaluators of neighborhood conditions when they track specific outcomes, though with digital surveys, "outcomes" are limited to predefined physical problems in the community. They may also take their evaluation to a deeper level, as they do in New York with help from FCNY, by reviewing survey results to determine which problems to report to agencies as the highest priorities to be fixed. This approach taps into citizens' day-to-day experience of their neighborhoods to make the project effective. The approach also involves the supporting organization in helping neighbors deliberate and reach consensus about which solutions—within the limits of physical streetscape or park problems—will make the most difference in improving life in their neighborhood. In this way, citizens' priorities, backed up by data gained through the use of digital surveys, influence government priorities in responding to neighborhood problems.

Involving Youth in Digital Surveys

The extent of youth involvement in digital survey projects has varied from none in some communities to others where a majority of survey hours have been provided by young people, generally of high school age. The use of young people to survey streetscapes or parks adds another dimension to the power of citizen engagement. Michelle Doucette Cunningham, former leader of the CPEC's City Scan project, said youth "generated substantial press coverage and public relation benefits that have helped us expand the program throughout a city." She also feels that "involving youth tends to get entire families involved, and holds the promise of connecting youth to their community by helping them see tangible results of their work." Several teens who conducted digital surveys for City Scan in Hartford bore her out. Priscilla, age fifteen, felt her involvement "made me more aware of things in the neighborhood. I notice things that I did not used to see." Nilda, age sixteen, explained, "There was a graffiti summit in the community as a result of our information. It showed people that teens would work on improving neighborhoods and that we're not self-centered." Eva, age sixteen, "felt like I got other people interested. My mom attended the graffiti summit because I was involved in the project." CPEC also uses youth to reduce the time adults spend surveying, allowing their adult volunteers to focus on using the scan data to improve city conditions, while the youth focus on data collection.

Increasing Survey Effectiveness Through Organizational Relationships

Partner with Grassroots Groups and Schools to Engage Volunteers. In New York City, several Connecticut communities, and Des Moines, Iowa, the lead intermediary organization with data capabilities has not directly recruited individual citizens to conduct surveys, but has relied on grassroots organizations to engage neighborhoods and residents. The Des Moines Digital Survey (DMDS) was organized as a partnership between the city government of Des Moines, including the city manager's office and the information technology department, and Des Moines Neighbors, an umbrella group of neighborhood associations throughout the city. Des Moines Neighbors identified neighborhood groups willing to try DMDS and able to supply volunteer citizen surveyors. In New York and Connecticut, FCNY and CPEC, respectively, worked directly with grassroots neighborhood groups to recruit citizens.

The use of grassroots partnerships leads to citizens' being engaged by groups that have already built trust in their neighborhoods and to neighbors' recruiting neighbors. As in New York and Connecticut, local high schools sometimes have recruited student surveyors. At first, a lead organization may have to spend significant effort on outreach to grassroots groups to get a digital survey project started, but as FCNY and CPEC have found, these compelling projects can eventually sell themselves. Success in one neighborhood breeds interest in another. The difficulty may be less in finding interested grassroots groups than in ensuring they can provide the volunteers with the time and commitment to complete the surveys, and preferably to do at least one follow-up survey so responsiveness can be gauged.

Build Relationships That Connect Survey Data with Accountability. To make digital surveys worth citizens' efforts, someone with some responsibility for addressing the problems identified must be willing to accept the survey data and take accountability for responding. In New York, the FCNY, which has a long history of working with city agencies, built on those past relationships to gain cooperation from responsible agencies and worked to provide them with digital data in a form they can use. The extent to which they built ComNET data into their priority service response plans has varied, but at least citizens' information on neighborhood problems was accepted by accountable agencies.

By contrast, the Connecticut Policy and Economic Council has operated since 1942 as more of an independent reviewer of government, having built its early reputation doing independent fiscal policy studies of Connecticut state and local governments. It has worked to build relationships with government officials from the start of each City Scan project, and willingness to cooperate has varied. CPEC quickly gained the city of Stamford's cooperation, for example, but in Hartford, the city administration originally refused to meet with citizens organized by CPEC or recognize the legitimacy of their process. Only after a new mayor was elected and a new city manager appointed did Hartford embrace City Scan, both responding to data collected by the initial City Scan neighborhood teams and helping CPEC expand City Scan to more neighborhoods.

In Des Moines, the organizational design of the project as a partnership between Des Moines Neighbors and the city government ensured a strong connection with accountability. The Des Moines Digital Survey (DMDS), which uses FCNY's ComNET palm-top technology, was designed for survey data to be directly downloaded into the city's electronic complaint tracking system. Based on results in the first two neighborhoods surveyed, Becky Morelock, president of Des Moines Neighbors, said they are "thrilled with the responsiveness of the city in handling the simple issues and working with the neighborhoods on addressing the more extensive issues." Because the city's complaint tracking system is Web based, citizens in the neighborhoods can constantly check the status of issues addressed in the surveys that qualify as manageable complaints. Issues that cannot be handled quickly through a complaint system are dealt with through meetings with neighborhood representatives and the city. In some cases, these may be reflected in budgets or capital planning processes.

Iowa Citizens Build Results-Based Partnerships with Government: Citizen-Initiated Performance Assessment

In nine Iowa cities, citizens have been directly engaged in creating service performance measures for use by their city governments under the Citizen Initiated Performance Assessment (CIPA) program. CIPA, launched in 2000 with a grant from the Alfred P. Sloan Foundation, has been managed by the Office of State and Local Government Programs at Iowa State University, along with partners at the University of Iowa Institute of Public Affairs and the Iowa League of Cities. These three groups were the mediating organizations to get CIPA started and to facilitate working partnerships in all CIPA cities, though they have generally not been data intermediaries, as it has been each city government's responsibility to provide needed data.

The CIPA project is designed to build partnerships between citizens and city officials, at both administrative and policy levels, to develop performance measures based on how citizens view services. The purpose is to use citizen involvement to build political credibility for performance measures so elected policymakers will be more likely to integrate the measures into their decision making. CIPA's designers saw inattention to performance measures by elected officials as a failing of past measurement efforts. For citizens like Jon Sampson in Carroll, Iowa, "A program like CIPA helps bring the voice of the citizens to the council, which can help the city council know what the citizens think is important in the delivery of services."

The nine CIPA cities, which range in population from 10,000 to 200,000, are Burlington, Carroll, Clive, Des Moines, Indianola, Johnston, Marion, Marshalltown, and Urbandale. In each city a committee called the Performance Team (PT) was created, including representatives of the city council and the city staff but with volunteer citizens constituting a majority of the PT. In many cities the city manager is on the PT. The idea was to give all three groups—citizens, staff, and elected policymakers—a stake in the process. Judy Tomenga, a citizen on the Johnston PT, observed, "A collaborative effort with citizens who are interested in being involved in their community can help build accountability in city government." CIPA has generally focused on citywide measurement, though Des Moines has used both citywide measures, and neighborhood data from the Des Moines Digital Survey.

Citizen Issue Framers Decide What to Measure

Citizens Select and Investigate Services. Once the PTs were formed, the citizen members started playing the role of issue framer by working with city officials to choose one or two services to measure. They mostly chose services they saw as critical to the community, but sometimes chose a service that had been the focus of recent controversy. Then each PT went on tours and was given staff presentations to get acquainted with these services. During these orientations, citizens raised issues and asked how the performance of the service was currently being measured, if at all. This step built the PT's knowledge of both the service and how to measure performance.

Citizens Identify Service Elements and Measures. The next steps of the PTs took citizens more deeply into their issue framer role: for each service they selected, each PT identified critical elements—things citizens feel define the service to them and suggest criteria for assessing service effectiveness. The critical elements enabled PT members to identify specific performance measures that reflect citizens' idea of the effectiveness of each service. Often the PT's performance measures were the same as those staff might design—for example, response times, citizen attitude measures, amounts of material used. However, citizen and staff opinions diverged on the need for better public information. In almost every CIPA city, the PT felt the government could improve how it informs citizens about activities and services. For example, they wanted city governments to follow up with citizens after responding to inquiries and complaints. The Des Moines Digital Survey, with citizens' neighborhood survey data downloaded into the city's complaint system, and online status checking available to citizens, is one city's response to these concerns.

Government Staff Advise the Process, Not Drive It. A concern at the outset of the CIPA project was that city staff might exploit their knowledge of government services to dominate the PTs' agendas, rather than limiting their role to providing technical expertise and information to support citizens. This did not prove to be a problem, according to the facilitators from CIPA's three external intermediary organizations. City staff generally played a helpful role by explaining the services and answering questions. They did influence the process by pointing out where measures were duplicative and by suggesting methods for collecting data. For example, some PTs initially identified a large number of measures, especially for police. Staff raised concerns about time and cost to collect data, leading the PTs to think about the need for each measure and the impact of data collection on service operations. The PTs then eliminated measures they felt were less useful.

Citizens Balance Practicality with the Need for New Information. Data collection options in each city were reviewed by the PTs after they picked specific performance measures. PTs were practical by accepting some collection methods already in use by their city governments. But where citizens felt new kinds of information were important, the PTs did not feel constrained to stick only with data already available. So they chose some new data collection methods, especially for gauging citizen attitudes about services, including citywide surveys, more targeted surveys of specific program users (for example, for recreation), and response cards to beneficiaries of specific services, such as fire and emergency medical services. Data collection proceeded, and CIPA performance information became available in each city.

Governments Begin Using Citizen-Initiated Performance Information

Citizens and Officials Discuss Using Data. In the summer of 2003, the focus shifted to integrating CIPA data into city council decision making. This process started in each city with a joint meeting between the PT and the entire city council and mayor. The interaction between the PT and council was intended to reinforce elected decision makers' awareness that the measures reflect what citizens felt was important. It also helped citizen PT members understand how the council uses information and that measures can still influence decisions even if council members rarely use raw data directly to make a decision. They are more likely to use the information in discussions leading up to their decisions—what might be called "data-influenced decisions" rather than "data-driven decisions." Council members responded well to early PT progress reports and meetings. According to Don Gloo, Urbandale assistant city manager, "After meeting with the Performance Team, the council was very enthusiastic about the CIPA process and seemed to have a renewed commitment to using performance measures." Chris Johannson, the Des Moines city manager's representative, described an unanticipated dynamic: "When the PT reported on their progress to the city council, I got calls from department heads the next day wanting to know more about the process."

Facilitation Helps Elected Officials Focus on Using Data. In some of the pilot cities, particularly those with little previous performance measurement experience, CIPA facilitators held orientation sessions with the city council to help council members think through how they might use measurements. Bill El, mayor pro tem in Burlington, saw this as a positive step to help the council begin to use information. According to El, "Raw data need to be formulated into assumptions and conclusions that the council can relate to, so they do not get overwhelmed with data." El's observation reflects a special double perspective: he started out as a citizen member of the Burlington PT and was elected to the city council in the fall of 2003.

Early Progress, Lessons Learned, and Future Challenges

Expanding CIPA to More Services. An early CIPA objective was for cities to decide to expand the CIPA process to more services, a sign they are starting to institutionalize the process. This objective was achieved in seven of the nine CIPA cities, which opted to take on new services and reach out to recruit more citizens to get involved, a decision supported by citizens and elected officials. As Carla Johnson, a downtown Des Moines resident on that city's PT, said, "I am looking forward to seeing this expand throughout the city." Les Asheim, mayor of Clive, felt CIPA led to benefits in police and fire services, which, he said, "need to be extended to the city's other five departments."

The two cities that did not continue based their decision on reactions of the administrative staff, who felt the measurement effort was not productive. In one case, a change in city manager influenced the decision. Losing those cities was disappointing, but CIPA was built on the premise that citizens, staff, and elected officials all have to be committed. Without staff support in a city, performance data reported may be suspect.

Streamlining the Process to Enable Expansion and Reduce Burnout. A lesson learned from the pilot CIPA experiences is that the length of the process led to frustration among participants, especially the citizen volunteers, and caused some initial members to drop out of the PTs. This led CIPA's management team to develop a much more streamlined approach that allows a service to be handled through two or three ninety-minute meetings. This should improve retention of citizen volunteers and keep the process from becoming overwhelming to staff as more services are added.

Intermediaries Remain Available While Shifting Organizational Ownership. During the initial years, the CIPA process was operated by intermediary organizations external to the participating governments, but it is designed to eventually become integrated into the normal processes of the city governments. The three organizations that initiated the process will remain involved to track future CIPA progress and will be available to provide occasional external assistance as the cities expand the process. The external help will be there if there is a need for a neutral convener or facilitator to assist at critical times, but ultimately the process has to belong to the citizens and local officials in each city.

Tracking the Influence of CIPA Data. So far, the CIPA process has demonstrated that citizens can and will get involved in developing performance measures and that building a partnership between citizens, their elected representatives, and city staff can be done with citizens, rather than staff or politicians, driving the process. The real test of CIPA's effectiveness will come in the next few years as the external organizations that initiated CIPA track participating cities to learn how influential the performance measures become, both for the initial services and those added in later years. Early anecdotal evidence is encouraging. For example, according to Mayor Asheim of Clive, "The data on response time by area within the city . . . helped the council with their capital planning by indicating where the best location is for any new fire facility and identifying when it is likely to be needed."

Future follow-up with CIPA cities will include looking for uses of performance measures in critical decision processes, such as strategic planning, budgeting, and formulating major policies. To be used for these purposes, measures must clear a high bar of politically credibility. If any of these cities goes beyond making individual decisions using CIPA's measures, to integrating citizen-driven measures into systematic results management cycles, then their citizens' reach for results will extend all the way to governing for results.

Data for Empowering Residents of Poor Neighborhoods: Nationally and in Denver

The National Neighborhood Indicators Partnership (NNIP), started in 1995, and the Annie E. Casey Foundation's (AECF's) Making Connections (MC) initiative, started in 1999, are national programs involving local nonprofit ventures that emphasize using a wide array of data to empower residents of poor neighborhoods to build a better future for their families and develop stronger, better functioning neighborhoods. The NNIP and MC have become intertwined. By early 2005, seventeen of the twenty-two NNIP cities were among the twenty-three sites in a Making Connections network receiving AECF investment for different kinds of improvement strategies, and nine of the ten comprehensive Making Connections sites engaged in "comprehensive family strengthening and neighborhood transformation efforts" were NNIP cities.[5] Local NNIP partners—nonprofit or university research organizations—often play a key role in local MC efforts. The NNIP is coordinated by the Urban Institute of Washington, D.C., and funded by AECF and the Rockefeller Foundation.

Intermediaries Democratize Information for the Community's Use. NNIP partners are data intermediaries who operate, or are building, extensive computer-based neighborhood indicators systems with integrated, regularly updated information on neighborhood conditions in their city. While they may use the data in their own reports, they see themselves as neither ivory tower research organizations nor as primary actors in planning and policy analysis. Instead, NNIP partners follow the NNIP principle of "democratizing information" to facilitate the use of data for local issues by stakeholders, such as residents, community groups, and nongovernmental leadership groups.[6]

Partnerships Use Data to Promote Learning, Connections, and Change. Making Connections (MC) is a ten-year AECF investment to improve outcomes for families and children in neighborhoods suffering from disinvestment and social isolation. MC aims to break that isolation by connecting families with economic opportunities (such as jobs, loans, tax credits), support networks, services (such as health, banking, transportation), and civic opportunities (a voice in city hall) available to stronger neighborhoods. MC also connects neighborhood residents with data for social change.

A key part of the MC strategy is the creation of a Local Learning Partnership (LLP) in each of the ten comprehensive MC sites. An LLP is a consortium of people and organizations with data-related expertise to help develop outcomes, measures, and strategies to achieve results. In many MC sites, the NNIP partner is also a partner in the LLP. As in NNIP, the MC LLPs have been established, as a first priority, to make data accessible and useful to others. Part of their charge is to create a learning community—to "build local capacity to use data to inform and propel change, by supporting continuous learning among community members, advocates and organizations and encouraging collaboration between data holders/traditional researchers and potential data users in the community." Those potential data users are not just intended to be advocacy organizations, but neighborhood residents themselves. LLPs are supposed to put "data in the hands of residents for practical uses and [take] the mystery out of data collection and use."[7]

A Cycle of Residents Using Data for Change

Both professional staff of data intermediary organizations and residents in NNIP and MC cities have examined their experiences and considered the steps residents go through to use data to achieve desired change in their communities. In November 2003 150 residents and intermediary staff from twenty-seven cities—more residents than staff—participated in a joint Making Connections-NNIP conference, or "cross-community learning opportunity," titled "Information *Is* Power: Resident Leadership in Using Data for Social Change," to explore these issues in depth, including both development of residents as influential data users and roles intermediaries play to support them.[8] Conference planners provided a starting point for consideration: a continuum of involvement of residents going through four stages to develop into leaders in using data, with residents' becoming more influential and taking greater initiative at each successive stage, as follows:

- Building relationships, in which organizations reach out to residents and build trust
- Residents as consumers of data, in which residents get access to available data
- Residents as participants in data collection, in which residents are involved in designing evaluations and collecting data they want (for example, doing their own neighborhood surveys) beyond what is available from traditional sources
- Residents as leaders in data collection and use, in which residents take ownership of data, control research funding, and make decisions on use of data[9]

Conference participants explored the implications of the continuum on their work at the local level and changed the model as they discussed it, resulting in the cyclical model shown in Figure 4.3 presented in the final conference report.[10] In Figure 4.3, "leadership" is in the center because conference participants realized that residents can take leadership at any point—"it is not a place you come to after you've been everywhere else. It is, instead, a point of view, a position about the role of residents that should be evident in all stages and activities."[11] For example, when thinking of resident leadership, "relationships" are not just a matter of reaching out to residents, but of learning the community's concerns, responding to resident-identified priorities, and, as in Figure 4.3, building resident skills to leave behind in the community to maintain resident leadership. And resident leaders are not just consumers of data; they analyze the information and interpret its implications for themselves, and they communicate it to the community.[12] In shifting from a linear to a cyclical model, participants recognized that communities and organizations work at different levels simultaneously and cycle through the stages repeatedly as new people and priorities enter the process. Participants also added two key ideas shown in Figure 4.3: that a mutually agreed-on purpose—the desired change—is needed to drive the process, and a larger goal of all their work is community power.[13]

The Making Connections-NNIP idea of residents taking on different leadership roles through a cycle of using data is consistent with one of the fundamental ideas of this book: that citizens play multiple roles in engaging in their community. As shown in Figure 4.4, all five of the major citizen engagement roles discussed in Chapter Two come into play in the MC-NNIP resident data use cycle. For example, when residents are leaders in relationship and skill building, they are not just *stakeholders,* but they also play the first two parts of the *issue framer* role (*foundation builder,* if they become engaged in determining a vision for their community, and *agenda setter* of issues to address) and they *collaborate* in their own learning to build skills for community change. Through the next two stages, they continue their *issue framer* role as they use data to define problems and, possibly, alternative solutions. They also become *evaluators* as they analyze and interpret data and may decide they need to collect and analyze more data.

FIGURE 4.3. CYCLE OF RESIDENT LEADERSHIP IN USING DATA

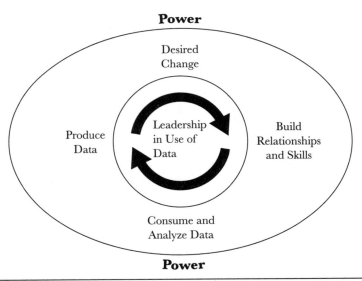

Source: Bailey, T. "Information IS Power" (unpublished report on the Nov. 2003 Information *Is* Power conference sponsored by the AECF Making Connections Initiative and the National Neighborhood Indicators Partnership, Apr. 2004).

FIGURE 4.4. CITIZEN ENGAGEMENT ROLES IN CYCLE
OF RESIDENT LEADERSHIP IN DATA USE

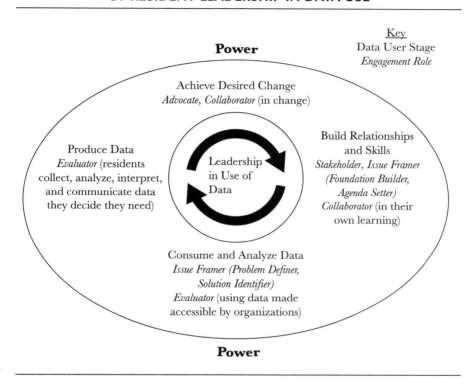

Then they become *advocates* as they use data to drive desired change, and they may also be *collaborators* with others in implementing change.

Residents as Data Leaders in Denver

Denver is a Making Connections and NNIP city where residents have become leaders in using data. Starting in 2000, residents from four Denver MC neighborhoods led the creation of the Local Learning Partnership, the Community Learning Network (CLN), to "take charge of our own learning agenda." According to residents, in the CLN, "We decide our priorities, issue grants or contracts to get the work done, and most often do the work ourselves. We developed our own principles—protecting human dignity, equalizing power, transforming institutions—to guide our work. Those principles require that residents be in leadership positions."[14] As MC resident and CLN member Linda Wurst said, "We've become empowered in a way we were never empowered before in other committees and boards."[15]

To Help Residents Become Leaders: First, Listen to Them. The Piton Foundation, a local Denver operating foundation, NNIP partner, and LLP partner, has supported the CLN from its creation. The CLN's partners, such as Piton, have been learning how to support residents participating in the CLN as the residents evolve through the stages of using data. Piton staff started by getting out into the community and listening, which got the attention of MC neighborhood residents, such as Gabriella Jacobo and Candace RedShirt. "You don't see that often," said Jacobo. "Many people have offered us their support but I never see them in my community. Never." RedShirt was amazed: "I couldn't believe there was someone there who was willing to listen to us. Staff didn't want to tell us what to do. That had never happened to me before."[16] Being listened to was so new to residents that staff worked hard at holding back their own opinions, but over and over said, "I don't know. What do you think?" Piton's Terri Bailey did not start with a mantra in mind, but realized that "repeating and reminding is huge" when she heard residents talk about how their reaction to the mantra changed. "They said that at first we would just piss them off because they thought, 'Well, if you don't know, who does?' But now they talk about how important that was."[17]

Put Residents in Charge, Build Their Skill, and Watch Them Lead. Piton provides financial and research assistance and has been passing on skills to CLN resident participants by helping them learn how to manage budgets, conduct research, and communicate using data. Through 2003, CLN resident leaders had taken control of an annual budget of $500,000, and residents from MC neighborhoods had been hired into two CLN staff positions. Funding decisions have given Bailey a window on how residents have grown as leaders. She reflected on an intense debate in which resident leaders did not rubber-stamp a grant request of a key MC-partner organization. Instead, they closely questioned the proposal and added conditions, such as quarterly reporting and data sharing, to the final grant. "The questions they asked the other night were about how to keep an organization accountable to the principles," said Bailey. "They realized that their role is not to give money to their friends. Their role is to advance learning and make sure that the learning advances Making Connections."[18]

By the end of 2004, the resident CLN staff had become co-coordinators of the LLP, a role formerly held by Bailey. They now relate directly to the Annie E. Casey Foundation and other organizations in developing the overall direction of Making Connections in Denver. Bailey's role has shifted from LLP coordinator to "coach on call" to resident CLN staff.

Use Data for Advocacy, and Keep Skills in the Community. Denver MC residents have not only become leaders through the CLN, they have also been building their skills and capacity to strengthen how they stay organized and use data for advocacy. Among the lessons learned cited by CLN resident leaders are "the need to build skills that remain in the community, the usefulness of data collected by and for the community . . . and the importance of deep and lasting relationships between residents and between residents and institutions and organizations that care about our communities."[19] The CLN's accomplishments in its first three years have involved:

• *Communication and engagement,* including developing a bilingual Web site, a four-color magazine, and an innovative "Story Circle" model that in 2002, its first full year of operation, engaged more than five hundred neighborhood residents, including non-English speakers.

• *Data collection and evaluation,* including conducting a comprehensive assessment of the MC neighborhoods' access to technology and resources; supporting a resident-conducted survey of crime in the Cole neighborhood, which uncovered a tremendous amount of unreported crime; evaluating models to tackle illiteracy; a survey of parents with children in a low-performing high school and its low-performing feeder elementary and middle schools identified by the community as in need of priority reform; and developing principles to guide CLN's fund to support research that meets neighborhood needs.

• *Neighborhood and resident capacity building,* including developing a tool kit for putting on a block party as an organizing method and helping to design a technical assistance program for residents who want to make a difference, including grant-writing training, peer-to-peer exchange, consultant availability, and a resource bank.

Service Organizations' Changing Relationships with the Community

As the CLN proves that residents of poor neighborhoods can get things done and take charge of their own agenda, AECF's Audrey Jordan sees a change in how social service staff, researchers, police, and others who work in poor neighborhoods view residents. "There has been a huge paradigm shift," Jordan believes. "They relate to residents differently. Before there was a sense of 'we need to take care of residents.' A sense of needing to do something *for* residents. But now they recognize that they have a lot to learn by hearing about and better understanding residents' experiences."[20] Jordan's paradigm shift can be seen as a mind shift by service providers from seeing residents as needy people requiring services to seeing residents as community assets that providers can support in improving conditions of families and neighborhoods.

At the November 2003 Information *Is* Power conference, Denver residents confirmed Jordan's observations, citing changes that resulted from conducting their own community survey, including new relations with police, new school programs, and the state's first community court in their neighborhood, which they thought would not have resulted from a survey conducted by outside experts.[21]

Partners Needed: Must Be Accountable to the Community

Participants from across the country at the Information *Is* Power conference had a lot to say about data intermediaries and other organizations that support community residents. For example, they observed that community residents need more than one type of organization as partners, as they need a range of skills that rarely exist in one organization, from skills in getting and using data, to very different skills in making change. They also observed the importance of seeing both sides of relationships: not just what a community needs from an organization but also what the organization's self-interest is in working with the community. They complained about foundations and policymakers who favor research by experts from outside the community who do not know enough about the community to interpret the data and focus on interesting research questions rather than critical community issues. Participants called for data intermediaries and other organizational partners to be willing to be held accountable to the community, not just to funders.[22]

Intermediaries Wanted: Must Respect and Learn with the Community

Information *Is* Power conference participants also identified characteristics of the best organizational partners for assisting communities in using data for social change. Many of these characteristics revolve around respect for community members and their different cultures, skills, and contributions, including the belief that residents should be at the core of decisions and actions, and a willingness to adapt the organization's agenda and practices to the agenda of the community. Some of the characteristics stress things organizations should do for residents, such as simplifying and demystifying data, teaching how to collect and communicate data, and creating space and opportunities for residents to grow and take the lead. Perhaps most interesting, other characteristics involved the organization's being willing to not approach its relationship with community residents as the expert, but being willing to listen to residents with an open mind and to grow and learn in the relationship along with the residents.[23]

Four months after the Information *Is* Power conference, Piton's Terri Bailey put her own learnings in personal terms when she spoke to the 2004 Quality of Life Conference of the newly formed Community Indicators Consortium. Bailey spoke about learning much in her role as a data intermediary, including learning "to be in relationship with those who need your data . . . to be as comfortable talking about data in a church basement or someone's living room as we are in our own office."[24] Because she has been in relationship with community people she supports, she has also learned that "there is no action without ownership. People own data that they've asked for, that they've produced, that they themselves analyze, that they themselves communicate. The more we do for them, the less it belongs to them and the less they are able to use it in meaningful ways. . . . [and] the task is even larger than one of creating data and tools. It is one of broadly diffusing the data, tools and skills . . . moving knowledge and tools from outside community to inside community. This is no small task. But at the end of the day, if more people do not know what we know and have access to what we have access to, then we will have failed."[25]

Learnings on Partnership and Accountability

The two regional quality-of-life indicators efforts explored in the next chapter were also featured at the conference where Terri Bailey spoke. So it is useful to conclude this chapter with learnings on partnership and accountability she spoke about that relate broadly to all citizens reaching for results projects, whether one is focusing on neighborhoods, cities, or whole regions. On partnerships, Bailey said, "We have in many ways moved from the concept of a single data intermediary to meaningful partnerships . . . between communities of data users, data providers, and policy-makers."[26] On accountability, Bailey not only mentioned holding others accountable for improving conditions measured by indicators but also spoke about the accountability of data intermediaries: "We must constantly be engaging citizens, defining and adapting indicators, and being accountable ourselves to whether those indicators are proven meaningful."[27]

CHAPTER FIVE

CITIZENS REACHING FOR RESULTS II

To Improve the Quality of Life in Their Region

I became involved in the JCCI indicators project because I saw that the indicators were gaining lots of respect in the city and that changes were beginning to happen because of them.

VANESSA BOYER, JACKSONVILLE CITIZEN

Vanessa Boyer was engaged as a citizen volunteer to improve how the Jacksonville Community Council Inc. (JCCI) tracks the quality of life in its northeast Florida region. She could see that JCCI's reports on quality-of-life indicators over the years were influencing community action, and she wanted to make the indicators even more effective at tracking results that matter to Jacksonville citizens. Boyer said, "I wanted to make my contribution to this effort because I feel certain issues, especially social and inclusiveness issues, were being overlooked and needed to be surfaced." So she and other citizens who joined a JCCI Quality of Life Indicators Task Force assumed the role of issue framer in reviewing and improving indicators that JCCI had been reporting for years to help make the results reported more relevant to issues of concern for citizens.

Citizens engaged with JCCI's community indicators provide an excellent example of citizens reaching for results, as do citizens engaged with Truckee Meadows Tomorrow's quality-of-life indicators. Citizens reaching for results is advanced practice 3 of the Effective Community Governance Model, in which engaging citizens and measuring results are aligned.

Advanced Governance Practice 3: Citizens Reaching for Results

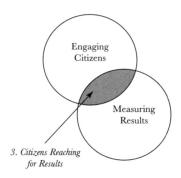

Engaging Citizens

Measuring Results

3. Citizens Reaching for Results

In the examples in the previous chapter, citizens were focused on results in either specific neighborhoods or small to medium-sized cities. In the two examples in this chapter, citizens are reaching for improving the quality of life in their region: JCCI's indicators cover a five-county region of northeast Florida with a population of about 1.2 million and an area of over thirty-two hundred square miles. Truckee Meadows Tomorrow (TMT) focuses on the Reno-Sparks-Washoe County region of northwest Nevada, with a population of about 373,000 but covering an area over twice that of the JCCI region. What the Jacksonville and Truckee Meadows region citizens in this chapter and the citizens focused on neighborhoods or smaller localities in Chapter Four all have in common is that in reaching for results, they are trying to use objective data on community conditions or public services to influence community improvement.

JCCI and TMT are different kinds of nonprofit organizations that work in different ways. What they have in common in helping citizens reach for results is that they are both intermediaries that compile data from various sources and produce community indicators reports. They also both go well beyond the intermediary role, to be advocates and partnership-builders for improving the quality of life in their region.

The Emergence of Citizen-Based Measurement of Community Well-Being

There have long been narrowly focused interest groups in communities, and nationally, that have used data to promote their specific policy agenda—for example:

- Taxpayer organizations that either want to reduce government or make government services more efficient so taxes can be lowered
- Advocacy groups for many different types of populations: the poor, racial or ethnic groups, the elderly, children and youth, the disabled, and others
- Advocacy groups for business interests

While many of these organizations have developed impressive research capabilities over decades, their use of quantitative information is usually narrowly focused on specific kinds of data that can most directly advance their group's narrow policy agenda.

A more recent phenomenon, which is more broadly citizen based and less focused on narrow interests, also involves the use of data in communities:

- Community organizations, often working from a base of citizen involvement to provide community-based direction, collecting and reporting data on a broad array of conditions related to quality of life or long-term community well-being

Citizen-based measurement phenomena have emerged for many reasons. Just a few are explored here. One is the microprocessor revolution. When JCCI, for example, started in 1975, its information technology consisted of typewriters and mimeograph machines. As the cost of computing power came down, JCCI could do more with data to empower the many citizens it engages, and by 1985 it produced its first annual report on indicators of community quality of life.

Community uses of data have also grown because many public and private organizations with different interests have come to see the value of tracking broad arrays of data on conditions relevant to community well-being. For example, regional business interests, as in Jacksonville and California's Silicon Valley, have found that traditional business and economic data alone are not sufficient to understand, improve, and market the business climate of their region, and they have supported reporting broader indicators of the quality of life, as in JCCI's annual "Quality of Life Progress Report"[1] and the "Index of Silicon Valley."[2] And as noted in Chapter Four, organizations that see community development from the perspective of poor families in disadvantaged neighborhoods have been gathering a wide range of community data to empower poor families and their advocacy groups.

Community-based thematic movements that have taken root across the United States have also spurred interest in community data. At least two of these movements, "healthy communities" and "sustainable communities," are related to worldwide movements aimed at long-term global quality-of-life improvement. An early regional sustainability effort in the United States, Sustainable Seattle, issued three reports in the 1990s on indicators of the Puget Sound region's cultural, economic, environmental, and social well-being. The effort grew from the interest of a group of citizens in fostering sustainable development, in which economic development proceeds at the same time as environmental conservation and social development.[3] In the 1990s, Sustainable Seattle generated worldwide interest in regional sustainability indicators, influencing scores of projects from Sustainable Calgary in Canada to Sustainable Penang in Malaysia, and received a 1996 United Nations award for excellence in indicators.[4]

John Kesler, of the Coalition for Healthier Cities and Communities, and Drew O'Connor, then of the National Civic League, identified seven strong thematic community movements in the United States, including healthy communities and sustainable communities. The other five themes they identified were "community building," "livable communities," "safe communities," "civic democracy," and "smart growth."

These movements have spurred interest in broad arrays of data on economic, environmental, social, and health issues in communities and regions. In 2000–2001, Kesler and O'Connor, funded by the W. K. Kellogg Foundation, facilitated dialogues around the United States among representative groups from these movements. They found that while the issues of these movements vary, they share a set of "operational and process themes," including inclusive, deliberative processes that engage citizens around shared visions and values.[5] These kinds of processes lead to community indicators that interest citizens and can empower them to stimulate action to improve conditions that concern them most: helping their communities achieve results that matter.

Key Ideas and Strategic Issues

The same key ideas and strategic issues explored at the start of Chapter Four apply to citizen-based community or regional indicators projects, which are broad-based examples of citizens reaching for results. The key ideas, in brief, are:

• *Citizens want results they care about, not just data, so citizen priorities should drive what data to collect, report, and use.* Citizen priorities have been key drivers of indicators in both the Jacksonville and Truckee Meadows regions.

• *Engage and support citizens in multiple roles to reach for results, including the roles of issue framer, evaluator, advocate, and collaborator.* Kesler and O'Connor's findings, noted above, about seven movements having common process themes of engaging citizens around shared vision and values, suggest that many community indicators efforts at least engage citizens as issue framers. In Jacksonville and Truckee Meadows, citizens are engaged in all four of these roles.

The strategic issues are, in brief:

• *Set the boundaries of community measurement to match the purpose of the endeavor.* JCCI's initial quality-of-life focus on Jacksonville-Duval County reflected its origins as an organization and the main focus at the time of its early indicators sponsor. Ten years later, the Northeast Florida United Way sponsored a set of JCCI health and human services indicators covering the five-county region, which became the focus of JCCI's merged quality-of-life reports, which brought the two indicator sets together (though for some indicators, only Jacksonville-Duval County data are available). TMT's regional quality-of-life focus comes from the regional planning process from which its initial indicators emerged. Sustainable Seattle, when frustrated with a lack of action on its regional indicators, switched to a neighborhood focus in 2000. After taking a few years to establish projects in several Seattle neighborhoods, Sustainable Seattle restarted its regional work and by 2004 was maintaining both regional indicators and neighborhood indicators projects, with its fourth regional sustainability indicators report planned for 2005.

• *Build partnerships that focus resources on desired results, and connect measurement with accountability.* JCCI's partnership with the Northeast Florida United Way has led to the health and human service subset of JCCI's indicators influencing resource allocation and strategic planning of United Way–funded agencies, and led to an outcome indicator focus for human service planning among other major funders in the region. And a measure of accountability for some of JCCI's indicators has been achieved through their adoption by another partner, the city of Jacksonville. In Nevada, TMT's quality-of-life compacts have drawn resources and accountability of major organizations behind trying to measurably improve the quality of life. Sustainable Seattle's move to a neighborhood focus in 2000 was due to its board's conclusion that local public officials were "reluctant to embrace some of the indicators because they did not want to be held accountable for results over which they had little control."[6] Working in neighborhoods, Sustainable Seattle partners with city government agencies, university programs, and citizens to measure and improve neighborhood conditions.

• *Build on an existing organization's credibility and relationships, or design a new organization to build relationships and credibility.* JCCI built on its existing credibility and relationships to help citizens reach for results, including its credibility as an impartial convener of community deliberation. TMT is an example of citizens' forming a new organization that has built relationships, in part through its design as a membership organization, and that has built credibility by reaching out to all interests in the region.

Citizens Focus on Improving Jacksonville's Quality of Life

By 2000, when Kesler and O'Connor were examining community movements, community indicators projects had proliferated across the United States. By 2004, anyone who was starting a new project might learn from any of thousands of community indicators researchers and practitioners gaining experience around the world. That March, 450 of them gathered at a conference of the newly formed Community Indicators Consortium[7] in Reno, Nevada, hosted by Truckee Meadows Tomorrow. A conference organizer, David Swain, a consultant who had recently retired from JCCI, gave welcoming remarks from his perspective of many years of managing JCCI's community indicators and giving advice on indicators to other communities. JCCI was a source of experience and inspiration at the conference, because in 1985, JCCI could not look to thousands of practitioners for guidance. It had to invent the wheel. Or, more accurately, it had to invent the first citizens' camera of community quality of life.

Citizens Design a Quality-of-Life Camera

When JCCI first ventured into community indicators reporting with the Jacksonville Chamber of Commerce, these partners sought a broader picture of the quality of life in Jacksonville than economic data alone would show. The chamber wanted that picture to market business development, and JCCI wanted to use it as a report card on community well-being. The initial JCCI Quality of Life Indicators Report in 1985 had annual data for 1983, 1984, and 1985, providing three comparative snapshots of how Jacksonville fared for those years on a wide range of issues.

The camera that took those snapshots was designed by citizens, as citizens selected the indicators reported, so the resulting picture mattered to people in the community. From the beginning, JCCI committed itself to developing long-term trends by gathering and reporting data for years into the future. Those snapshots became the first three frames of a motion picture, updated annually, of how the quality of life has been changing in Jacksonville. Over the years, JCCI reporting has evolved into an increasingly sophisticated camera, used by citizens to keep the focus on critical issues of community well-being. The quantitative pictures of these issues in the annual indicators reports inform JCCI's citizen policy study and advocacy processes and have been recognized and supported by important public and private institutions in the community.

Developing JCCI's Community Indicators

Citizens Have Been Involved from the Start. In 1985, a steering committee was formed of about a dozen volunteers who combined civic involvement experience with knowledge of key aspects of Jacksonville's quality of life. Working with JCCI staff, the committee defined the quality of life as "a feeling of well-being, fulfillment, or satisfaction resulting from factors in the external environments" and developed a framework of the following nine "elements" (or "external environments") of quality of life to help define indicators:

- Achieving Educational Excellence
- Sustaining a Healthy Community
- Growing a Vibrant Economy
- Maintaining Responsive Government
- Preserving the Natural Environment

- Moving Around Efficiently
- Promoting Social Wellbeing and Harmony
- Keeping the Community Safe
- Enjoying Arts, Culture, and Recreation

More than one hundred citizen volunteers representing a broad base of the community were then recruited in an open process to serve on nine task forces of ten to fifteen people each, to develop up to ten indicators for each element. Task forces were informed by staff research on what might and could be measured and by invited stakeholders and experts. Over several months, citizens on the task forces played issue framer roles as they developed indicators. JCCI staff used the task forces' work to prepare a draft first report, which was reviewed by the steering committee, revised, and published by JCCI with a media release cosponsored by the chamber of commerce. Since then, publication of each annual report has been overseen by a committee of citizens who act as evaluators to ensure the emphasis in interpretation and presentation of the report is a citizen emphasis, and the report is kept relevant to the community.

In 1995, when the United Way of Northeast Florida partnered with JCCI to develop indicators focused on health and human service issues, JCCI again used citizen committees to develop them. These have been reported annually in a separate report and amalgamated with the quality-of-life indicators into a combined report starting in 2002, titled *Indicators for Progress: A Guide for Building a Better Community.*[8]

Citizens Improve JCCI's Indicators, Increasing Their Relevance and Sophistication.
Through special projects in 1991, 1995, 2000, 2001, and 2002, JCCI has engaged citizens in major efforts to enhance its indicators, keeping citizens involved as issue framers who keep making the indicators more relevant and useful. In each case, variations of the first task force process to develop indicators have been used. With each upgrade, citizens have added new lenses to their quality-of-life camera, enabling them to use the indicators in more ways. For example, in 1991, citizens set targets for the year 2000 for the quality-of-life indicators, giving themselves a lens to see their desired community future. They also set priorities among the nine elements of quality of life and among indicators within each element, and started an annual process of awarding "gold stars" and "red flags" to selected indicators based on their trends and distance from targets. This added "close-up lenses" to focus community attention selectively on important progress and critical problems. In 1999, citizens also added targets, gold stars, and red flags to the health and human service indicators.

With staff assistance, citizens have enthusiastically dug into indicators upgrade projects. Bill Kwapil was a citizen volunteer in the 2000–2001 efforts to review and revise the quality-of-life indicators to keep them relevant after fifteen years and to set new targets for 2005. To Kwapil, "The process was fun because of two challenges.

First, we had to try to quantify concepts of the community's quality of life to determine the best indicators, balancing what we were actually able to measure against what we wanted to measure. Then we had to try to set targets that reflected both our ideals of the quality of life and our practical sense of what improvements could reasonably be accomplished in just a few years. This was all very meaningful for me—and is very important for the good of the community—because it creates real-life meaning from numbers, which can guide influential leaders and decision makers toward meaningful community improvement."

In 2000 and 2002, citizens used information provided by staff and stakeholders to identify "very important linkages" among indicators: how changes in one indicator were expected to affect other indicators. They identified "reinforcing" linkages, for example, a positive trend in student achievement test scores is expected to have a positive influence on net employment growth.[9] They also identified potentially "undermining" linkages, for example, how an increase in housing starts, desired for a vibrant economy, can have a negative influence on the number of good air quality days if added housing leads to increased traffic congestion.[10] These linkages are like special lenses that increase the resolution of citizens' pictures of their community's well-being, allowing them to see more finely grained connections between important issues, and informing how they learn in the policy study process and use their findings in JCCI's implementation process in their role as advocates for change.

Using Indicator Trends to Inform Citizen Policy Studies

JCCI's annual update reports have provided long-term indicator trend data, changing JCCI's reports from snapshots to "moving pictures" of an evolving quality of life in Jacksonville. That has helped citizens working as issue framers and evaluators in JCCI's policy study process, described in Chapter Two, learn to be more nuanced in designing and conducting studies of complex problems. For example, JCCI first conducted a citizen policy study on teen pregnancy in 1982, before the indicator projects had started. By 1995, citizen interest in the issue, driven at least partly by the availability of indicator information, led JCCI to consider the issue for study again. Indicator trend data showed slow but steady improvement, leading the volunteers and the JCCI board of directors to decide not to repeat or update the 1982 study but to tackle a closely related issue: the well-being of teen single parents and their families. They wanted to study results when the preferred outcome, prevention, failed. When they got down to work, the citizen policy committee went beyond this agenda and also examined prevention. In effect, the citizen study committee's response was to acknowledge prevention progress but want the community to do even better, reinforcing a strong community value of preventing teen pregnancies. But they also learned that they had to look deeper into this complex problem, to consider how to improve community solutions for those teens who do give birth.

An Integrated Process to Stimulate Community Improvement

Although they were developed separately, JCCI has come to understand how its indicators and its citizen policy study and implementation processes (described in Chapter Two) perform related roles in the context of an overall, integrated process of community improvement. In this circular process, measurement through the use of indicators is important in two ways, shown at two different points in Figure 5.1. First, the quantification of key aspects of a community vision through a set of indicators aids in understanding important issues, which translates to improved learning by citizens in JCCI's policy study process, which informs their policy recommendations. Then, after the JCCI implementation task force advocates for change and monitors community action, changes in the indicators over time inform future evaluation of whether the action was adequate to achieve the vision.

In Figure 5.1, the primary citizen engagement role is noted below each step in the community improvement process. Mostly, citizens are issue framers, evaluators, and advocates in this process. If, in the "monitoring of action" step, citizens not only track actions as advocates seeking change, but also take action themselves through voluntary coproduction, compromise, or partnership building, they will also play a collaborator role at that time.[11]

FIGURE 5.1. JCCI INTEGRATED COMMUNITY IMPROVEMENT PROCESS

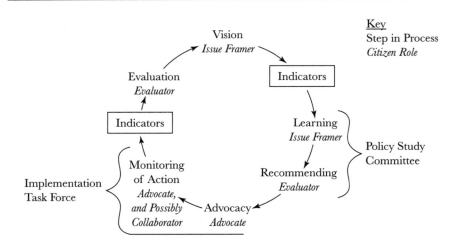

A Work in Progress: Applying the Process to Education Reform

Jacksonville citizens have voiced concerns about public education since the 1960s. They have seen persistent deficiencies in their countywide school district of almost 130,000 students. In 1991, JCCI volunteers ranked education the highest-priority quality-of-life element and the high school graduation rate the most important education indicator. In later years, citizens corroborated the importance of high school graduation when they identified "very important linkages." They noted how the graduation rate affects indicators of a "Vibrant Economy," "Social Well Being and Harmony," "Arts, Culture, and Recreation," a "Healthy Community," "Responsive Government," and "Keeping the Community Safe."[12] It is perhaps JCCI's most "linked" indicator. But high school graduation had been disappointingly low for years, hovering between 66 and 76 percent from 1983 to 1990.

In 1991, citizens set a goal of a 90 percent graduation rate by the year 2000, and JCCI started an education policy study in 1992, in which fifty citizens took part. Their June 1993 report, *Public Education: The Cost of Quality,*[13] was enthusiastically received by the school superintendent. JCCI then immediately started a citizen implementation process to advocate for recommended improvements, but it soon bogged down. As volunteer implementation chair Penny Christian put it, "We became increasingly frustrated by the lack of responsiveness on the part of administrators throughout the system, despite evident support for our recommendations from the superintendent. After two years of this frustration, we turned to the elected school board but found that they felt as limited as we in their ability to control the bureaucracy." In the meantime, the high school graduation rate behaved erratically, peaking at 84 percent in 1993 but then declining steadily to 71 percent by 1996.

JCCI issued a negative citizen implementation report, and the business community, interested in workforce development, took note. A group of business leaders published a "manifesto" in the local newspaper, based on the 1993 JCCI study recommendations, calling on the school board for major reform. The school board responded, establishing the New Century Commission, which conducted a participative inquiry (consistent with a JCCI recommendation) that involved more than a thousand citizens and led to 155 recommendations. A new superintendent was hired to lead the reform, and new efforts were made to involve citizens and the business community in assisting schools. Despite all that effort and promising early increases on Florida's standardized achievement test, the high school graduation rate continued to decline.[14]

By 2002, JCCI volunteers were concerned enough to launch another citizen study. While the new study started out assessing implementation of the New Century recommendations, it branched out into a broad assessment of public education as a two-year, two-phase effort. The phase one study committee found that the school system had implemented productive reforms over ten years, and many students did well. But they also found a large, "deplorable" achievement gap: the system failed many other students. They noted that the gap had not only been attributed to schools but also to factors such as low family income, racial prejudice, low parental involvement, high mobility, or low household literacy. In its charge to the phase two study committee, the phase one committee observed that "the social and economic issues that interfere with a child's ability to learn represent the failure of a community, not the school system. At the same time, student achievement will not improve if schools wait for the community to provide them with only well-adjusted, middle-class children to teach. . . . Therefore, Phase Two should study the issue: How can the community and the Duval County Public Schools eliminate the gap in individual student achievement by ensuring that all students achieve at the highest levels possible."[15]

In keeping with that charge, the phase two committee took a comprehensive look at reasons for an achievement gap from early child development issues to family, community, and in-school factors that affect children's learning from grade school through high school. Their recommendations, released in the summer of 2004, specified actions to be taken by the school system, many other community organizations, and community leaders such as the mayor, were passed on to the next implementation task force for advocacy.[16]

Education reform in Jacksonville continues to be a work in progress, illustrating that major improvements of complex community systems do not occur quickly and easily, even with the help of indicators. But JCCI's community improvement cycle combining indicators and citizen studies is still going, incorporating learnings from education reforms attempted between the 1993 and 2003 JCCI study reports. Interim efforts benefited from the attention and energy of the business community and the New Century Commission. Once others' energies had dissipated, however, JCCI citizens were again on hand to take the lead in studying and advocating for improvement.

Recognition for the Indicators Increases Their Influence on Results

In addition to JCCI and its citizen volunteers using the indicators, other institutions have recognized the indicators, increasing their credibility in the community. This has further encouraged volunteers, such as Vanessa Boyer, quoted at the start of this chapter.

JCCI's initial indicators partner, the chamber of commerce, has gotten what it wants of the indicators: to document Jacksonville's quality of life to corporate leaders considering investing in the region. Chamber president Wally Lee said, "Quantitative answers to questions about our schools, recreational and cultural opportunities, and the environment help market the community. Since JCCI began reporting its indicators, we have used them every year as one tool to help promote Jacksonville to the world."

Government Recognition of Indicators Increases Accountability for Results. The city of Jacksonville, a combined city-county government, has made the JCCI quality-of-life indicators a source for improving its own performance measures. The city also became a major funder of JCCI's reporting. While the city has not committed to acting on JCCI's indicators wholesale, it has tracked selected JCCI indicators as part of city outcome measurement, including police, fire, and rescue response times, and public satisfaction with the leadership of elected officials. This is significant because, for those indicators, the city government has implicitly taken accountability for results.

JCCI volunteers have also interacted with city officials to improve data made available, so community conditions can be better understood. For example, JCCI volunteers succeeded in getting the city to report acreage separately for "passive" and "active" parks, and for "neighborhood" and "regional" parks, instead of just reporting one undifferentiated number.

Partnership with Nonprofit Investors Links Resources to Indicators. JCCI's other major indicators partner, the United Way of Northeast Florida, used JCCI's quality-of-life indicators for strategic planning in the late 1980s and early 1990s, before approaching JCCI in 1995 to develop health and human service indicators to document unmet needs and desired outcomes. As planned, the regional United Way has been using this indicator set, called the Community Agenda, to guide volunteers who help determine allocation of nearly $20 million in annual contributions. As a result, service agencies now refer to Community Agenda indicators to justify funding requests and use the indicators in their own strategic planning. Meanwhile, recognition and use of the indicators has expanded to all member organizations of the Human Services Council (HSC), a collaboration of major public and private funders in northeast Florida, and to the service providers they support. The HSC funders, finding value in the Community Agenda indicators, recently decided, for their own purposes, to begin collectively tracking a larger, more detailed set of outcome indicators that includes the JCCI Community Agenda indicators. In a relatively short time, the region's landscape for health and human services funding has changed significantly to become more outcome oriented and more informed by indicator data.

Building Trust and Community Energy Through Impartiality and Deliberation

JCCI's Impartiality Adds to the Indicators' Credibility. While JCCI advocates for community actions, these are not predetermined actions based on narrow interests, but emerge from citizen studies. This helps make JCCI's indicators, and priorities that citizens set among them, highly credible in Jacksonville. As volunteer Bill Kwapil explains, "It's especially important that this kind of thinking comes from a group like JCCI, which is seen as representing the impartial consensus of the community. JCCI has no self-interested axes to grind because of its broadly based citizen involvement.

Decision makers and the media take the indicators seriously, although they don't always respond with action, so our efforts are helping to define the community's preferences and are having some influence, at least, on defining public issues."

Fostering Deliberation Sustains Citizens' Energy. Another critical role JCCI plays is that of convener of community deliberation. An essential JCCI staff role is facilitation of the group process of volunteer committees, including working with volunteer leadership on agendas, inviting stakeholders and experts to meetings, facilitating meetings, and maintaining a written record. JCCI staff research and analysis also helps guide citizens. But perhaps most essential is JCCI's promotion of openness to stakeholders with different interests and perspectives, and facilitation of thorough deliberation before conclusions are reached, to ensure decisions will be respected in the community. JCCI also often convenes decision makers and stakeholders in attempts to move community improvement processes along and has become trusted as an impartial—if not always neutral—convener.

For issues that seem intractable, such as education reform, it could be easy for the community to give up in frustration. However, the respect JCCI has built as a convener of deliberation keeps citizens coming back to participate and keeps institutions and decision makers paying attention, which helps keep the community working at difficult issues for decades. JCCI, as a deliberative institution, sustains the community's energy to keep reaching for results.

Making a Difference and Measuring It in Truckee Meadows

The people of the Truckee Meadows region in northwest Nevada did not have an organization like JCCI to turn to when they wanted to support a system of regional quality-of-life indicators. So they formed their own organization, small in budget and contract staff, but big in volunteer energy, partners' support, and community spirit.

From Stalemated Planning to Bottom-Up Commitments

Truckee Meadows's quality-of-life indicators were conceived to help break a regional planning stalemate between rapid-growth and constrained-growth advocates. The Truckee Meadows region includes the cities of Reno and Sparks and unincorporated areas in the Truckee River Valley in Washoe County, Nevada. The idea was to track indicator trends over time as feedback to suggest whether or how regional plan revisions should regulate growth to protect the quality of life. This was the crux of a compromise that enabled the first Truckee Meadows Regional Plan to be adopted in 1991. Indicators were developed, and annual reports on them have been published since 1994. But they have not become a driver of state-mandated updates of the regional plan, which have been driven by other considerations. However, although the region does not yet have top-down quality-of-life mandates, a bottom-up movement has been growing of citizens and organizations committed to improving outcomes. The catalyst for these commitments is not a large government or private organization, but Truckee Meadows Tomorrow (TMT), a small community nonprofit that was not even formed until after indicator development was underway and depends on a dedicated membership of citizens and organizations from across the region.

Broad-Based Participation Leads to Indicators Citizens Support

A citizen-based process to develop indicators was initiated by a 100-person task force formed by a government planning agency and a private, nonprofit economic development organization. The task force was broad-based, combining professional planners and community representatives. They started by learning from Jacksonville, borrowing JCCI's model of identifying major elements of community well-being, which led the task force to form nine committees (for example, on public safety and on the environment). The committees did initial research and took a working list of 180 indicators out to the public. The task force first met with numerous groups, discussing two major issues per meeting and playing the Quality-of-Life Money Game with citizens placing ten "quality-of-life dollars" on indicators they felt best defined an issue. The task force then conducted mail and newspaper surveys and held forums targeting ethnic communities not yet well represented in the process. The task force also conducted a "Youth View" event to get youth input on indicators.

The approximately two thousand citizens who took part in discussions and eleven hundred who answered surveys were engaged as issue framers in defining quality of life in the Truckee Meadows region. Their ideas enabled the task force to select sixty-six indicators of broad citizen interest in 1993, used for the first quality-of-life indicators report in 1994. The indicators were revised in 2000 to the current "30 Top Indicators for the Future," organized to measure six major issues: Economic Vitality, Health and Wellness, Natural Environment, Education and Life Long Learning, Land Use and Infrastructure, and Public Safety and Welfare. Reno resident Alice Heiman was not involved in developing indicators but says, "The indicators are pretty much right on. TMT picked things people really care about, because of all that citizen input."

An Organization Built on Engagement, Trust, and Collaboration

TMT did not exist at the start of the initial process to select indicators. By its end in 1993, members of the initial indicators task force had incorporated TMT as an independent nonprofit organization to maintain and report on the indicators. The people who started it had already demonstrated that they listened to citizens, which gave TMT a good start on engendering community trust.

After having virtually no direct budget for two to three years, TMT received a grant of $750,000 from the Washoe Health System, which sustained its work for several years and helped TMT build its name in the community and establish credibility for the indicators and related projects. Since that grant ran out, TMT has kept going on membership fees and in-kind support.

TMT Members Provide Energy, Support, and Relationships. TMT developed as a membership organization, with both individual citizen and organizational members, a good blend for "an authority, change agent and advocate in improving the community's quality of life through collaboration and partnership," as former TMT president Karen Foster called TMT.[17] Individual members provide energy and personal commitment. Organizational members from government, business, and the nonprofit sector provide in-kind and financial support.

Members also provide important relationships for TMT to build on. Individual citizen members provide relationships with friends, neighbors, business associates, and resident, school, professional, and other affiliative groups across the region—grassroots connections that build awareness of TMT and provide a base for drawing on citizens as assets who can act individually or in small groups to improve the quality of life. Organizational members provide relationships with decision makers who control resources and influence policies, and with similar decision makers in other organizations they work with, to provide a ready-made base of partners who can get things done. "Getting things done" can mean helping TMT get its work done, such as issue its indicators report, or lining up resources and actions of organizations in the region behind improving the quality of life.

Members include the governments of Reno, Sparks, and Washoe County, whose elected officials were not able to agree on using indicators for planning. Some of the staff of those governments, such as Washoe County community relations director Kathy Carter, have been leaders of TMT's efforts to build support for the indicators in the community. Carter, TMT president in 2004 and a long-time board member, has been instrumental in gaining county cooperation with TMT initiatives.

Wide Consultation Keeps Indicators Relevant. TMT's inclusive, engaging style helped lead to the current set of indicators, revised in 2000 from the initial set to stay consistent with citizen preferences yet also reflect indicators commonly used by other organizations in the region such as business and economic development groups and the United Way. In developing the current indicator set, TMT surveyed several thousand people from groups using various indicators to help find which would have the broadest application. TMT executive director Karen Hruby notes how TMT's current indicators "do not reflect a single viewpoint, like that of business," but can gain support from many organizations and citizens in the region. TMT's biennial quality-of-life indicators reports make its members evaluators who are tracking outcomes for their region.

Focusing on What *Can* Be Done to Improve the Region

Once TMT was started, its early members did not wait until the first indicators report was published to become advocates for improvement, as they began engaging citizens as collaborators in improving the quality of life. Even when the indicators did not become a driver of top-down policies enacted in regional plans, TMT kept on going with its bottom-up, collaborative approach to keep citizens engaged and find new ways of engaging organizations, always focusing on what *can* be done to improve the quality of life.

Keeping Citizens Engaged. In 1993, TMT's first year, it launched the Adopt an Indicator program. Most "adopters" are residents, though some are businesses and public officials. Here are just three examples:

- Susan Lynn adopted Truckee River Water Quality. She organizes an annual Truckee River Cleanup Day. Also, through her river improvement group, the Truckee River Yacht Club, adopters of sections of the river keep watch, looking for illegal campers and trash buildup.
- Washoe County district attorney Dick Gammick adopted child abuse and domestic violence, making those problems high priorities of his office and implementing special programs to combat them.
- Alice Heiman adopted the high school dropout and college attrition rates and lifelong learning, which she works on as an officer of Women Executives Accelerating Change Today, which mentors women in high school, college, and the workforce. She also adopted parental involvement in schools and has volunteered in her son's school, and on the Washoe County Middle School Task Force for Special Populations.

Citizens rarely commit to big initiatives. Former TMT president Lynn Atcheson calls it "a program more geared to engaging citizens in improving an indicator in some small way." As TMT board member Elisa Maser explains, "A lot is built on things that are already being done, but it helps for people to understand their piece of the puzzle and that someone else is working on it." TMT asks adopters for feedback on their progress, but does not correlate their actions with indicator trends. Adopt an Indicator works well at building awareness of the indicators. Opportunities to engage thousands of citizens in big issues, such as defining quality of life, do not occur every year. But Adopt an Indicator keeps hundreds of citizen-collaborators engaged as co-producers of quality-of-life solutions at any given time. TMT's slogan, "You make a difference. We measure it," reinforces citizens' roles in improving the quality of life.

Moving Up to Larger-Scale Collaborations That Link Indicators with Resources and Accountability. When the regional plan was updated in 1996 without strong influence from the quality-of-life indicators, TMT still kept Adopt an Indicator going. In 2001, it started its quality-of-life compact initiative, focusing on organizations' making large, measurable commitments. Participants sign a legal contract that spells out stakeholders, indicators they will try to improve, plans to measure their contributions, the time period for the compact, and reporting requirements. While they may not measure specific items in TMT's data tables for an indicator, they will measure things they do that should contribute to improvement in the indicator. For example, Washoe County's compact to improve the natural environment did not include TMT's air quality measures, such as numbers of good, moderate, and unhealthy days, but it did include a commitment to increase and measure the number of county alternative fuel vehicles, which increased by 50 percent in a year. The county accepted accountability for a measurable achievement and used significant resources to accomplish it. The Washoe County quality-of-life compact was recognized by the International City/County Management Association.

From 2001 to 2004, TMT arranged five quality-of-life compacts. The Washoe County compact on the natural environment came first. The other four are:

• The United Way of Northern Nevada and the Sierra's Community Wide Indicators Compact, with a plan to tie community funding to outcomes and indicators in use.

• An Open Space Compact focused on environmental stewardship that brings together five business and nonprofit organizations that do not normally work together, including the Sierra Pacific Power Company, the Girl Scouts of the Sierra Nevada, and the Nevada Land Conservancy.

• The Washoe County School District and Washoe Education Association's compact to improve parental involvement includes producing a best practices booklet and commitments to measurable increases in parent volunteer hours, attendance at parent conferences, school participation in a National PTA certification program, and professional development for teachers and staff to better use parent volunteers in classrooms and schools. Toward the last goal, the National PTA, hoping to encourage similar partnerships around the country, trained 231 teachers and staff from sixty-one school district sites at no cost to the district in summer 2003.

• A Voter Turnout Compact with the New Voters Project, Nevada Museum of Art, Washoe County Registrar of Voters, and Washoe County Library.

Another compact was under development in 2004, a Healthier Lifestyles Compact targeting outreach and education on obesity and diabetes with the Washoe Health System, St. Mary's Health Network, District Health, and the University of Nevada, Reno.

The compacts are an important advance in TMT's scope, expanding the advocate and collaborator roles of TMT's citizen members and the partner role of its organizational members. When organizations sign compacts committing to specific, measurable actions, they are making themselves accountable for their actions and putting substantial resources behind improvements that can make a difference in the quality of life. Elisa Maser feels that "since the compacts are so large, over time they will have an impact on the indicators. Compacts should be able to move the needle."

Using Leverage and Making the Most of Opportunities. TMT leverages in-kind contributions from organizational partners and compact participants, and tremendous energy from its members to accomplish much more than might be expected, given its very small contract staff. TMT should gain added secondary leverage from the regional United Way's Community Wide Indicators Compact by leveraging the efforts of United Way–funded agencies to contribute to improving quality-of-life indicators.

When opportunities arise, TMT has also leveraged popular support and organizational commitments for large gains. For example, it built popular support for a sustainable quality of life, contributing to Washoe County voters' approving a $34 million bond issue specifying sustainable design to build libraries, trails, and open spaces. Then the county signed the Natural Environment Compact confirming its commitment to conserve energy in existing and planned facilities. TMT's Kathy Carter used the opportunity of these events to reinforce the county board of commissioners' initial consideration of a sustainable design for a new library. The board approved the sustainable design despite the higher initial cost, as operating savings would pay back the added investment in seven years. Based on the final design, the county projected a savings of over $400,000 in a twenty-year period in utility costs alone, just one benefit of having an environmentally friendly new public building.

Keeping the Community Aware and Active

TMT's leaders know the value of keeping the spotlight on its indicators and on opportunities to improve the quality of life. They also know the importance of giving public credit to those who act on their opportunities, encourage others to do so, and keep people and organizations in the community actively pursuing improvement.

Celebrating Accomplishments and All Who Play a Role. Every two years, TMT draws about fifteen hundred people to its "Accentuate the Positive" event to celebrate quality-of-life contributions of indicator adopters, TMT members, compact participants, and about thirty award winners. Their first celebration was Alice Heiman's first exposure to TMT. She called it "such an uplifting event, so inspiring. It showcased all the good stuff going on in the community. I just got so jazzed." Heiman soon started adopting indicators.

Using Times of Appreciation for Public Education. TMT includes an educational day before the awards luncheon to ensure all who play a role, large or small, feel appreciated, and to educate the public on quality-of-life indicators and initiatives. Elisa Maser calls the process a "quality-of-life showcase," similar to a trade show, with exhibitors who interactively tell their story on how they are improving quality of life in the region. They also highlight quality-of-life issues that have lacked attention, to draw interest in compacts and indicator adoptions on those issues. While their big celebration is biennial, every year TMT thanks all their active indicator adopters, using the opportunity to further adopters' educations and build support for quality-of-life compacts among organizations that adopt indicators.

Continually Getting the Message Out. Some of TMT's most important partnerships help it communicate with the public. Every two years, TMT partners with the daily newspaper, the *Reno Gazette-Journal,* and the three local television stations, to feature award winners and their quality-of-life contributions. Before 2003, the *Gazette* ran inserts each year featuring highlights from TMT's annual Community Well Being Report. Then *Nevada Living,* a regional magazine in the *Gazette's* publishing group, printed the entire report in its April 2003 issue, circulating it to eighty thousand people in the region. Before then, TMT could mail the report to only twenty-five hundred people per year. In another in-kind effort, Washoe County has been making educational videos for TMT. Through these efforts, the celebrations, and marketing campaigns, TMT works hard with its partners to keep beating the quality-of-life drum and educating the public. District attorney Dick Gammick sees great benefit to TMT's publicizing a broad picture of the quality of life: "It is immeasurable. It tells you everything as a community. All of us get in our little world—fighting crime is mine. TMT lays it all out. TMT is invaluable in that."

Learning, Changing, and Staying Focused on the Future

TMT was not fazed when elected officials did not use the initial indicator set for its original purpose in regional planning. Elisa Maser said, "This has been an evolution. In the beginning, they wanted decision makers to use all the indicators to make good decisions. But this is too much information for many decision makers to use. They have to focus on specific topics." So TMT learned to get public agencies that report to some of these same decision makers, as well as other organizations in the region, to adopt indicators, and then to sign compacts committing to larger-scale improvements. Maser calls the compacts "a way to arrive at a self-reinforcing system."

Maser also observed, "What's good about TMT is they continually ask, 'How do we take this to the next level?'" TMT wants to build on the compacts and become more systematic in linking plans and actions to indicators. The challenge of increasing the indicators' influence on policymakers' decisions, including growth strategies, also remains. Kathy Carter noted, "We know you don't give away the farm just to have growth, because the quality of life will go away if you don't take care of it." And TMT has the indicators to measure how much quality of life is lost, or gained, depending on how growth is accomplished. Finally, TMT faces a challenge in just staying afloat, with a small budget based on member contributions and a minimal contract staff, and its high dependency on in-kind support. TMT's members and partners, and the citizens they inspire, will need to continue to focus their great energies to keep the organization moving ahead.

Connecting Indicators with Resources and Accountability and Making Those Connections Stronger

Citizens reaching for results through community measurement and improvement efforts are bound to run into disappointments along the way, especially if they stay at it for a while. That has happened in Jacksonville, the Truckee Meadows region, and Seattle. The Jacksonville Community Council Inc., Truckee Meadows Tomorrow, and Sustainable Seattle have all been pursuing their community indicators efforts for over a decade—for two decades in Jacksonville. All three have been disappointed, at one time or another, when resource or accountability connections have not been made to their indicators or failed to lead to improvement.

In response to failed education reforms, JCCI rolled out its citizen policy study process again, but changed the focus of study based on learnings from indicators and past reforms. Sustainable Seattle could not get local public officials to accept accountability for improving regional sustainability, so it put its regional indicators on hiatus for a few years until it could establish neighborhood indicators and improvement efforts with partners willing to accept accountability and commit resources on a smaller scale. TMT faced a lack of top-level accountability for improving regional indicators. TMT's response was to become a catalyst for bottom-up action and accountability, with the Adopt an Indicator program and especially the quality-of-life compacts. Although all three responses are different, they all make sense in their own community and organizational context. All three organizations were willing to learn, change, and respond in ways that improve the chances that citizens will reach results.

One of the challenges citizens—and the organizations that support them—face in reaching for results is that the use of their indicators for community improvement is not assured. It is possible for citizens to gain commitments of resources and accountability for efforts to improve some indicators, as is clear from the JCCI and TMT examples. But citizens have to work hard on their advocacy and expend a lot of energy to win those commitments. While such advocacy is well worth the effort, citizens' energy can be used more effectively if it is channeled into a systematic performance feedback cycle used by government or private organizations that commit substantial resources to improving community results.

Strong connections of measured results with resources, actions, and accountability are possible in managing-for-results cycles that include systematic feedback of measured performance. When citizen engagement is aligned with such cycles, as it is in the next three chapters, they become governing-for-results cycles, in which citizens can become even more effective in reaching for results.

CHAPTER SIX

COMMUNITIES GOVERNING FOR RESULTS I

An Introduction to the Practice and to Interpreting the Case Examples

In advanced practice 4, communities governing for results, the three core community skills of citizen engagement, measuring results, and getting things done are well aligned with each other, as suggested in the graphic below, to enable a community to systematically, measurably, and continually achieve results that matter for its citizens.

Advanced Governance Practice 4: Communities Governing for Results

Four case examples of communities governing for results are presented in some depth in the next two chapters. Chapter Seven has three examples of results-driven community governance organized and managed by local governments: Prince William, County, Virginia; the City of Rochester, New York; and the District of Columbia (the city government of Washington, D.C.). Chapter Eight has an example of results-driven governance of nonprofit community development in many neighborhoods of the bistate Greater Kansas City metropolitan region. First, this chapter describes and analyzes communities governing for results as an overall concept and references the examples in the next two chapters to help illustrate that analysis.

This chapter provides a context for the examples in the next two chapters, to help you learn things from those communities that can enable you to make progress toward governing for results in your community. Advanced practice 4 is analyzed here

Advanced Governance Practice 4: Communities Governing for Results

4. Communities Governing for Results

by comparing it with the three other advanced practices of the governance model. Part of that comparison includes how the three-way alignment of communities governing for results builds on the strengths of the other advanced practices and resolves key issues that can lessen the benefits of each of those other practices. The issues and ideas presented here are meant to guide your interpretation of the community examples in the following chapters, so you may more likely find ideas or processes from those examples that may be adaptable to your community.

Turning Managing for Results into Governing for Results

The basic ideas behind communities governing for results are straightforward. One or more organizations in a community that make decisions that can have a significant impact on the well-being of the community and its people are systematically driven by two things in the decisions they make: the desired outcomes that community citizens say are most important and measurable performance in achieving those desired outcomes. The systematic nature of governing for results is of paramount importance. It is not enough to be responsive to citizens in solving one problem after another. Governing for results goes beyond solving individual problems to feeding measurable results back into community decision making, so the community will know whether solutions attempted are leading to desired outcomes and will have useful performance information to determine adjustments needed to get better outcomes. Communities using advanced practice 4 must have a systematic performance feedback cycle working so they can learn and keep making better decisions from day to day, month to month, and year to year. This is essentially the same as the managing-for-results performance cycles explored in Chapter Three, with one important addition: citizens are engaged to ensure the results sought and achieved by the community are the results people most care about, in other words, results that matter.

Comparing the Advanced Governance Practices

Communities governing for results is the most complex of the four advanced governance practices, and it encompasses elements of each of the first three practices. So, it is useful to approach advanced practice 4 by examining the strengths and weaknesses of the first three advanced practices and then exploring how governing for results builds on the strengths of the first three practices and resolves issues related to their weaknesses. Strengths and weaknesses of the first three practices are described below as they relate to three key community improvement themes that recur throughout this book: citizen roles, performance feedback, and collaborations. A fourth key improvement theme—linking desired results to resources and accountable organizations—also comes up in these discussions of strengths, weaknesses, and comparisons of practices.

Advanced Governance Practice 1: Community Problem Solving

Community problem solving, advanced practice 1, is particularly strong in the many roles citizens can effectively play and in collaborations citizens forge among themselves and with community organizations to leverage community assets and solve problems. Its chief weakness is the lack of systematic, measurable performance feedback on results. Without performance feedback, the community cannot know if solutions really result in desired outcomes over time. Also, without results measurement, the community lacks useful measures of conditions that can help citizens and decision makers determine the most strategic issues to address.

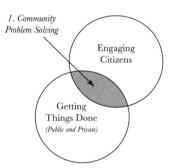

1. Community Problem Solving

Engaging Citizens

Getting Things Done
(Public and Private)

Advanced Governance Practice 2: Organizations Managing for Results

Organizations managing for results, advanced practice 2, has as its signal strength the systematic feedback of measured performance information, both to influence the use of an organization's resources to achieve results and create strong accountability for results. Collaborations across organizations to get better results can be quite strong,

Advanced Governance Practice 2: Organizations Managing for Results

*2. Organizations Managing
for Results*

as multiple organizations can adopt a clear, measurable focus for cooperating to achieve a common strategic goal. The weaknesses of this practice lie in not making use of all the ways citizens can strengthen community improvement. Organizations that manage for results primarily engage citizens as stakeholders—usually as customers. While citizens are sometimes engaged as collaborators as a matter of program design (usually as coproducers, as in Citizen Schools in Chapter Three), engaging citizens beyond their stakeholder role is not essential for managing for results. So the results measured and achieved may not be the results that are most important to a community's citizens. Also, with only limited involvement of citizens, identification of community assets beyond well-known organizations is likely to be limited, as the skills and resources of citizens, small businesses, and lesser-known groups are not tapped.

Advanced Governance Practice 3: Citizens Reaching for Results

Citizens reaching for results, advanced practice 3, has strengths related to each of the three themes examined. Citizens are effectively engaged in many roles, citizen-driven measurement keeps the focus of what is measured on results that most matter to citizens, and collaborations tend do be formed as a matter of necessity in order to marshal at least some community resources behind desired outcomes. But there are also

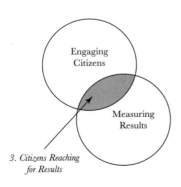

*3. Citizens Reaching
for Results*

limitations to these strengths, due to the chief weakness of this practice: the lack of systematic links between measured results and community resources and between measured results and organizations accountable for achieving those results. Citizens may have success in getting community organizations to commit resources and take accountability for measured results, but it is not inherent in advanced practice 3. Citizens have to work at it.

How Governing for Results Builds on the Strengths of the Other Three Advanced Practices

Advanced practice 4, communities governing for results, shares the strengths of the other advanced practices with respect to performance feedback, citizen roles, and collaborations, as shown in Table 6.1. This practice also builds on the strengths of the other three advanced practices with respect to these three key community improvement themes, as described below, including brief examples from the cases in the next two chapters on Prince William County, Virginia; Rochester, New York; Washington, D.C.; and Greater Kansas City.

Use of Performance Feedback. Communities governing for results combine the biggest strength of organizations managing for results (advanced practice 2)—systematic measured performance feedback to improve results—with a key strength of citizens reaching for results (advanced practice 3)—citizens influence what gets measured. These communities have systematic performance feedback cycles that influence resources and actions, and they build on this strength through citizen engagement to ensure results measured and achieved are results that are important to citizens—results that matter.

Like the managing-for-results cycles shown in Chapter Three, governing-for-results cycles can take different forms, with varying levels of complexity. All the community examples in Chapters Seven and Eight involve some form of systematic feedback of measured performance. The Prince William County, Virginia, example in Chapter Seven and the Greater Kansas City nonprofit community development example in Chapter Eight provide the most explicit depictions of governing-for-results cycles and how they influence resources and actions. Prince William County provides an example of systematic enterprisewide results management, using a complex cycle similar to that of Sunnyvale in Chapter Three, with the strong influence of multiyear strategic planning to determine shorter-term budgeting decisions and service-level (performance) targets. Citizens' active and frequent engagement in governance processes, especially in developing the strategic plans that drive results-based governance, advance this managing-for-results cycle to governing for results.

Nonprofit community development in Greater Kansas City is also driven by a complex governing-for-results cycle—really two interrelated cycles. One cycle works primarily at the level of individual community development corporations (CDCs) in specific neighborhoods, where most citizen engagement occurs, and where CDCs plan and implement specific community improvements responsive to citizens in the neighborhoods they serve. A nonprofit service organization in any community—no matter what services it provides—can learn from this inner cycle alone, as the Kansas City

TABLE 6.1. COMPARISON OF THE ADVANCED GOVERNANCE PRACTICES

Advanced Practices	Use of Performance Feedback	Citizen Roles	Nature of Collaborations
Advanced practice 1: **Community problem solving**	No systematic feedback of measured results.	Citizens participate in many roles and are involved early.	Citizens collaborate with each other and with organizations and identify community assets to add to collaborations.
Advanced practice 2: **Organizations managing for results**	Organizations use measured performance feedback to influence use of resources and achieve results.	Little integrated citizen involvement in organization's decision making process. Citizens seen mainly as stakeholder-customers.	Collaborations are mainly across organizations that adopt a measurable focus to achieve a common strategic goal.
Advanced practice 3: **Citizens reaching for results**	Citizen-driven measurement focuses on community-relevant results but is not linked to accountable organizations.	Citizens effectively engaged in many roles, but may not have much influence over organizations' use of performance data or resources.	Citizens work with data intermediaries to advocate for collaborations focused on desired outcomes.
Advanced practice 4: **Communities governing for results**	Citizens influence what gets planned, measured, and fed back to accountable organizations to keep resources and actions focused on desired results.	Citizens are engaged in several roles early in the governance process and stay engaged, as citizens' influence is a systematic part of the process.	Collaborations are forged among citizens, organizations, and other community assets to drive broad-based community governance for results that matter.

CDCs adapted a straightforward system of results-based targets and milestones for this cycle that has been used for many nonprofit services besides community development. The other cycle involves how investments in nonprofit development throughout the bistate metropolitan region are determined, including a performance-based approach to determine funding levels for all CDCs in the program. While neighborhood residents are not engaged in the regional investment cycle, several criteria used for assessing CDCs for investment reinforce citizen engagement by requiring various kinds and levels of engagement for a CDC to get the best "grades" on these criteria.

Citizen Roles. A key strength of both advanced practice 1 (community problem solving) and advanced practice 3 (citizens reaching for results) is how citizens are engaged in multiple roles. Communities governing for results share this strength, as citizens in those communities step well beyond their stakeholder roles to serve also as advocates, issue framers, evaluators, and collaborators, as should be clear from the full range of examples in the next two chapters. Communities governing for results build on this strength by reinforcing the influence citizens have in these roles in various ways. This is perhaps most dramatic in the way thousands of citizens of Washington, D.C., come together every two years in Citizen Summits to influence the strategic direction and budget priorities of the District of Columbia, their city government. But it is also apparent in the way citizens of Rochester, New York, Washington, D.C., and Greater Kansas City influence the planning and implementation of improvements in their own neighborhoods.

In Prince William County, while most citizens participate in strategic planning as issue framers, other citizens strengthen public trust by playing collaborator roles in running the process by cofacilitating strategic planning focus groups with county staff. Citizens also participate as evaluators in annual reviews of how the county is doing against its strategic plan, when they get a chance to review measured progress, ask questions, and provide their own interpretations for county officials to consider. In Greater Kansas City, some citizens are advocates for their neighborhoods while also playing issue framer and evaluator roles as board members of a neighborhood CDC. There are many more examples of citizens playing multiple roles in the cases of communities governing for results in Chapters Seven and Eight.

The Nature of Collaborations. Collaborations are an important way communities derive benefits from the first three advanced governance practices, as many of the examples in Chapters Two through Four demonstrate. In community problem solving (practice 1), citizens collaborate among themselves and with organizations to compromise and reach consensus to solve problems. Citizens also collaborate by identifying community assets and playing coproducer roles to enhance services and implement more improvement than organization budgets allow. Organizations managing for results (practice 2) tend to collaborate mainly with other organizations in the community to cooperate in achieving measurable results, focusing resources of several organizations on common goals to improve measurable outcomes. Citizens reaching for results (practice 3) need to be resourceful as collaborators, both to contribute to desired outcomes themselves as coproducers and to forge collaborations with organizations to get them to commit resources and voluntarily accept accountability for achieving measurable results.

Communities governing for results build on the collaborative strengths of all of the first three practices by combining some of the best features of all their collaborative tendencies. For example, Rochester's Neighbors Building Neighborhood (NBN) program involves many of the best aspects of collaborations that often occur in community problem solving. Citizens not only collaborate with each other and with city departments to plan improvements to their own neighborhoods, they also reach out to identify and engage other citizens and community organizations as assets in the community who can provide resources, expertise, and effort to help implement the plans, resulting in improvement efforts that go well beyond what the city government could pay for on its own. Citizens' collaboration with city government goes further, as city departments make sure resources are budgeted for those improvements to be implemented by the city, and they are held accountable for implementing results both through quarterly performance reporting to the mayor and through the automated NeighborLink Network that allows citizens to track implementation activities.

Prince William County benefits from a wide range of collaborations. As with organizations managing for results, Prince William forges many results-based collaborations among organizations. For example, county officials collaborate with forty nonprofit social service providers in the Coalition for Human Services to coordinate needs assessment, planning, and services. The county government budgets resources and contracts for many of the planned services and then holds the nonprofit providers accountable for achieving targeted results just as they would county government agencies. The county also collaborates for results with the school district by coordinating five-year financial and capital plans, which enabled the opening of new schools and renovation of existing schools ahead of schedule when growth exceeded projections. Prince William County goes well beyond these kinds of organization-to-organization collaborations to the kinds of citizen-citizen and citizen-organization collaborations more prevalent in advanced practices 1 and 3. For example, citizens with different views on development have collaborated in reaching compromises to complete economic development plans and comprehensive land use plans. One collaboration combines aspects of collaborations among organizations and collaborations between government and citizen coproducers: the collaboration among the county government's paid career fire service and the volunteer fire companies in the county, including volunteer firefighters and volunteer chiefs. This is also a strategic, performance-based collaboration as the volunteer fire companies' resources are planned together with paid career staff to meet service objectives such as the percentage of time emergency response targets are met.

Greater Kansas City also makes use of a wide range of collaborations in non-profit community development, including the collaboration of many local private and public organizations that pooled their resources and attracted matching national funds to create the largest community development fund in the Kansas City area's history. The local collaborative group of investors drives the overall performance-based focus of community development, including the performance criteria, noted above, that both keeps CDCs focused on results (as in advanced practice 2) and reinforces citizen engagement at the neighborhood level (as in advanced practices 1 and 3). Greater Kansas City CDCs forge collaborations with neighborhood associations as one of their most effective ways to bring citizens into collaborative efforts to improve their neighborhoods. CDCs see citizen collaboration in improving their neighborhoods as so important that they help build grassroots neighborhood organizations where they do not exist or where they need to be strengthened. The CDCs also collaborate with each other, neighborhood associations, neighborhood residents, and local police departments and other public agencies on community safety collaboratives to make neighborhoods safer.

How Governing for Results Provides the Missing Links

The first three advanced governance practices can all benefit communities. However, each has a weakness—a missing link that limits the community's ability to continually achieve results that matter to citizens. Advanced practice 4, communities governing for results, adds the missing links to resolve issues that limit governance effectiveness, as summarized in Table 6.2 and described below with further illustrations drawn from case examples in the next two chapters.

Adding Performance Feedback to Resolve Limits of Community Problem Solving. The weakness of community problem solving (advanced practice 1) is a lack of systematic performance feedback involving regular measurement of results. So even if collaborative solutions are implemented, the community will not know if those solutions really lead to desired outcomes. Also, the community, its government, and its other service providers are likely to focus most on problems that elicit the strongest negative response from engaged citizens. Many of these may be important problems to solve, but without measures of community conditions to guide them, decision makers will not know if they are addressing the most strategic improvements needed in the community.

Communities governing for results have what is missing from advanced practice 1: regular, systematic performance feedback of measured results. This performance

TABLE 6.2. COMMUNITY GOVERNANCE ISSUES AND THEIR RESOLUTION

Advanced Practice	Issues Limiting Effectiveness of Community Governance	How Governing for Results Resolves the Issues
Advanced practice 1: **Community problem solving**	*Lack of results measures and performance feedback:* • Cannot be sure important conditions really improve and that solutions work over time. • The most strategic issues may not be addressed, because of a tendency to focus on problems that elicit a strong emotional response by concerned citizens.	*Adding performance feedback on results:* • Informs community how well solutions really work and how much progress is being made toward desired outcomes, so organizations can make adjustments and improve results over time. • Performance feedback on important issues helps citizens and decision makers focus on the most strategic issues.
Advanced practice 2: **Organizations managing for results**	*Limited citizen engagement means:* • Results measured and achieved may not be what is most important to citizens. • Not making use of the full range of ways citizens can be engaged fails to harness the full energy possible from citizens.	*Adding robust citizen engagement in various roles ensures:* • What gets measured and implemented is what matters to citizens. • More citizen engagement in collaborations adds more assets beyond traditional government and nonprofit services.
Advanced practice 3: **Citizens reaching for results**	*Lack of systematic cycle tying resources and accountability to results:* • Resources to achieve results that matter not assured—citizens have to advocate for it. • Accountability by organizations for results not assured—citizens have to work at getting them to voluntarily accept accountability.	*Adding systematic governance cycle with performance-based resource allocation and accountability:* • Makes resource allocation part of systematic cycle focused on results. • Organizations see accountability for results as part of their role in community governance.

information will keep the community informed about how well solutions really work and how much progress is made toward desired outcomes, so they can make needed adjustments to improve results over time. For example, the system of targets and milestones used by CDCs in Greater Kansas City keeps CDC managers and boards, including neighborhood resident board members, informed about CDC progress toward their performance targets, so they adjust their efforts before they get too far off course and get better results for their neighborhoods. Performance feedback also helps citizens and decision makers better understand what issues are of high strategic importance, and act accordingly. A dramatic example was the 1996 decision by the elected board of supervisors of Prince William County to add a strategic goal on human services midway through a four-year strategic planning cycle because they saw that indicators related to social conditions in the county, such as homelessness and substance abuse, were deteriorating.

Adding Robust Citizen Engagement to Resolve Limits of Organizations Managing for Results. The weakness of organizations managing for results (advanced practice 2) is that citizen engagement is limited. Citizens may be engaged as customers and coproducers, but they have few opportunities to influence decisions about what gets planned, measured, and implemented. So even impressive gains in measured results by community organizations may not achieve the improvements that are most important to citizens, and the full energy of citizens is not likely to be harnessed.

Communities governing for results have what is missing from advanced practice 2: citizen engagement, starting early in community decision processes so they can influence what is planned, measured, and improved and continuing in a variety of roles to make greater use of citizens' energy and leverage more community assets to improve the community. All the examples in Chapters Seven and Eight involve robust, early citizen engagement that drives priorities on a communitywide level (for example, Prince William County, Washington, D.C.) and on a neighborhood level (for example, in Rochester, Washington, D.C., and Greater Kansas City). As the examples cited above make clear, a tremendous amount of citizen energy is harnessed to assist in implementing plans and evaluating performance and in leveraging assets beyond traditional government and nonprofit service providers. In Rochester, citizens engaged in neighborhood planning are even referred to as "asset managers" to describe their role in identifying and engaging community assets beyond government.

Another effect of adding citizen engagement is to keep the natural tendency of a well-run organization to maintain efficiency and control costs from overriding the extra quality or effort that may be needed to respond to citizens' priorities or to community needs as citizens, rather than managers, see them. For example, rather than build where it would be less costly to add new homes, the CHWC CDC of Kansas City, Kansas, built on South Ninth Street where it cost $150,000 extra to improve the infrastructure because neighborhood residents said it was most important to develop that site. In

Rochester, the City Department of Environmental Services reduced the quantity of street designs produced to increase their quality, from citizens' perspective, by putting in the extra time and effort to engage citizens in neighborhood charrette processes at the front end of planning for major street improvement projects. Also, without citizen engagement, even well-managed organizations tend to keep doing what they are used to doing. Engaged citizens can bring a focus on new priorities and stimulate new initiatives, as Washington, D.C., citizens did when they spurred creation of a whole new focus on youth, including creation of the Youth Advisory Council of young people from across the city to keep youth issues, and the effectiveness of youth programs, high on the government's agenda.

Systemically Link Performance Feedback to Resources and Accountability to Resolve Limits of Citizens Reaching for Results. The weakness of citizens reaching for results (advanced practice 3) is that measured results are not systematically linked to significant community resource commitments or to organizations accountable for achieving results. Citizens influence what is measured, but they have to expend a lot of energy advocating for service providers or other organizations to focus significant resources on achieving desired measured outcomes.

All the community examples in the next two chapters involve commitments of resources to what gets measured and planned and organizations that readily accept accountability for results as part of their role in community governance. The governance cycles in these communities make resource commitments and performance accountability part of a systematic process to help ensure results that matter are achieved. These approaches are not free. They involve costs to government or other community organizations as well as significant volunteer citizen effort. But the organizational costs and volunteer energies are good investments in using the much larger amounts of community resources generally spent on service delivery and improvement projects more wisely—in getting better results that matter to citizens.

The Washington, D.C., Citizen Summits involve significant costs by the district government and many citizen volunteer hours. These up-front planning and engagement costs and efforts have proven well worth it, as the District of Columbia has shifted tens of millions of dollars in budget allocations so its resource commitments will better match citizen priorities. In Rochester neighborhood planning, citizens spend time negotiating with city agencies concerning which improvements they will support. But once an agreed improvement plan is set, agencies include the planned improvements in their budgets. In each planning cycle, as citizens come to understand the limits of the city government's resources, they can focus part of their energy on identifying and engaging other community assets so a higher percentage of their priority projects will be implemented. Over time, as city agencies have shown they are accountable by implementing improvements, participating citizens have held themselves accountable for doing their part, as Rochester resident Glenn Gardner explains in Chapter Seven.

Systematic cycles that tie measured results to resources and accountability do not reduce citizen advocacy. There are still plenty of citizen advocates in communities where government or nonprofit organizations follow governing for results cycles, such as Paul Moessner, a volunteer advocate for human services in Prince William County, or Carole Diehl, an advocate for improving her Strawberry Hill neighborhood in Kansas City, Kansas. As is evident with the wide range of volunteer efforts in Prince William County beyond public decision processes, citizens in these communities do not take responsive governance for granted and sit back and wait for organizations to come to them and ask them to participate. A responsive, accountable system should generate greater citizen involvement, not less, as citizens have greater expectations that their efforts will make a difference for their community.[1]

Community Governance as a Form of Community Learning

The end of Chapter Three discusses how a managing-for-results cycle should be part of a learning process, and suggests that organizations managing for results learn how to get better results. In fact, all four advanced governance practices involve some form of learning in the community. However, there are differences among the advanced practices concerning tendencies of who learns, and what they learn to do. Broadly speaking, it is useful to think of "who learns" as referring to two main groups:

- *Citizens* engaged in the community, including the grassroots citizen groups, more formal citizen boards or organizations, and the advocacy and intermediary organizations that assist them
- *Organizations* (government or private) in the community that commit resources to services or community improvement projects

Broadly, two main types of learning can be associated with the four advanced practices of community governance:

- *Process learning:* Learning to use and improve decision processes
- *Performance learning:* Learning to use information on measurable results

Learning in Community Problem Solving

In advanced practice 1, community problem solving, the main form of learning is process learning, and in the best case, both citizens and organizations learn. For positive learning to happen, citizens and organizations must be committed to open deliberative processes and want to make them work well. Government or nonprofit organizations that make up their minds on their own about what they want to do, and only go through the motions of involving citizens in decision processes because a law or funder requires it, will learn only how to disappoint citizens and make the participative processes ineffective at incorporating citizen concerns and priorities. In the best cases, both citizens and organizations will learn from each other to solve the problems at hand, and both will learn how to use participative decision processes effectively and improve these processes over time. Mutual process learning is extremely valuable; it builds trust in the community among citizens with different interests and between citizens and the organizations that serve the community. The drawback of process learning alone is the same as the weakness cited for advanced practice 1: without feedback of performance information, citizens and community decision makers cannot be sure the solutions they develop really improve desired outcomes or that they are addressing issues of the greatest strategic importance.

Learning in Organizations Managing for Results

In advanced practice 2, organizations managing for results, the main type of learning on a week-to-week or quarter-to-quarter basis is performance learning, as organizations learn to improve results from performance data fed back to them in managing for results cycles. As the Phoenix example at the end of Chapter Three shows, in the best cases, process learning also takes place over longer periods of time, as organizations learn to make their managing-for-results processes more effective at delivering strategic results. The drawback here is that all—or almost all—the learning is being done by organizations, not by citizens. Inevitably, some citizen advocates and coproducers in these communities learn about performance and about working within established processes, but many fewer citizens will likely be learning these things than in communities that openly encourage citizens to become engaged as issue framers. Also, the relatively few citizens who take it on themselves to learn will not be learning to improve the decision processes or the overall governance system. When only organizations manage for results, systemic learning is up to the organizations that serve the community.

Learning Where Citizens Are Reaching for Results

In advanced practice 3, citizens reaching for results, both performance and process learning occur, but citizens, rather than government and other service organizations in the community, are the primary learners. Intermediary and advocacy organizations will likely learn about performance and community processes along with the citizens they assist, but these do not include the organizations that control resources to provide services and implement community improvement projects. The process learning can be particularly interesting here; citizens may learn not only how to navigate existing community processes but also how to invent and improve new community processes, as many of the citizens and intermediary organizations featured in Chapters Four and Five have done, such as the resourceful members of Truckee Meadows Tomorrow who invented Adopt an Indicator and quality-of-life compacts. If citizens (and their intermediaries and advocates) are the only learners, little is likely to improve in the community. Citizens have to work hard to call attention to what they learn to get organizations to take action. In effect, engaged citizens have to force organizations to learn some of what they—the citizens—have learned, so the organizations will act to improve results in the community. But organizations are not systemic learners under advanced practice 3, where it is the citizens who are reaching for results. As citizens (and their intermediaries and advocates) are the only systemic learners in advanced practice 3, there is an inherent limit to how much community learning will occur in a given time and how much that learning will lead to community improvement.

Learning in Communities Governing for Results

In the best cases of advanced practice 4, communities governing for results, both citizens and organizations experience performance and process learning. And both types of learning can happen systemically, as community governance processes play out. If citizens and organizations are authentic in their desire to make community governance work,[2] then well-designed governance processes will inevitably lead to some learning by citizens and organizational officials who participate about how to improve performance, how to make the process successful, or both. However, long-term systemic learning to continually improve community governance and results over time will not happen automatically. Community leaders need to examine their governance processes and be willing to take the risk of making changes from time to time, even if the processes appear to be working well.

Why tamper with something that already works and risk making it less effective? Because community conditions change over time, and citizens' interests, priorities, and the citizens themselves change. Processes that worked well for making decisions and improving results for one set of community conditions or interests may not work as well for different kinds of problems or interests that surface later or for a different mix of engaged citizens. For example, new demographic groups may become prominent in the community over time, whose culture, language, level or type of education, or life experiences may make them less effective participants in processes in which other groups have participated effectively. Also, any process, no matter how well designed, will inevitably have flaws in either design or delivery that can be learned only from the actual experience of carrying out the process. After a governance process has been implemented, it is always worth a review to determine what worked well and what did not with respect to how effectively citizens were engaged and the community was able to learn from the process to make better decisions and improve results. For example, when City of Rochester staff found that the new NeighborLink computer network for tracking implementation of neighborhood plans drew only limited citizen use, the city launched a training program to develop resident "technology leaders" to use the system to track progress and report it to their engaged neighbors. Even if a process has worked well, it is useful to look for opportunities to make it better, as Prince William County did. The county built on citizens' trust and experience working with government to run its strategic planning focus groups differently in 2003 by having citizens cofacilitate the groups along with county staff.

None of the examples in the next two chapters involve communities that developed governance processes and stayed with them without change. Washington, D.C.'s first Citizen Summit worked well. Still, with each successive summit, organizers have changed the agenda not only to be more relevant to the issues of the day, but also to advance the development of community governance by, for example, having citizens work on strategic neighborhood action plans in Citizen Summit II, and putting "partnerships" on the agenda for Summit III. They also developed a more thorough follow-up approach for Citizen Summit III, convening follow-up meetings in all eight wards of the district rather than the single citizen review meeting held in the past, to check whether district staff properly interpreted what citizens said at the summit. In Greater Kansas City, leaders of the Community Development 2000 program have also been willing to change and learn over time. In 2002, for example, they revised the performance metric for evaluating CDCs and determining each CDC's funding range. In 2003, they began experimenting with an index of neighborhood health and improvement and intend to link part of future CDC investments to index gains in neighborhoods served by each CDC. Community Development 2000 investors know this is a risk, as many factors in addition to CDC efforts determine neighborhood conditions. But they think the risk is worth taking to create an incentive that may stimulate CDCs' creativity to improve outcomes even more in inner-city neighborhoods of the Kansas City region.

Trust, Accountability, and Results-Focused Learning

The stories in Chapters Seven and Eight involve government and nonprofit institutions that trust citizens enough to engage them in their performance management processes, making them performance governance processes. Citizens return that trust with their continued engagement. They know the time they invest will be well spent. Performance feedback in these communities serves two important purposes: it provides accountability of these institutions to their communities, and it provides information for organizations and citizens to learn from to improve results. As the case examples in Chapters Seven and Eight show, community learning can go beyond learning to improve results, to learning to improve community governance processes that lead to better results. When a community opens up its learning process to its citizens, that community becomes even more capable of achieving results that matter.

CHAPTER SEVEN

COMMUNITIES GOVERNING FOR RESULTS II

Local Governments Engage Citizens in Results-Based Systems

Citizens know the board really takes the strategic plan seriously, so hundreds of them come out to participate in strategic planning.

SEAN CONNAUGHTON, CHAIRMAN,
PRINCE WILLIAM COUNTY, VIRGINIA, BOARD OF SUPERVISORS

Citizens in Prince William County, Virginia, have learned that engaging in community affairs is well worth their time and effort, as public officials listen and give them an opportunity to make a difference. The county's elected board of supervisors appreciates the power of a strategic plan built on citizen participation from across the county to give their decisions legitimacy. What makes planning and engagement even more powerful in Prince William County is how they fit into a results-based governance system that feeds back measured performance information in several ways to keep the county focused on achieving results that matter for its citizens.

Prince William County's system is an excellent example of advanced practice 4 of the Effective Community Governance Model: communities governing for results. This chapter starts with an in-depth look at results-based governance in Prince William County, including many ways that performance feedback, robust citizen engagement, and collaborations are used to focus the community's energy on desired outcomes. Then, examples of governing for results are presented that feature citizens engaged in neighborhood planning and improvement in Rochester, New York, and Washington, D.C. The Washington, D.C., example also includes an engagement approach used every two years that brings thousands of citizens from across the city together in technology-enhanced town meetings that have an important influence on strategy and budget decisions of the city government.

Advanced Governance Practice 4: Communities Governing for Results

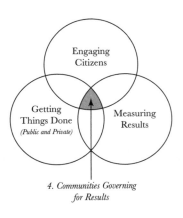

4. Communities Governing
for Results

See Chapter Six for a broader discussion of what governing for results is about, with references to the examples here and in Chapter Eight to help you interpret all of these examples. As you read the examples that follow, keep in mind relevant processes and practices in your community that get at least part of the way to governing for results, and consider what may be missing to keep your community from getting all the way there. See if you can find a few things done in the communities featured here that your community may be able to adapt to get closer to having its own results-based approach to community governance.

Prince William County Stays Focused on Citizen-Driven Strategy

Prince William County's approach to performance-based budgeting was presented in brief in Chapter Three. Performance budgeting is only one part of an enterprisewide results-based approach—what Prince William County calls its "results oriented government system."[1] Not only do county officials manage the government to get results, but effective community governance reaches beyond the county government, through many collaborations with other governments, with the private sector, nonprofit organizations, and citizens. Citizen engagement is robust in Prince William County, with citizens playing many roles throughout the governance process. As citizens have learned that their effort makes a difference, they have become engaged in many ways to help their community achieve results that matter.

The County's Governing for Results System

Prince William County refers to its four-year strategic plan as "the foundation of the system of results oriented government. . . . It provides policy guidance for service delivery and resource allocation during the Board of County Supervisor's four-year term."[2] The strategic plan is shown at the top of Figure 7.1 as the driver of governing for results in

Prince William. Similar to Sunnyvale (Chapter Three), Prince William County has an enterprisewide integrated system, with multiple results-based cycles completed when measured results are fed back (as in Figure 7.1) to inform (1) how managers improve service delivery day-to-day and month-to-month; (2) the annual performance budget and budget adjustments made during the year to help services achieve desired results; (3) annual updates of the strategic plan by the board of supervisors; and (4) major updates of the strategic plan every four years, approved by a newly elected board of supervisors, and characterized by extensive citizen engagement, including outreach to many different interests and groups across the county.[3]

Figure 7.2 superimposes a sampling of major citizen roles at various points in the governance cycles. As shown in Figure 7.2 and described throughout this example, citizens take advantage of many opportunities to become engaged in governance in Prince William County, including annual updates to the strategic plan, resource allocation, land use planning, service coproduction, and numerous boards and commissions. But it is in the major update of the strategic plan every four years in which citizens are engaged in building the foundation for county decision making.

FIGURE 7.1. GOVERNING-FOR-RESULTS CYCLES IN PRINCE WILLIAM COUNTY

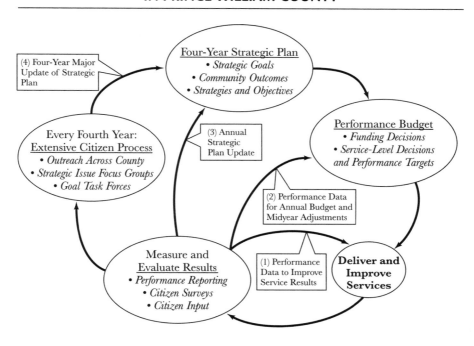

FIGURE 7.2. MAJOR CITIZEN ROLES IN PRINCE WILLIAM COUNTY'S GOVERNING-FOR-RESULTS CYCLES

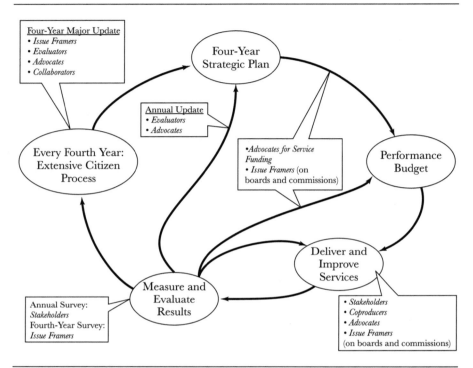

Note: Citizens' roles are in italic type in the boxes.

Citizen Priorities Drive Strategic Planning

A 1994 Prince William County ordinance mandates a major strategic plan update every four years, timed so a newly elected board of supervisors can decide its strategic goals and approve the plan near the start of its term. In implementing the mandate, the county gives citizens early and ample opportunity to influence strategic priorities.

The County Engages Citizens as Issue Framers to Start Strategic Planning.
Before the fall election, citizens get at least two opportunities to play issue framer roles, voicing their priorities for issues the county should stress in the strategic plan. In the spring, the county conducts an annual citizen phone survey. The 2003 survey reached a random sample of 1,484 residents. Most years, the county survey addresses citizens in their stakeholder roles, asking about their perceptions of aspects of the quality of life

in the county and about their satisfaction as customers of county services. Every fourth year since 1995, when a major strategic planning update process is starting, the county has included a section on strategic planning goals, in which citizens are asked to rate the importance of twenty-four potential strategic goal statements. Results have been fairly stable. For example, in 1995, 1999, and 2003, citizens ranked "Making the County Safe from Crime" and "Improving the Quality of Public Education" first and second in importance. But there have been significant changes. For example, from 1999 to 2003, "Improving the County's Road Network" moved up from sixth to fourth place, "Making Sure Tax Rates Don't Go Up" dropped from fourth to seventh, and "Meeting Basic Needs of Low Income Residents" moved up from fourteenth to ninth place.[4]

The citizen survey is only the start of the issue framing process, as the survey results are provided as resource information to diverse groups of citizens from across the county who respond to county outreach to participate in a series of focus groups conducted in the late summer and early fall. Citizens deliberate among each other in the focus groups and advance the thinking in strategic issue development. As county executive Craig Gerhart explains, "They use a blank sheet of paper to frame issues in ways that mean more to them" than the preset goal statements of the survey.

In 2003, 485 citizens participated in thirty-one strategic planning focus groups held across the county. Participants came from home owner associations, school groups, business groups, and employee groups, among others. Steve Ryner, a citizen volunteer, said he saw "a broad spectrum of income range, age, educational backgrounds, geographic region, and interests" in the seven focus groups he cofacilitated with county staff. Ryner also saw members of the county's growing Hispanic population in his sessions, participating in English. Ryner's knowledge of Spanish from an international business and diplomatic career enabled him to assist those who occasionally had trouble working in English.

Staff and Board Consolidate Citizen Priorities. Staff consolidate the focus group results to present to the board of supervisors with survey results, showing different ways issues have been framed and ranked. The board then asks staff to research and prepare white papers for ten to fifteen issues, likely to include all or most of the top consolidated focus group issues and some of the top survey issues, with a few adjustments based on board experience and priorities. For example, the board may see that citizens emphasized crime, fire safety, and emergency medical services as high priorities and may ask staff to combine them in a white paper on public safety.

Board of supervisor elections are held by the time the staff completes white papers on potential strategic planning issues. The new board considers the staff research and the survey and focus group results when designating five or six strategic goal areas, some of which may combine several survey or focus group priorities into one broader goal area. For example, for the 2004–2008 strategic plan, the board combined issues identified under priorities for "Affordable Housing," "Community Maintenance," "Quality Development/Land Use," and "Tourism/Historic Preservation"[5] into a single "Community Development Strategic Goal."[6]

Citizens Develop and Propose Goals, Outcomes, and Strategies. The board appoints citizens to strategic issue study groups and strategic goal task forces to study and develop each goal area and prepare specific goal statements, desired measurable four-year community outcomes, and a series of strategies with specific objectives to achieve the outcomes. Staff assist the citizen goal task forces in this process. The board then considers and adopts the citizen task force proposals in one or more formal resolutions, including any revisions desired by the board. By developing measurable outcomes, citizen foundation builders bring the community vision for a goal into sharp focus. In getting there, citizens not only play issue framer roles, but are also evaluators of performance information staff provide them to inform the process. And as Steve Ryner describes below, they also must be effective collaborators who compromise to reach consensus on the plans they will submit to the board.

Board of supervisors chairman Sean Connaughton sees citizens as being primary drivers of the strategic plan and sees the board, besides having the final decision, as playing a "vetting role." Connaughton explains, "People often raise an issue but don't understand the real problem behind it. We try to identify the underlying problem and what the county government can really do about it." For example, he notes, "We've made great strides improving transportation within the county. We effectively move people to mass transit and onto the interstate highways. But we get complaints from people about transportation because they are getting stuck on the interstates, which are state and federal responsibilities and over which we have little control." That does not keep such issues out of the strategic plan, but the citizen task forces learn to put them in context, such as phrasing parts of strategic objectives about interstates as "encourage VDOT"[7] to act (VDOT is the state transportation department), rather than directing the county to act on its own. Table 7.1 provides a sample community outcome for each strategic goal in Prince William County's 2004–2008 strategic plan.

Citizen Collaborators Find Common Ground on Goals They Propose. Citizens often come to strategic goal task forces as advocates for different interests, but as Steve Ryner explained, they find a way to come together around common outcomes and strategies. In describing his experience on an economic development task force for the 1996 strategic plan, Ryner said, "There was a lot of disagreement at first" among the diverse citizens, including people from different kinds of businesses with different interests. Then, according to Ryner, "We used the old facilitator's approach of saying, 'let's agree on what we don't agree on.' Amazingly, as one person states what he thinks are his differences, someone else says, 'Oh, I really agree with you on that.' We ended up with a pretty good report and got good results."

TABLE 7.1. SAMPLE COMMUNITY OUTCOMES IN PRINCE WILLIAM COUNTY'S STRATEGIC PLAN

Strategic Goal Area	Sample Community Outcome
Community Development	Increase new owner occupied residential units that are affordable to County citizens as defined by 30 percent of median family income.
Economic Development	Increase the average wage per employee by 12 percent at the end of four years as measured in constant dollars.
Education	90 percent of all 11th grade students will pass the English research paper on first submission. *(This was a performance measure in the School Board's Plan, which was submitted to the County Board of Supervisors for consideration of accepting it as a County plan as well.)*
Human Services	Serve in the community no less than 92 percent of youth at-risk of out-of-home placement.
Public Safety	Attain a witnessed cardiac arrest survival rate of 10 percent or greater.
Transportation	Increase the percentage of County citizens who telecommute to 20 percent, as measured by the Citizen Survey.

Source: Prince William County Office of Executive Management, *2004–2008 Board of County Supervisors Strategic Plan* (Prince William, Va.: Prince William County Office of Executive Management, 2004). www.co.prince-william.va.us/oem.

The process Ryner described helps citizen advocates bridge their different interests by finding they have more goals in common than they think and quickly narrowing their differences to a few key issues. Citizens then become collaborators who compromise on those issues to reach a consensus plan. To get there, they may have to engage in some creative issue framing in how they articulate outcomes, strategies, and objectives so a reasonable balance of interests is achieved. Once citizens know they have some common goals, they have an incentive to compromise as needed so they can complete the plan and see the county put its resources behind achieving those goals.

Performance-Based Budgeting Reinforces the Citizen-Driven Plan

Prince William County's annual budgets include quantitative service-level objectives for all services, developed by staff and approved by the board of supervisors. Board members appreciate the performance information provided to help them make budget decisions. Former county supervisor Ed Wilbourn describes how "department heads bring all performance-based budgets to the board. When they ask for more employees, they must justify them by service expectations, for example, what the caseload will be with added staff." Wilbourn adds that performance-based budgeting helps the board be "vigilant in watching the growth of county government." He explains that while staffing and services have increased with the county's growing population, "we reduced the number of positions per capita." In addition to helping the county lower its property tax rate, these staffing trends have enabled Prince William to increase employee salaries to the level of nearby wealthier counties. Wilbourn says that as a result, "We're holding onto employees longer, and not just training them for higher-paying jobs in other counties."

Performance and Strategic Priorities Drive the Budget. All county services have performance objectives in their budget, and many of those objectives align with the outcomes and strategies in the strategic plan. But not all services align with the plan because, as county executive Craig Gerhart explains, "We decided early on that our strategic plan would not be a 'corporate business plan' that includes all programs. Our strategic plan determines our *top* priorities, even though we still have to do a lot of other things." The limited number of strategic goals strengthens Gerhart's performance-based budget rubric, described in Chapter Three.

Figure 7.3 is a variation of Figure 3.6 and comes closer to the reality of how strategic budget decisions are made. According to Gerhart, programs and services targeted for funding cuts are really those that fall under a movable curve, as shown in Figure 7.3, rather than those that neatly fit into the lower left-hand box of Figure 3.6 (outlined here in thin dotted lines). During economic downturns, when less revenue overall is available for programs and services, the curve moves up and to the right, as in the broken-line curve in Figure 7.3. So during difficult times, some programs that perform reasonably well but are less strategic will fall under the curve, and their budgets will be cut.

As Gerhart explains, in years "when the economy went south, we went after a lot of things to cut that were good things, but were not strategic. Parks got cut those years, for example. So did consumer affairs. That exercise solidified the importance of our strategic plan. A professional policy analyst wouldn't always like what we cut, but it was consistent with our citizen-driven plan. It was important for the board to use the power of the plan."

The Process Provides Strategic Discipline for the Staff and the Board. Mary Beth Michos, chief of the Prince William County Department of Fire and Rescue, who came to Prince William from another county in 1994, said, "It was a shock for me when I got here that everything had to be aligned with the strategic plan and really had to have performance numbers. I couldn't just say that 'houses will burn and babies will die' to get additional funding. But then I learned I could make data work for me to justify what we proposed."

FIGURE 7.3. USE OF STRATEGIC GOALS AND PERFORMANCE RESULTS IN PRINCE WILLIAM COUNTY BUDGET DECISIONS

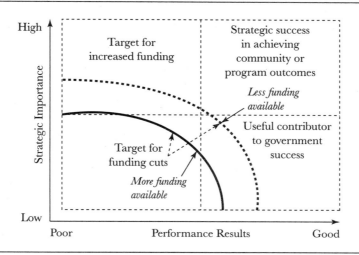

Board of supervisors chairman Sean Connaughton appreciates the focus and discipline this approach has given the board. He explained, "When people stand up and say, 'Why aren't we spending more on this program?' I can say, 'We have to focus on what's strategic. It's all there in the plan. Citizens said what should be in the plan.' We budget to it, and we measure it." He added, "The beauty of it is, it keeps you focused on what you need to do, not what the media push you to do."

Performance Feedback to Keep on Course and Learn When to Change Course

Periodic performance reporting closes the loop by feeding back information to county leaders to determine if strategies and programs are working as planned to achieve results and make needed adjustments. At certain times of year, the board of supervisors especially scrutinizes performance information. From February to April, during initial presentations for the next fiscal year's budget (which starts July 1), departments report how they are doing against current year performance targets and past trends, to help supervisors understand if next year's targets are realistic for the funds requested. As Ed Wilbourn said, "They don't get to arbitrarily say what they'll achieve." A key public document prepared by the internal auditor in February, in time for budget deliberations, is the Service Efforts and Accountability Report. The report has multiyear performance trends for major services and comparisons with other local governments comparable to Prince William County for each service.[8]

A Performance Focus on Strategic Priorities and Citizen Satisfaction. All through the year, the board considers performance concerning strategic services or issues. According to supervisor John Jenkins, "The second Tuesday of every month is set aside for board work sessions, open to the public, in which we get feedback on ongoing programs. We review strategic goals at these sessions, and from time to time get updated performance information on services of special concern." For example, public works director Robert Wilson described how his department "reports monthly to the board on key indicators of development regulation, such as turnaround time, number of inspections per inspector, backlog." The board does not want its strategic economic development goal to be hindered by a slow regulatory process. Assistant public works director Thomas Bruun says, "Performance measurement has worked well in development regulation. The board has put money into the process. They can see we're reasonably efficient, so they add staff and consultants when the workload goes up to keep our review times down." Developer fees, not taxes, pay for the staff, so these are not tough board decisions. But without periodic performance reports, they would not have the information needed to make the decisions.

Each summer includes special reviews by the board because the annual citizen satisfaction survey results become available and because the board does an annual progress review against the strategic plan. Supervisor John Jenkins says, "We want to know what citizens think of us. In the annual citizen survey, citizens grade us. We take a close look at anything below 90 percent satisfaction. Then we look for causes." Part of the search for causes involves county staff working with the survey contractor to analyze data geographically and demographically, to see if a targeted focus is needed on special populations or sections of the county to resolve some issues, while countywide improvement efforts may be needed for others. For example, in 2003, residents in older, denser communities were complaining of community maintenance issues concerning neighborhood property upkeep and proper use, suggesting that a targeted zoning enforcement approach was needed rather than a countywide effort.

Performance Feedback Helps the County Adjust Funding. Whether part of an annual review process (involving the budget, strategic plan process, or citizen satisfaction) or a more frequent review of special issues, the board makes program and budget adjustments based on performance, usually to improve progress toward the established county strategic goals. "By having well-established goals and objectives," Chairman Connaughton says, "we avoid wild mood swings in government based on the politics of the moment. Our budgeting process is simple and objective. We get years of performance data and we shift funds among priorities because we see what's working and what's not. We make funding shifts each year—usually not major shifts—to better achieve our goals. But our goals stay the same."

Citizens do not disappear from the governance process after strategic planning. A representative sample of them gets the opportunity to respond to the annual citizen survey as stakeholders. Also, as in many other jurisdictions, some citizens will advocate for more funding for their particular interests. And others, particularly those who were most engaged in strategic planning, will be there to hold county officials accountable for following the priorities they approved in the plan and attempting to achieve desired outcomes. Occasionally citizen advocates become evaluators who use performance feedback to convince the county to change its plans.

Performance Feedback Tells the County When to Change Course. With its emphasis on keeping the county focused on a few strategic goals, by reviewing performance information, the board has also learned when it needs to change its set of goals between major strategic planning updates. In the 1996 strategic plan, the board decided not to include a strategic goal related to human services. Supervisor Jenkins looked back on that decision as a "disaster," as county funding did not keep up with social needs growing with the population. But it would have been more of a disaster had the board waited four years to take corrective action.

Citizen advocates for human services, such as Paul Moessner, a retiree who sits on a half-dozen nonprofit human service boards, evaluated performance information showing worsening conditions and made sure the board paid attention to these trends during an annual review to update the strategic plan. Moessner recalls that the board of supervisors could see, for example, that "waiting times were going up for people to see mental health professionals, and to get food stamps; youth problems such as substance abuse were rising; homelessness was rising," among other concerns for which data were available. So the board added a human services goal to the strategic plan in 1998 rather than wait two more years for a major update. Moessner sat on a citizen advisory board to recommend outcome goals and said "the board accepted most of our goals" and followed through where it could make a difference. Moessner points out, "The board went back to a focused effort to reduce homelessness. They spent more on programs to get kids off the streets, for example, increasing support for Boys and Girls Clubs. They funded a nurse in every school—instead of nurses splitting time among schools; that's important because kids often talk to the school nurse about child abuse, nutrition problems, substance abuse, when they won't tell others about it."

Paul Moessner did not agree with the board's 1996 decision not to have a human services goal in the strategic plan. But he gives them credit for paying attention to worsening conditions and performance, listening to citizens, and making a midcourse correction. Moessner describes how the board holds its annual summer review of the strategic plan on a Saturday, making it easier for citizens to attend, and many do. He notes how "county staff come in and say, 'This is how we're doing on these indicators.' They show us the numbers. Citizens ask questions, and we provide our own interpretations for the staff and board to consider. Our county government wants that. They don't say, 'Oh my god, public input.' They actually look for it."

Citizens Take Advantage of More Opportunities to Participate

Citizens do more than become involved just in the formal parts of Prince William County's governing for results process. They become involved in their community in countless other ways. The county executive's office has a citizen participation coordinator who helps citizens find volunteer roles they can play in some fifteen county agencies, often as coproducers to augment government services to reach more people and communities. The nonprofit community provides similar volunteer opportunities, as Paul Moessner can attest. Also, at any time, about five hundred to six hundred citizens sit on various county boards and commissions, usually appointed by the board supervisor for their district. Some are standing commissions or advisory boards, and others, such as the strategic planning committees, are engaged less frequently for multiyear planning.

Citizens Collaborate in Land Use Planning and Advocate to Enforce the Plan.
One of the committees with a multiyear focus is a citizens' advisory committee, which reviews the county's comprehensive plan on land use and public facilities at least once every five years. George Shamer, an active citizen on development issues, says, "Boy, is that a good food fight every time." Shamer points out that some open disputes in the process are raised by "people who want to get elected by beating up on developers." But citizens with different interests on the committee do get down to business as collaborators and, as Supervisor Jenkins puts it, "a lot of compromise goes into where those dotted lines are drawn." Shamer feels public deliberation has led to better planning and development: "Our developments are now more environmentally sensitive than they were twenty years ago. We take care of the land better, trying to avoid soil erosion into the Potomac River. We've been planning clustered development with smaller lots, narrower streets, more public green space. We put developments near public transportation nodes to make our bus and rail transit more viable." And citizens who worked for such provisions are vigilant in following up on them.

As Supervisor Jenkins points out, "You'll see citizens who participated in development of the plan get involved in public hearings later to see that what was decided in the process gets enforced. They remind supervisors that they have to make land use decisions consistent with the plan." In that way, they are similar to Jacksonville citizens who participate in JCCI policy studies and then advocate for implementation of the study recommendations. But in this case, Prince William citizens have the advantage that the land use plan they developed was approved by the board of supervisors. They are then advocating for enforcement.

Strategic Citizen-Staff Collaboration in Fire Protection.
One citizen coproducer role in Prince William County involves a venerable rural institution: the volunteer fire company. Although volunteer fire and rescue staff are not paid, their companies'

operating and capital expenses are paid by the county, which helps keep volunteer companies' business practices aligned with the county's. As Prince William has grown and attained more of a commuter population, it has built a paid career force to ensure adequate fire and emergency medical protection at times when volunteers are not available. Even as the county has become more dependent on career staff, the volunteers have maintained a tight alignment with county planning practices, including the use of performance data.

Brian Hickerson, chief of the Nokesville Volunteer Fire Company, is one of twelve volunteer chiefs in the association, which is chaired by the paid chief, Mary Beth Michos, who heads the career service and the department. After the board of supervisors has adopted a strategic plan, Michos notes that she "goes on a retreat with all the volunteer chiefs to develop the fire-rescue service plan for the next four years with goals, objectives, strategies, and action steps." Hickerson described how they also worked together, using computer mapping and analysis software with historical data and projected growth patterns "to map where we would need new fire stations for the next twenty years to meet performance goals of responding to 90 percent of fires within eight minutes, and 90 percent of basic life support emergencies within eight minutes." Hickerson added that as a result, "Last year, we opened our first new station in fourteen years, and have a plan for a new one every two years for twenty years" if county growth keeps up with projections.

Many Kinds of Collaborations Fuel the County's Success

In addition to citizen-citizen and citizen-staff collaborations, many other kinds of collaborations help make performance-based governance effective in Prince William County. Fire and rescue chief Michos talked about her former fire department, in another county, as being "pretty isolated. Here, we're always working with other departments." Among others, she mentioned the county attorney, office of information technology, police department, public works, and health department. She also talked about "working on a daily basis with the Planning Department on comprehensive plan issues." Also, county supervisors have been active in stimulating and serving on regional collaboratives with other local governments to develop new roads and mass transit systems, such as Virginia Railway Express.

Collaboration Enables Accelerated Results for Schools. Another collaboration is between the county government and the separately elected county school board. Volunteer George Shamer said, "I've heard the relationship between the county and the school board is so good, it's envied throughout the state." The county executive and school superintendent agreed to prepare five-year budgets for the same periods, with annual adjustments. Ed Wilbourn explained, "Both boards approved the agreement.

It's important because about half of the taxes collected by the county go to the school board." That agreement is essential for the two entities to coordinate financial and capital planning while keeping tax rates stable as the county grows. County board chair Sean Connaughton said the five-year plan enabled them to "take advantage of opportunities, do things faster when extra revenue came in. We could build schools faster, because we already had the plan. We built twelve new schools and renovated nine schools" ahead of schedule.

Public-Private Collaborative Development. Prince William County has also benefited from public-private collaborations, especially in economic development and human services. A prominent collaboration is the county's "Innovation" industrial development site. In 1996, notes Wilbourn, "the board of supervisors took a risk of buying five hundred acres of land in bankruptcy, and worked with the owner of an adjoining five hundred acres to assemble and develop the site as a public-private development." Wilbourn credits good marketing by the County Economic Development Department and county planning decisions, such as to build and renovate schools, for attracting businesses to Innovation at a rapid rate, from such giants as America On Line and Eli Lilly, to smaller firms, many focused on technology. They also attracted a campus of George Mason University, including a biotechnology center, to provide a supporting research base. Wilbourn said, "We paid off the county's loan to buy the site in one-third the time projected because of the rapid development."

Performance-Based Partnerships and Public Investment in a Nonprofit Service Network. Paul Moessner, an active county and nonprofit volunteer, says, "This community is extremely representative of the view that government doesn't do everything. There is a huge amount of human services done by public-private partnerships. Nonprofits are the main service providers, on a fee-for-service basis. The county gets a good buy in services addressing homelessness, transitional housing, anger management, domestic violence, and more." The County Department of Human Services oversees their work. Assistant county executive Melissa Peacor notes that "we measure nonprofit human service providers' performance just as we do county agencies."

Public officials see nonprofit human service providers in the Prince William area as not just a collection of contractors but as critical partners in meeting human needs and maintaining the quality of life. County officials participate with the Coalition for Human Services, an umbrella group of about forty nonprofit agencies that addresses service coordination, needs assessment, and planning and also plays an advocacy role. Recently, according to Moessner, public officials demonstrated their awareness of the importance of maintaining a strong network of human service partners by agreeing to use government funds (from Prince William County and the city of Manassas) to make up for most of an unusual one-year $800,000 shortfall in funds that Prince William area nonprofits normally receive from the major regional United

Way. According to Moessner, "Some of our smaller agencies would have had to close, and larger agencies would have had to close down whole programs." With the endorsement of the Coalition for Human Services, Moessner said that he and other citizen advocates "made presentations at budget hearings so policymakers would understand the good value these agencies were for citizens, and why they needed to act to preserve our human services system. We got 80 to 90 percent of what we asked for."

The county's public-public and public-private collaborations are not random efforts. These collaborations, like others in the Prince William community, relate to commonly desired outcomes, often specified in the county strategic plan or implied by the comprehensive plan. Once outcomes are adopted by the county, many organizations participating in collaborations align their efforts to support achieving those outcomes. The county's discipline in aligning its budget with strategic plan goals helps drive that.

Learning and Improvement as the Governance System Evolves

Prince William County, its citizens, and its public and private partners have learned a lot and have improved governing-for-results processes over time. The learning started early in the evolution of these processes, when the county saw the power of merging them into a self-reinforcing results-based governance system. "I wish I could say we started with a 'grand design,'" says county executive Craig Gerhart. "But really, our system evolved on two parallel tracks." Strategic planning evolved from a late 1980s community visioning effort, involving thousands of citizens. Gerhart recalls that "a great report came out of it. Staff concluded that it could be the 'vision element' of strategic planning, which should be community driven, not staff driven." In 1991, with strong support from the board of supervisors chair at that time, Kathleen Seefeldt, the county launched its first citizen-driven strategic planning process, leading to the board's adopting five strategic goals in 1992.

Also in the late 1980s, the county started to reform its budgeting, especially encouraged by Supervisor Jenkins and Bill Becker, who was then a supervisor. But the new budget process lacked evaluation data. So in 1992, the county went on a crash course to develop performance measures. The two tracks came together as a governance system when performance budgeting was used to shift resources to the plan's strategic goals. Since then, learning and improvement have proceeded on many fronts.

Organizations Learn to Plan and Perform Strategically. County agencies and external service providers have learned how to make the county's performance-based processes work better for themselves and for advancing the county's strategic goals. For example, county departments have learned to be more strategic in performance reporting, easing their reporting burden and helping decision makers. Nokesville volunteer fire chief Brian Hickerson recalls that in fire and rescue, "We started out very analytical, trying to measure and report everything, even how many miles we drive in a year. Now we're much more focused on strategic measures, such as the percent of time we make our response time goals." Board chairman Connaughton said some organizations in danger of funding cuts have learned to refocus their efforts to support county strategic goals. He particularly mentioned the Cooperative Extension Service, which "saw the county's agricultural base diminishing, and its traditional services becoming less strategic. So they shifted into great nutritional programs, and savings programs to help low-income people buy homes. Now they're getting more funding from us." The learning by some organizations may be a matter of survival, but, nonetheless, it strengthens the overall community focus on results.

Citizens Learn and Develop Along with the Organization. Assistant county executive Melissa Peacor recalls that "the first strategic plan had goals but no measures." By the time the county went about its second major strategic planning process, staff had learned the power of performance alignment, which they leveraged by strengthening citizen roles in determining outcomes that matter. Peacor goes on, "We gave citizens a little performance measurement training, and they developed measurable outcomes for the 1996 plan." George Shamer, a citizen who participated, said "training was key. We started out saying, 'Outcomes, what's that?' But citizens could work through it and do the plan with outcomes."

The county has learned to trust citizens more and more in the process. For the 2003 strategic planning focus groups, the county used citizens as cofacilitators with staff. Selected citizens and staff went through the same facilitator training. Peacor said the citizen and staff facilitators "melded so well, you could not tell who was staff and who was a citizen facilitator. They were absolutely equal." Steve Ryner, a citizen cofacilitator, called it "a marvelous process. I'm totally sold on it." Elected officials, including board chairman Sean Connaughton, reported getting extremely favorable feedback from constituents who attended the 2003 focus groups.

Early on, the county learned the power of engaged citizens and became determined to help citizens learn more about government and the community, to have better-informed citizens involved, to empower them more by helping them understand governance processes, and to encourage more citizens to become engaged. To do so, since 1994 the County has developed not one citizen education program, but three, as discussed in Chapter Nine, where the Community Leadership Institute is highlighted.

Staff Keep Learning to Make the Process Better. As Prince William County's results-based governance system has evolved, it has survived several elections and major changes in the board. Yet the process has gotten stronger over time. Supervisors Connaughton and Jenkins credit the county staff for strengthening the system. As in Phoenix (in Chapter Three), most of the approaches used for each part of Prince

William County's results-based system had been used earlier in other communities. But the county staff has tweaked other jurisdictions' approaches to adapt them for their own setting and added new wrinkles over the years as they learned from experience to develop a system that is uniquely Prince William's own and keeps evolving to work better. Jenkins praises the staff for borrowing good approaches from other communities and levels of government and adapting them to Prince William County. He said, "The not-invented-here syndrome does not exist here. We don't care where it was invented." They only care about achieving results that matter.

Rochester Citizens Govern Neighborhood Improvement for Results

The project to redesign University Avenue in Rochester, New York, exemplifies how the city government's Neighbors Building Neighborhoods (NBN) initiative has put citizens in charge of improving their own neighborhoods. Ed Doherty, city of Rochester commissioner of environmental services, said that "originally there was tension between traffic engineers and neighborhood people." Local residents wanted a narrower street—not usually what traffic engineers have in mind for a busy arterial. The citizens also had an idea of creating an "art walk" to add character to the avenue. Not only did the citizens' vision prevail, but, according to Doherty, "by the end, the local chapter of the American Society of Civil Engineers contributed funds for the first piece of artwork" and the project won a U.S. Conference of Mayors City Livability Award.[9] In Rochester, it has become the norm for citizens' visions to guide neighborhood improvement. Since the public rollout of NBN began in 1994, the city government has engaged citizens in many roles, through several governance processes, not only to develop neighborhood visions but to achieve results and track progress toward making their visions real.

Governing for Results in Rochester

Figure 7.4 depicts Rochester's Neighbors Building Neighborhoods initiative as a governing-for-results cycle. During sector planning (top of Figure 7.4) in ten geographic sector areas of the city, citizens engage as issue framers who identify priority neighborhood improvement goals, as advocates for those goals, and as collaborators who negotiate commitments for public and private action. During this process, citizens also identify and map assets in the community that can be a source of improvement beyond the government's resources. The assets they map are often private organizations or individual citizen coproducers with capabilities or resources to help implement citizens' sector plans.[10]

FIGURE 7.4. NEIGHBORS BUILDING NEIGHBORHOODS GOVERNING-FOR-RESULTS CYCLE

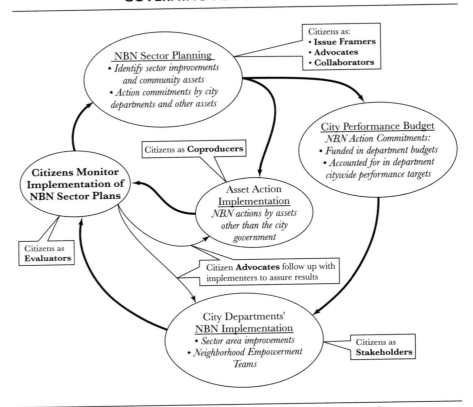

Note: The thinner lines show performance feedback to improve implementation.

The citizens' NBN sector plans also drive improvement actions implemented by city departments (bottom of Figure 7.4) that are backed by resource commitments in the city budget—a performance budget that includes department citywide performance targets. Department performance targets are adjusted when the sum of NBN sector commitments will require a net change in the performance level of a service across the city. Citizens have their own electronic NeighborLink Network to monitor change as evaluators of improvement efforts (left side of Figure 7.4) which empowers them with information as advocates to follow up with implementers to assure responsive improvement. In addition to city departments implementing sector plan actions, city-staffed teams help control neighborhood problems, serving citizens as stakeholders. The mayor's Neighborhood Empowerment Team (NET) Office assigns city property inspectors and police officers to each sector to resolve and prevent chronic quality-of-life, nuisance, and disorder issues. NET also provides property complaint services.

To understand how Rochester is a community that governs for results, it helps to see how NBN fits in a broader context of management and governance processes. As shown on the left side of Figure 7.5, the Rochester city government monitors department performance quarterly against targets set in the budget, as part of a broader results-based cycle that includes NBN. Another influence on getting results in Rochester neighborhoods is the city's comprehensive plan, Rochester 2010: The Renaissance Plan (sometimes referred to as "Renaissance 2010," "R2010," or just "2010") was approved by the city council in 1998. Citizens on the Mayor's Stewardship Council, which guided the plan's development, now monitor plan implementation and recommend how to guide future implementation as conditions in the city change (top of Figure 7.5).

FIGURE 7.5. NEIGHBORS BUILDING NEIGHBORHOODS IN ROCHESTER'S BROADER GOVERNING-FOR-RESULTS CYCLE

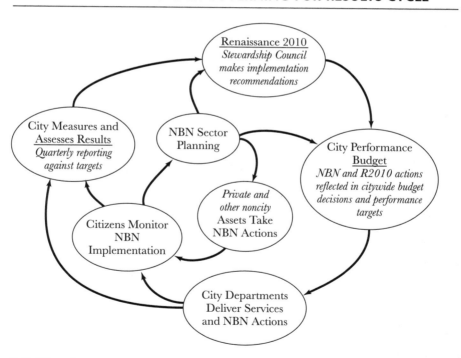

Note: Feedback loops and Renaissance 2010 leveraging of outside assets are omitted for clarity.

Resident leaders from all ten NBN sectors sit on the Stewardship Council, enabling them to ensure that local citizens' visions and sector plan priorities are considered in their implementation recommendations. This has become more important as Rochester 2010 has begun to influence the overall city budget through the plan's eleven "campaigns" (for example, "Involved Citizens," "Environmental Stewardship," "Economic Vitality," "Healthy Urban Neighborhoods"). Assistant to the mayor (and former city budget director) Rick Hannon said, "Initially, we just linked a lot of what we already do to the 2010 plan. But after three years, we've gotten a lot more driven by 2010," by making marginal budget shifts each year to 2010 priorities. Hannon cited as examples the city's committing an extra $5 million to lead paint remediation and abatement, a citywide priority in the 2010 plan, and committing to demolishing more abandoned vacant properties rather than leaving them boarded up for a long time, based on a "strong hue and cry from neighborhoods."

NBN: Built on Neighborhood Assets and Embraced by a New Mayor

Rochester has had grassroots neighborhood associations since at least the 1960s. Former city community development commissioner Tom Argust recalls that by the early 1990s, "we had thirty-six neighborhood associations, but many were burned out" due to a lack of staff support and poor relations with government. They mostly focused on narrow issues in their own neighborhood, without a larger purpose or broad community picture. The associations were neighborhood assets that were not being used to their potential. In 1993, Argust and his staff reached out to the neighborhood associations to begin revamping community planning from the neighborhoods up, first by grouping neighborhoods into larger sector areas to create stronger citizen planning entities and enable better city support. In defining NBN sectors, staff considered the geographic distribution of resources and assets to ensure each sector area had enough community organizations and businesses to contribute to developing and implementing a plan. After some negotiation and adjustment with neighborhood associations, the boundaries of the ten sectors were set.

Whether the start-up program would go any further was uncertain, as Mayor Thomas Ryan did not run for reelection in 1993. But the new mayor embraced NBN. As Mayor William Johnson related, "Because of my background as a community activist who had been constantly struggling with city hall, NBN presented an opportunity that was way too good to pass up." He went on, "I came not with a political base but a community base. That was a big invitation to people to invest their time."

When he took office in 1994, Mayor Johnson encouraged city managers to put resources behind the NBN goal "to establish and maintain stable, healthy, and diverse neighborhoods" which, added the mayor, "are developed and sustained by citizens." The city created an NBN support staff—now the Neighborhood Initiatives Bureau under the Department of Community Development—and supported the formation in each sector area of a sector group, a consortium of residents, businesspeople, schools, churches, and nonprofit representatives to lead the development, monitoring, and management of their NBN sector action plan. The initial planning horizon was three years. The second set of sector action plans covered a two-year period: six months to update the plans and eighteen months to implement the proposed activities. By 2003, during Mayor Johnson's third term, sector groups were working on the fourth series of sector plans.

Citizens Govern Planning and Negotiate Implementation Actions

Rochester's NBN program is remarkable for truly being the citizens' own process that they largely govern themselves.

Citizens Plan Their Own Neighborhoods. The city government has not just involved residents in planning but has made them planners of their own neighborhood improvements, as they were in the redesign of University Avenue. In working through the process, citizens are both issue framers to decide what neighborhood problems and opportunities their plans should address and collaborators among themselves to develop a plan that addresses them. Tom Argust emphasizes that "city staff do not write the sector plans for citizens. The volunteers write the plans. We had to spend a lot of time training professional architects and planners to *not* do the planning for people, but to be facilitators and resource providers to help neighborhood volunteers write the plans." Mayor Johnson recalls, "Early on, we committed that staff would be facilitators, not convene or run meetings, or direct the content of the conversations. We told staff, 'If the residents are doing okay, you just have to turn off the lights when they're done.'"

Each Sector Consortium Determines Its Governance. The city does not dictate one approach to sector governance. Some sectors set their own rules for operating their groups; for example, residents, heads of neighborhood associations, community councils, nonprofits, or business representatives may have ex officio roles. Others are less formal. However, they all reach out to engage many citizens into their process of meetings. Neighborhood Initiatives director Vickie Bell explains that allowing each sector group to use its own model increases the groups' local ownership of their sector action plans. Before each major plan update, however, each sector group must submit an outreach plan and what Tom Argust calls a "plan to plan" that describes how they will make the process inclusive of the full diversity of sector residents and organizations. The city provides a guidebook to help each sector organize, identify leaders, meet city inclusion requirements, and work through the planning process.[11]

Stakeholder Meetings Convert Plans to Projects. In 1999, issue-specific consulting meetings were added to the NBN planning process, bringing together the sector groups and others with a stake in specific activities, such as city departments, nonprofits, and businesses, to develop a detailed implementation plan that all agree on. All parties work out details, including scope of actions, time line, stakeholders' roles in projects, how projects will be monitored, and end products. Citizens on sector consortia participate in these NBN "stakeholder meetings," as they are called, in several roles. While they are stakeholders themselves, they are also advocates for their consortium's plan to address the issue, and they are collaborators with government departments and private organizations to agree on realistic projects that can be implemented.

For street improvement projects, Department of Environmental Services (DES) commissioner Ed Doherty said that before NBN stakeholder meetings, "We would meet with neighborhoods after a street improvement plan was set, but before construction. Now, residents work with DES on the street design way up front, and staff work with them to manage the process." Only then are engineers hired to prepare technical designs based on what residents want.

The city even developed a neighborhood charrette process where citizens, often supported by the local chapter of the American Institute of Architects, work together to develop a design for their neighborhood. From 20 to 150 people have participated in each charrette. They fill a hall, work in committees, and publish their proposals for the neighborhood development projects. DES staff act as moderators to ensure that residents, not the architects and engineers, design the streets. Doherty says, "The design charrettes have been uplifting. People can put in pen and pencil what they want."

The City's Performance Budget Backs Sector Plans. During each NBN plan update period, staff from city departments meet with sector groups to keep abreast of sector issues and desired projects and bring evolving sector proposals back to their departments. Staff then inform sector groups which projects are feasible and which are not within department mission and funding constraints and which may become feasible with marginal funding increases. Sector groups then negotiate with departments to get as many of their priorities funded as possible, and departments must include all projects they agree to in their budgets.

Department Performance Plans Are Adjusted to Reflect NBN Commitments. Since before NBN, Rochester has included department performance indicators with annual targets and past results in the city budget, and departments have reported quarterly against targets to the budget bureau. Departments explain major quarterly variances to the mayor's cabinet, including budget implications to correct problems.

These are citywide performance targets, not sector targets. But when departments agree to NBN or Renaissance 2010 actions, if actions across all sectors will change citywide results, such as an increase in vacant properties demolished, they need to include those changes in their targets. NBN efforts can sometimes cause service outputs to be reduced in order to do a better job. For example, according to Ed Doherty at DES, "We reported a small reduction in the number of miles of streets designed. In part, this reflects the increased workload for each project," because of the increased effort to work with citizens. "In other words," Doherty continues, "we increased quality at the expense of quantity." Because it is usually decades before a street is rebuilt again, extra time to ensure neighborhood-friendly designs is not a bad trade-off.

For summary reporting on promised city actions in sector plans, the citywide total number of "NBN Plan Activities Implemented" is targeted in the budget under the Neighborhood Initiatives Bureau and reported quarterly.[12] Quarterly reports of affected indicators against targets provide one level of accountability of departments to the mayor for promised results. Departments are also directly accountable to citizens for specific sector actions.

Citizens Tap Assets Outside the City Budget to Achieve Goals

Citizens in sector groups have learned to go beyond the city budget to find resources for their plans. Their "asset mapping" is essential to realize many of their goals. Vickie Bell explains, "Residents often serve in the role of asset managers. They conduct an inventory of assets in their neighborhoods: nonprofits, businesses, schools, churches, neighborhood residents, etc. and ask, 'What resources are available to get the things we want done?' For example, they might enlist a professional gardener who lives in the sector area to help build a community garden." Asset mapping helped Sector 1 organize a senior citizen safety plan. "We wanted police to go out and talk about home safety and telephone scams to seniors," Sector 1 leader and resident Glenn Gardner explained. He noted that "we had identified this need through surveys and community input." But the Police Department can visit only a limited number of seniors. So, Gardner went on, "the sector obtained a grant from a local business to buy a portable VCR, TV, and public safety videos, which are used by local groups in the sector to reach many more seniors."

Rochester sectors tap their assets in many ways. According to Vickie Bell, "Some residents have bought parcels of land to be maintained as open space. Others have been creating 'monumental art' for their neighborhoods." Several grants were obtained to fund the University Avenue Art Walk. Also, property owners sometimes agree to an added tax to get additional embellishments as their streets are redesigned and rebuilt. Glenn Gardner called identifying all potential assets "a challenge, but very worthwhile, because there is more out there than you think."

City Seed Money Leverages Other Resources. In 2000, the mayor gave sector groups an incentive to leverage outside resources. One million dollars of city funds—$100,000 per sector—was allocated for economic development or physical improvement projects, with no time limit, if a sector raised at least a one-to-one match for a project. The sector groups decide on the types of projects to fund. The city has provided technical assistance and access to people who can help find resources, including, said Mayor Johnson, "people on the Stewardship Council who can open doors to funding sources." By 2003, $800,000 of city funds had been committed, leveraging several times that in other resources. Mayor Johnson noted that "Sector 10 found it to be a gold mine. They have taken that $100,000 and raised over $2 million, from the Kellogg Foundation and HUD, for example. They have worked the system better than most."

When asked if encouraging sectors to raise noncity funds just means "the rich get richer" because they can draw on more assets and connections, the mayor replied, "The irony is that Sector 10 is the poorest sector of the ten. It has the most problems. They got over their internal issues real fast. They attracted skilled people to work with them. They even found two acres of farmland hidden in their sector and got high school kids to learn how to plant and grow produce. Then they opened a market so those kids could make some money. The same group is finding new opportunities. They're creating community gardens from vacant land and turning vacant commercial buildings into restaurants. They got the Enterprise Foundation to come in and invest." The Enterprise Foundation, which has an office in Rochester that serves Upstate New York, is a national organization that supports local community development efforts across the country, similar to the Local Initiative Support Corporation, which is involved in the Greater Kansas City community development example in Chapter Eight.

Asset Budgets Take Sector Improvements Further Than City Budgets. Vickie Bell called tapping non–city budget assets "win-win for everyone," adding that "government resources only made up 30 percent of contributions to sector plans." In reaching out to community assets, citizens engaged in sector planning take on more responsibility and also gain more independence. As Sector 1 resident Glenn Gardner puts it, "We know we have a budget. But it is more about our asset budget" than the city budget. "The city budget does not make or break what we do. If there were a pullback on the NBN budget, the planning process would continue anyway. People are involved, and it has created a whole new way of looking at community improvement."

Citizens Monitor Performance and Receive Technology Support and Training

To monitor early sector plans, volunteers tracked implementation data manually. "It was frustrating," said Vickie Bell. "The information was obsolete and often inaccurate." To enhance accountability, the city introduced an information management system, the NeighborLink Network, to track activities and prompt discussion among neighborhood citizens, city managers, and other partners. This more timely and accurate information strengthens citizens as evaluators of implementation and enables them to be better advocates for their neighborhood and sector in following up with city departments and others, holding them accountable for living up to commitments in the sector plans.

Each sector area now has a neighborhood site with a computer link to an NBN database of sector plan activities. City government departments and the Rochester City School District can update progress in completing their planned actions, and sector volunteers update information on other community activities such as nongovernmental projects. As of 2003, NeighborLink was accessible only at specific public sites in all sectors, generally library branches open long hours for public access to the system, including evenings and weekends. At these sites, anyone from the community can view the NeighborLink information, run data queries, and generate reports. NeighborLink also provides virtual space, through the city government intranet, for citizens and city staff to discuss sector issues on line. A reason for limiting the system to these locations, rather than making it available widely on the Internet, was to encourage citizens to meet and network at NeighborLink sites.

Because early use of NeighborLink by citizens was limited, the city launched the Community Technology Leaders Training Program in 2003 for residents to learn to use software for NBN data entry, three-dimensional virtual planning, and mapping using geographic information systems. The training is intended to make more resident "technology leaders" available, who will be expected to track progress on a regular basis and produce deliverable products for their sector group, including performance reports and maps indicating progress implementing sector plans.

Plans for a Participatory Evaluation of NBN

After ten years of NBN and six years since Renaissance 2010 was approved, the city of Rochester started asking, "How does the planning process make a difference in people's lives?" For answers, the city is planning a participatory evaluation, with roles for volunteers from each sector, other stakeholders, and evaluation professionals. They will also reach out to include the full diversity of each sector in focus groups and other methods to involve or collect data from people. Each sector will develop indicators for nine evaluation criteria: sector plan progress, number of volunteers, use of nontraditional resources, new neighborhood organizations, visual impacts, new working partnerships, capacity-building opportunities, community health and wellness, and related NBN initiatives. The city also plans to examine the impact on the whole city and region, and compare each sector's results against the others and against the region.

Convinced Management, Empowered Citizens, Stronger Public Leaders

When Ed Doherty of DES sat on a state advisory committee, he heard residents of other communities complain that their local governments had failed them. "It was then that I realized the importance of the planning process we use in Rochester," said Doherty. "Sometimes the process can make results-oriented people impatient. But collaborations with citizens aren't the best way to succeed; they are the *only* way." Rochester resident Glenn Gardner would not disagree: "We have come to expect that our ideas will be solicited, heard, and acted on. The city has helped define and build neighborhood capacity. They are accountable to follow through on implementation. We are accountable and so are they." When empowered citizens, like Gardner, are willing to share responsibility for improving their community, they in turn empower public officials. Mayor Johnson knows that. Tom Argust puts it this way, "By empowering citizens, the mayor became more powerful. He gave up power to get it."

Washington, D.C., Citizens Focus the City Budget and Neighborhood Actions on Results That Matter

The District of Columbia city government has a citizen-oriented, neighborhood-based performance management approach that, from thirty thousand feet, looks much like Rochester's. The District has organized 133 "named" neighborhoods into 39 clusters and engaged citizens in developing improvement plans for each, called Strategic Neighborhood Action Plans or "SNAPS," similar to Rochester's sectors and sector plans. The District's citywide strategic plan is driven by priorities similar to the "campaigns" of Rochester's Renaissance 2010, and like Rochester, the District has a performance budget and department performance targeting and reporting. District departments are held accountable, through electronic reporting, to neighborhood residents and the mayor, for performing their committed actions in the SNAPS, as Rochester departments are for sector plan commitments. The District also has a Neighborhood Services Initiative to address persistent quality-of-life and disorder problems, as well as more routine service and nuisance complaints, similar to the responsibilities of Rochester's Neighborhood Empowerment Teams.

Many details on the ground differ from Rochester, as befits the different local situation. Two of the biggest differences concern how the cities' citizen empowerment efforts got started and the pattern of citizen engagement and influence that has emerged in Washington, D.C., since then.

Citywide Citizen Summit Launches New Empowerment

In 1994, in Rochester, a new mayor with a community action background took office and built his reforms from the neighborhoods up. Five years later, in Washington, D.C., a new mayor took office who had been the District chief financial officer. He was elected mayor after he had balanced the budget and restored fiscal accountability to a District government whose past problems had caused the U.S. Congress to establish a financial control board to oversee District budgeting and financial management. In 1999, Mayor Anthony Williams took the helm of a government widely perceived as poorly managed and unable to provide decent services or respond to residents' needs. He wanted to build confidence quickly—to generate interest and excitement citywide and give people a sense that their priority concerns mattered and would influence their government. His first empowerment initiative was a dramatic one—a Citizen Summit that engaged three thousand citizens from across the city on one day in November 1999 in the Washington Convention Center.

Those citizens who participated in the summit played a powerful issue-framing role. They were foundation builders who helped set strategic priorities that would drive District policy and governance for years to come. The top five priorities they identified that day were "Strengthening Children, Youth, Families and Individuals," "Building and Sustaining Healthy Neighborhoods," "Promoting Economic Development," "Making Government Work," and "Enhancing Unity of Purpose and Democracy."[13]

The 1999 Citizens Summit also represented the launch of Neighborhood Action by Mayor Williams, which led to the neighborhood-focused planning and improvement initiatives started in the following months to meet the sustainable neighborhoods priority from the summit. The summit created a promise. The new neighborhood initiatives were one way to keep it. Another way was to make major shifts in the District budget to reflect citizens' priorities.

Citizen Summits as Semiannual Capstone Events. After the 1999 summit, a pattern emerged of ongoing neighborhood-level citizen engagement, punctuated every two years by a large-scale citywide Citizen Summit to update strategic priorities and advance the District's community governance practices. Through 2004, three Citizen Summits and one Youth Summit had been held. The summits and Strategic Neighborhood Action Plans that citizens helped develop have also become key drivers of what the District calls its strategic management cycle (not shown) by influencing the citywide strategic plan, the annual performance-based budget, and agency performance scorecards. The District government has called its strategic management cycle "a two-year process in which Citizen Summits are the capstone, serving as both the starting and ending points."[14] The citizen influence in the process makes it a strategic governing-for-results cycle.

The Citizen Summits' Basic Process. All the Citizen Summits and the Youth Summit have used a process for technologically enhanced town meetings developed by America*Speaks*, a nonprofit organization based in Washington, D.C. America*Speaks* also facilitated the summits. The America*Speaks* process combines the reasoned, respectful discourse and listening that works best in small groups, with the inclusiveness and representativeness possible in large groups. People deliberate around tables of up to ten participants plus a trained facilitator and communicate their shared ideas—and strongly held minority views—using computers connected by a wireless network to a "theme team" of neutral content analyzers, who pull out the most common ideas from all tables for reporting back on large screens. Participants use wireless keypads to indicate their preferences among emerging themes. The one aspect of the process that resembles voting or opinion polling takes place only after thorough, facilitated discussions in small groups and is mostly focused on issues that emerge from those discussions. America*Speaks* president Carolyn Lukensmeyer likens the process to updating the centuries-old New England town meeting to the scale and pace of the twenty-first century by engaging hundreds or thousands of people while preserving authentic, democratic face-to-face deliberation.

America*Speaks* has used this model across the country, for public deliberations on local, regional, and national issues. Because of their size, these meetings tend to generate substantial media attention, giving added weight to what citizens say at the sessions. For example, media attention was worldwide for America*Speaks'* largest application to date of its process in one time and place, when forty-three hundred people deliberated in New York City on July 20, 2002, about planning and design issues for rebuilding the World Trade Center site after the September 11, 2001, terrorist attacks.

Essential Preparation: Crafting the Agenda and Getting a Representative Group in the Hall. Careful preparation is crucial to the Washington, D.C., Citizen Summits, and all other events America*Speaks* facilitates using its process. For example, it is important to carefully craft the meeting agenda and deliberation questions with decision makers to meet the public objectives at hand, be credible to participants, and generate citizen responses useful for the governance process the meeting is contributing to.

Perhaps the most important preparation is extensive outreach to attain the broad representativeness of participants that these large meetings make possible, including special efforts to attract people to the meeting from groups that tend to be underrepresented in public processes. For the Citizen Summits, the District government reaches out to people from all races, to all education and income levels, and to neighborhoods throughout all of the city's eight political wards, to attain participation that is geographically and demographically representative of the district's population.

Summit Follow-Up Ensures Decision Makers Hear What Citizens Said. After each Citizen Summit, two important further steps are taken that enhance the influence of citizens' deliberative ideas. First, all recorded comments from all citizens' tables—not just consensus themes—are documented by America*Speaks* and reviewed by District staff. According to Doug Smith, director of strategic planning and performance management, "We pore through detailed reports and look for the sense of the room" beneath or beyond the big themes. The second extra step is to hold one or more smaller follow-up meetings in which District staff feed back their interpretation of citizen priorities from the large summit to representative groups. People in the smaller forums confirm whether staff heard citizens correctly and offer revisions to ensure citizen priorities are interpreted accurately for incorporation into district plans and budgets. Citizen Summits I and II were each followed by a single forum attended by about a thousand citizens. After the November 2003 Citizen Summit III, eight Neighborhood Citizen Summits were held, one in each ward, in February 2004, creating opportunities for greater representation in the follow-up process and for the District government to learn more about how priorities differ across the city.

Neighborhood Engagement, Planning, and Service Improvement

Mayor Williams's neighborhood empowerment initiatives provided a way to fulfill the promise of Citizen Summit I close to citizens' homes, where they will notice change. Beverley Wheeler, director of the Mayor's Office of Neighborhood Action, said these initiatives were intended "to get people to trust the government again. To give voice to neighborhood residents, find out what they want, and give them quality services." The initiatives also kept up the momentum of citizen engagement stimulated by Summit I.

Citizens Bring Different Perspectives and a Variety of Roles. Since its 1974 home rule charter, the District of Columbia has been divided into eight political wards, each of which elects a district council member and thirty-seven Advisory Neighborhood Commission (ANC) districts, which are associated with the wards. Citizens are elected to the ANCs as volunteer commissioners from very small districts similar to the many Dayton citizens elected to priority boards (see Chapter Two). The thirty-nine neighborhood planning clusters, devised in 2000 for development and implementation of the SNAPS, are meant to build long-term cohesion, so they were not drawn to ANC boundaries, which shift when district council ward boundaries are redistricted. However, another key improvement effort, the Neighborhood Services Initiative, is organized by ward. The result has been a broader mix of citizen perspectives drawn into participation than had been experienced in the past. Elected ANC members and others who worked through the ward-ANC structure remained engaged, while citizens from neighborhood associations, business associations, and other community groups have also been drawn into the process.

Grace Lewis, who has been a Ward 5 ANC member and president of the North Michigan Park Civic Association, has participated from multiple perspectives. In Lewis's view, citizen involvement in neighborhood planning "enables you to be a part of what is going on, part of the bigger picture. You have a voice in decision making." People like Lewis may come to SNAPS planning sessions as advocates for their neighborhood or business group, but they move on to frame the issues for their neighborhood cluster and collaborate with each other and district planning staff to determine what will be in the SNAPS. Citizens can track the progress of SNAPS initiatives, giving them the opportunity to be evaluators of SNAPS implementation and advocates for the district to follow through on actions if they feel more progress is needed.

Service Improvement Collaborations Address Persistent Problems. The Neighborhood Services Initiative (NSI) provides service coordination staff in each ward who serve citizens as stakeholders facing persistent problems in their neighborhoods. NSI staff often forge collaborations across agencies and between agencies, citizens, and private organizations to solve difficult problems that can fall between the cracks of the bureaucracy. For example, Ward 2 Neighborhood Services coordinator Clark Ray brought together efforts of the Metro Police, the health department, consumer and regulatory affairs, zoning code enforcement, the courts, and local businesses to close down illegal massage parlors along the Fourteenth Street Corridor, where prostitution was endangering development.

Effects of the Citizen Summits

District Funding Priorities Driven by the First Two Citizen Summits. Major changes in District spending priorities due to Citizen Summit I became clear in the fiscal year 2001 budget (which started October 1, 2000). That budget added $70 million to education and $10 million to improve senior services. It funded a thousand new drug treatment slots, approved new neighborhood supermarkets, and funded continuing neighborhood-based planning and participation in governance.[15] It also funded a Youth Summit and Youth Advisory Council. Citizen Summit II also affected District budget priorities, reflected, for example, in the allocation of $10 million to renovating aquatic and recreation centers and expanding after-school programs.[16]

Summits Advance the Governance Process and Promote Citizen Learning. In addition to influencing District budgets, the Citizen Summits have advanced the community governance process. Citizen priorities and concerns expressed in Summit I led to major new neighborhood engagement and improvement processes and to new forms of engagement and governance for youth, starting with The City Is Mine: Youth Summit, a November 2000 event facilitated by America*Speaks* in which fourteen hundred youth, ages fourteen to twenty-one, engaged in a discussion with Mayor Williams. Youth Summit participants' desire for changes in how youth interact with government led the mayor and district council to create the D.C. Youth Advisory Council to keep youth issues at the forefront of the District's agenda. The council, made up of thirty-two youth from the District's eight wards, the juvenile justice system, and foster care, has a $250,000 annual budget and comments on legislation, recommends how to improve young people's lives, monitors the effectiveness of youth programs, partners with neighborhood youth organizations, and conducts workshops for youth and adults.[17]

Citizen Summit II in 2001 was specifically designed to contribute to two of the District's governing-for-results processes. In the first half of Summit II, citizens reaffirmed the five top strategic priorities from 1999 (while making some revisions, such as adding "Elders" to the "Strengthening Children, Youth, and Families" priority) and developed more specific goals under each one for a new citywide strategic plan. In the second half-day of Summit II, citizens regrouped into thirty-nine neighborhood clusters to work on updating the SNAPS, which were developed earlier through participatory planning. Part of Citizen Summit III was used to boost a new partnerships initiative started by the District, with people from businesses, civic and community organizations, and other nonprofits invited, to explore with citizens problems where solutions must go beyond government efforts.

The summits also help advance community governance by contributing to citizens across the city learning from each other. As Grace Lewis, from Ward 5, said, "From the summits, I learned that we have the same common problems and goals in my ward as in others. We have the same issues as Wards 2 and 3. It lets you know you're not the only one with this concern, giving it more impact."

Challenges, Progress, and Learning

Dramatic budget shifts demonstrate a strong link between high-level District strategies and citizen summit priorities. However, District staff have seen a need to improve finer-grain linkages across neighborhood planning and performance management processes, such as between agency and citywide strategic plans and between the SNAPS and agency budget and performance plans. These finely grained linkages can take years to develop, as they did in Rochester, which started its neighborhood-based reforms six years before the District started similar reforms under Mayor Williams. But District staff also report progress. For example, deputy director of planning Julie Wagner mentioned difficulties funding early SNAPS actions: "Initially, it was difficult to obtain funding commitments to individual neighborhood improvements. Working with the mayor's office, we were able to establish a formal process where agencies were asked to commit to specific improvements as part of the annual budgeting process. The city administrator, the mayor's chief of staff, and the deputy mayors approved additional resources to complete additional improvements." She added, "Today, agencies are held accountable to their commitments, as this is one of the measures on their agency scorecards." The mayor uses the scorecards to rate the performance of agency executives.

Patrick Canavan, director of Neighborhood Services, wants better feedback to neighborhoods. "Did we accomplish what we set out to do? Are we responsive to citizens? I'm a bureaucrat. I feel a difference. But are citizens feeling the difference?" He added, "We need to celebrate all the things we are doing, but we do not do that well. This coming year there will be more focus placed on celebrating achievements."

Several District staff have noted a need for more nongovernment effort to enhance and sustain improvement efforts. For example, Ward 2 Neighborhood Services coordinator Clark Ray described the District's four-stage approach to solving persistent neighborhood problems as "Mobilize, Reclaim, Revitalize, and Sustain." Ray and his counterparts in other wards mobilize District agencies and neighborhood people to reclaim and revitalize, but, he adds, "the sustain part is tough. We need residents and businesses to do it. But a lot of people expect the District will do it all." The District has been learning here, too, with its new partnerships initiative, for example. And the District recently started a "Neighborhood College" to develop more volunteers with knowledge, skills, and confidence to work with government and other partners to improve their neighborhoods. Its first class graduated in 2003.

Governing for Results Can Be Led by Nongovernment Organizations or Collaboratives

This chapter featured three communities where citizens are engaged in results-based governance processes run by local governments that can strategically target resources and services to achieve results that matter. Governing for results can also be led by nongovernment organizations or collaboratives (which may include some government participation) that can amass substantial resources for community improvements in which citizens have important roles. That is the approach used for nonprofit community development in the bistate Kansas City region, described in the next chapter.

CHAPTER EIGHT

COMMUNITIES GOVERNING FOR RESULTS III

Citizens Engaged in Results-Based Nonprofit Community Development

Most of my board wanted to tear it down; use the lot for a yard. But neighborhood residents were adamant. They said they had to save that house or the lot will be a dumping ground.

MICHAEL SNODGRASS, PRESIDENT, CHWC,
A COMMUNITY DEVELOPMENT CORPORATION IN KANSAS CITY, KANSAS

No one knows a neighborhood like the people who live there know it, and they will let a community development corporation (CDC) know when it is important to go the extra mile and do work they might otherwise avoid. As Michael Snodgrass explained about the Pacific and South Ninth Street house, on a lot too small to build a new house, "The house was in horrible shape. We had to prop it up with crisscrossed two-by-fours while we did a full gut rehab. We lost $15,000 on that house. But we sold it to a great family with six kids from Togo, Africa. They came here as political refugees, but they were being taken advantage of by a slumlord. The house changed their lives and helped change the neighborhood." Because CHWC was working from a sound strategic plan, it could adjust the already difficult South Ninth Street project to include one more house, and take a loss on that house, to make the project more successful for the neighborhood and its residents.

CHWC[1] and the fifteen other CDCs in two states in the Greater Kansas City Community Development 2000 (CD2000) program are part of a metropolitan region-wide collective enterprise tied together by a string of collaborations, a common vision, pooled investment resources, and a common performance framework. They use a system of targets and milestones, aligned with a strategic work plan and regular performance reporting, to manage for results. But it is not just CDC managers like Snodgrass who develop strategic plans and determine details of community projects. Citizens—residents and other stakeholders of the neighborhoods served by each CDC—are built into decision making at several stages, so CDCs produce results that matter.

CD2000 is an excellent example of advanced practice 4 of the Effective Community Governance Model, communities governing for results. It is an especially interesting example because it is not led by a single organization but by a broad-based collaboration dedicated to making nonprofit community development more effective in low-income neighborhoods across the metropolitan region. The nonprofit Greater Kansas City Local Initiatives Support Corporation plays a key role as a management intermediary organization that administers CD2000. Citizen engagement is at the neighborhood level with each CDC, not at the metro-regional level. But the performance criteria used at the regional level to determine investments in each CDC recognize citizen engagement as critical to several aspects of CDC performance. Those criteria also emphasize the importance of CDCs achieving community development results. And participating CDCs are required to plan and manage their development and citizen engagement efforts using results-based systems. All in all, regional management and governance of CD2000 reinforces governing for results at the neighborhood level.

Advanced Governance Practice 4: Communities Governing for Results

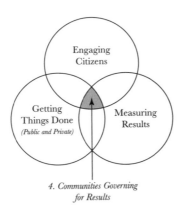

4. Communities Governing for Results

See Chapter Six for a broader discussion of what governing for results is about, with references to the examples here and in Chapter Seven to help you interpret all of these examples.

The Greater Kansas City CD2000 program is especially strong in all four community improvement themes: use of performance feedback, robust engagement of citizens in many roles, the use of collaborations, and linking measured results with accountability and resources. As you read the Greater Kansas City example, keep in mind relevant processes and practices in your community that get at least part of the way to governing for results, and consider what may be missing to keep your community from getting all the way there. See if you can find a few things done in the example that follows that organizations and citizens in your community may be able to adapt to get closer to having its own results-based approach to community governance.

CDCs, Citizens, and Collaborators Work for Results That Matter in Greater Kansas City Neighborhoods

In the late 1990s, local foundations and other investors in low-income neighborhood development in the Kansas City area teamed with the Greater Kansas City Local Initiatives Support Corporation (GKC LISC) and the Kansas City Neighborhood Alliance (KCNA) to develop the Kansas City Community Development Initiative (KCCDI), a results-focused approach to nonprofit community development that started operating in 1999. They sought not only to improve delivery and management of development projects (affordable housing and commercial development) but also to strengthen the engines of development in these neighborhoods—their nonprofit community development corporations (CDCs). The CD2000 program, the largest component of KCCDI, was designed to measure and continuously improve how CDCs perform in:

- Implementing affordable housing and other community development initiatives
- Engaging citizens so community development initiatives will be responsive to the needs and priorities of residents and other neighborhood stakeholders
- Building their capacity to improve as organizations to serve neighborhoods better

The other major components of KCCDI, started earlier and brought under KCCDI, are the Neighborhood Self-Help Fund, which channels resources to grassroots volunteer groups, and the Neighborhood Preservation Initiative (NPI), which focuses special investment to reverse trends of disinvestment and disrepair in targeted neighborhoods. The components of KCCDI are not managed directly by investors, but by intermediary organizations experienced at working with CDCs, residents, and others who work in neighborhoods. KCNA is the intermediary for the Self-Help Fund and for NPI in Missouri. GKC LISC is the intermediary for NPI in Kansas and for CD2000 throughout the bistate metropolitan region. CD2000, as managed by GKC LISC, implemented by the CDCs, and overseen by local investors, is the main focus of this example.

GKC LISC is one of thirty-five local programs of the New York–based Local Initiatives Support Corporation (LISC), which also has a national rural program. LISC raises funds nationally to support CDCs across the United States, including funds to match local KCCDI investments. A local investor Donor Advisory Board (DAB), chaired by a prominent local business or foundation executive, oversees all of KCCDI.

Like all other LISC local programs, GKC LISC has a local advisory committee of corporate, philanthropic, and community leaders, which also oversees CD2000. Mayor Carol Marinovich of the Unified Government of Wyandotte County and Kansas City, Kansas, and Mayor Kay Barnes of Kansas City, Missouri, whose governments invest in KCCDI, are on the DAB. Mayor Marinovich sees "the Unified Government in partnership with the CDCs to revitalize our older, urban core neighborhoods."

Self-Reinforcing Governance Cycles Improve Performance and Engagement

CD2000 is a systematic, self-reinforcing approach to measurably improving the performance of CDCs in engaging residents and achieving results for inner-city neighborhoods in the Kansas City metropolitan region. It has two main governing-for-results cycles: one for each CDC working in the neighborhoods it serves and a broader cycle for performance-based investments in each CDC from the overall regional investment pool. Linkages between the two governance cycles, and performance criteria (in the form of a performance metric) to determine investments in each CDC that reinforces desired outcomes and practices, make CD2000 an effective collaborative regional enterprise seeking common goals in each neighborhood served by participating CDCs.

Governing for Results at the Neighborhood Level. Figure 8.1 shows the neighborhood-level results-based governance cycle. Each CDC develops a strategic work plan (top of Figure 8.1) that looks ahead up to three years and is revised annually. The work plan uses a series of targets and milestones to set explicit performance expectations for the CDC in each neighborhood it serves. The citizens most engaged in strategic planning are the residents and other stakeholders of neighborhoods served who are members of the CDC's board of directors. They play roles as advocates for their own neighborhood, issue framer for what the CDC will try to accomplish, and collaborator with others on the board to approve the plan. Some CDCs also use broader resident engagement, beyond their board, when they develop or update their strategic work plan.

The most extensive citizen engagement generally comes in the next two stages of the neighborhood-based governance cycle, when residents are engaged as stakeholders in improvement of their own neighborhoods. First, they are given the opportunity to collaborate in planning the details of improvement, for example, by suggesting specific blocks to be redeveloped, or as with the Pacific and South Ninth Street house noted at the start of this chapter, recommending what should be done with a specific property. GKC LISC emphasizes helping stakeholders with different interests compromise, where needed, to reach consensus at this stage of neighborhood improvement planning. Then residents are engaged in implementation of improvements, often

FIGURE 8.1. CDC GOVERNING-FOR-RESULTS CYCLE IN NEIGHBORHOODS

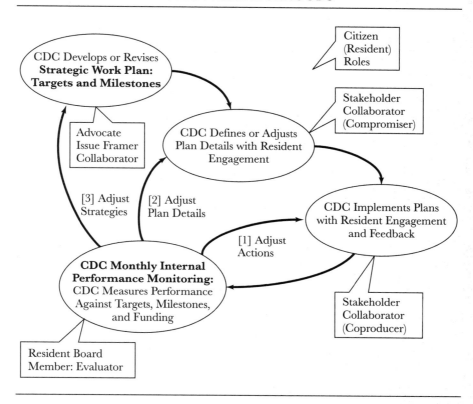

as coproducers of efforts to organize their neighborhood, reduce crime, clean up lots or parks, or other collaborative efforts to improve the community.

In its internal monthly performance reporting against planned targets, milestones, and budgets (bottom of Figure 8.1), each CDC engages its neighborhood resident board members as evaluators of CDC progress. The monthly performance monitoring becomes a source of information for three performance feedback loops, to adjust (1) implementation actions, (2) details of planned projects, and (3) strategies, including targets and milestones, to improve results. Specific ways residents are engaged vary by CDC and neighborhood.

A Performance-Based Investment Cycle Linked to Neighborhood Results-Based Governance. Figure 8.2 adds to the previous figure the broader regional program cycle that determines the performance-based investments made in each CDC.

Neighborhood-level governance used by each CDC is shown as the inner cycle in Figure 8.2. The program investment cycle—the outer cycle (with thicker arrows) in Figure 8.2—involves the planning and implementation of each three-year phase of CD2000, informed by program evaluations by a national community development consultant and data-tracked and analyzed by local university researchers that go beyond CDC-by-CDC results, to examine conditions in entire communities.

The cycle for a new phase starts (top center of Figure 8.2) when the investment partners led by the DAB assemble a funding pool and establish, in consultation with GKC LISC and CDC executives, the nature of the main outcomes sought for the next phase. For phase 1 and the start of phase 2, a CD2000 performance metric has been used to translate desired outcomes and practices into an objective tool for GKC LISC to use to assess the performance and capacity of each CDC. That assessment becomes a key part of the evaluation of each CDC for the range of CD2000 funding it will be eligible for.

FIGURE 8.2. CD2000'S TWO REINFORCING GOVERNANCE CYCLES

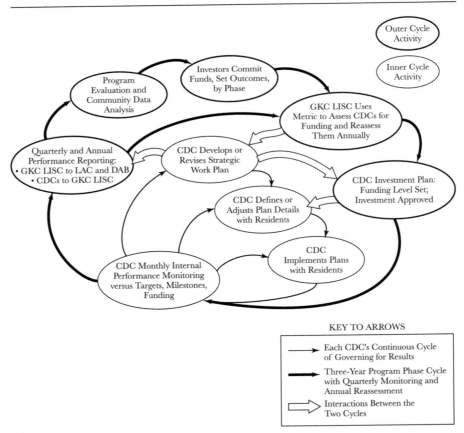

Next comes the first of several reinforcing links (the white arrows in Figure 8.2) between the outer investment cycle and the inner neighborhood-level governance cycle, as that performance-based funding range determines the overall scope a CDC can build into in its CD2000 strategic work plan. The CDC's strategic work plan then becomes the basis for a CD2000 investment plan for the CDC within the allowable funding range.

The monthly reporting that CDCs do internally to their boards turns into quarterly and annual external performance reporting by CDCs to GKC LISC and by GKC LISC to its local advisory committee (LAC) and the DAB, which again reinforces CDC efforts toward desired outcomes. Mayor Barnes of Kansas City, Missouri, appreciates the rigorous performance monitoring of KCCDI and CD2000. She said, "KCCDI has brought a discipline to the CDCs. I'm impressed with the attention to detail—going over the same questions and issues over and over—every month with the CDCs and every quarter with the DAB." That performance information helps GKC LISC reassess each CDC annually against the CD2000 performance metric.

The Performance Metric at the Investment Level Reinforces Governing for Results in Neighborhoods.
The CD2000 performance metric is a performance-based investment tool that strengthens the common focus of CD2000 as a collaborative results-driven enterprise for the bistate Kansas City metropolitan region. The use of the performance metric to help determine a CDC's funding for each phase of CD2000 and reassess CDC performance annually gives CDCs a powerful incentive to achieve desired outcomes and improve their practices.

The CD2000 performance metric provides criteria to grade each CDC from A to D for six major performance dimensions: Board Governance, Planning, Resource Development, Internal Management, Community Connection, and Program Delivery. Each dimension is broken down into specific performance characteristics for which a four-point descriptive scale has been devised to determine if the CDC gets an A (for "Excelling"), B (for "Advancing"), C (for "Operational"), or D (for "Developing") for that characteristic. The characteristic grades are combined, in a weighted scale, to form the dimension grades. For example, the "Planning" grade consists of grades for "Strategic Plan," "Mission and Neighborhood Change Results," and "Strategic Partnerships." All the dimension grades are then combined on a weighted scale to form an overall grade for the CDC.[2] Each overall grade is associated with a specific funding range.

The performance metric especially reinforces desired outcomes and practices by spelling out specific performance characteristics under each dimension, to tell CDCs what they have to do to maintain or improve their grade, and thus protect or enhance future funding. For example, here are descriptions of requirements to get an A on just two of several performance characteristics that reinforce resident engagement:

- *To get an "A" on Neighborhood Representation (under the dimension "Board Governance"):* Board members must consist of at least 51 percent neighborhood/core city/target area residents or stakeholders, with at least three resident leaders.
- *To get an "A" on Community Engagement and Communication (under "Community Connection"):* CDC must expand its circle of community input and cooperation by recruiting new community representation on advisory or ad hoc board committees. CDC creates communication exchange with community stakeholders annually.[3]

Grade descriptions for other characteristics reinforce outcomes for new physical development, such as new homes; managing existing assets, such as rental properties; and practices that build CDC capacity in planning, resource development (raising funds), and financial and organizational management.

Assessment against the performance metric indicates each CDC's opportunities to improve, so each CDC can target specific ways to build its capacity in its strategic work plan. Each CDC's strategic work plan is specific to the needs of the neighborhoods it serves and to its own capacity and growth objectives. However, the use of common performance criteria for overall CDC evaluation helps drive consistency and alignment of CDC outcomes and practices across the region. For example, all CDCs know they will be rated on community engagement in several dimensions of the CD2000 performance metric, which ensures all will pay attention to, for example, neighborhood organizing and local resident representation on their boards.

Targets and Milestones Help CDCs Build Capacity and Achieve Outcomes. Each CDC's strategic work plan provides the basis for a neighborhood-level governing-for-results cycle (Figure 8.1) and is influenced by the detailed assessment of the CDC in the outer investment cycle of CD2000 (Figure 8.2) based on the performance metric. CDC strategic work plans are built on a system of targets and milestones used to specify details of all the ways the CDC expects to improve neighborhoods and build its own capacity. For each type of development outcome sought in each neighborhood (for example, housing, jobs), for each type of citizen engagement outcome (for example, blocks organized), and for each capacity-building goal (for example, improve financial management systems), the CDC sets a target of what it will try to achieve and specifies milestones it will reach on the way to each target.

The nonprofit Rensselaerville Institute of Rensselaerville, New York, helped GKC LISC adapt the institute's "outcome framework" to the development of low-income neighborhoods. Rensselaerville's outcome framework had previously been—and still is—used for many other public and nonprofit services, particularly human services.[4] GKC LISC has helped CDCs articulate measurable targets for outcomes to be achieved in one to three years.

For example, for a given year, a CDC may set three of its targets to be:

- Complete development of thirty units of new or renovated housing in three specific neighborhoods, occupied by mixed-income home owners (including a minimum percentage low income) able to maintain the property physically and financially
- Get twelve neighborhood residents to complete leadership development training to increase their engagement in community improvement
- Organize twelve neighborhood blocks to engage residents in block clubs, neighborhood associations, public safety committees, or other community-building activities

The CDCs then develop milestones of interim accomplishments they must achieve over periods of weeks and months on the way to achieving the targets. For example, for the first target above, milestones may include:

- Project financing obtained and redevelopment sites acquired
- Design and construction contracts executed
- Homes designed and sites prepared for construction or renovation
- Families of the desired income mix recruited as home owners
- Prospective new home owners qualified for mortgages and have knowledge in maintaining homes and managing financial obligations
- Six housing units a month completed, sold, and occupied by qualified families of varying incomes

CDCs also document how they will verify accomplishment of each target and milestone and more specific action steps they will take that they assume will help them reach each milestone—for example: provide training and technical assistance to new home owners in establishing credit, obtaining mortgages, and maintaining homes. All of a CDC's targets, milestones, verification approaches, and action steps become part of its strategic work plan, which becomes the basis for performance monitoring in both the neighborhood-level and program-level governance cycles (see Figures 8.1 and 8.2).

The point of the target-and-milestone approach is not only to provide measurable outcome targets, but to provide dates for interim accomplishments along the way—the milestones—so managers can determine, month by month, whether they are on course to reach their targets. Then they can more quickly learn what is working about their programs and what is not, question their assumptions in program designs, and improve programs' ability to achieve results while they are implementing them.

Often when an organization first uses the model, it does not know what it can accomplish in one to three years, as CDCs in Greater Kansas City have been learning during CD2000. Mike Clarke, president and CEO of the CDC Neighborhood Housing Services of Kansas City, Missouri (NHS-Missouri), explains, "A CDC might have a production target of completing one hundred houses in a year. If nine months pass, and only ten houses are completed, there is obviously some problem with the planning and target setting." By tracking milestones, the CDC's managers may learn in the first few months that they could not produce required financial reports in time to secure loans on schedule, or they did not have legal support needed for site acquisition. They could then take corrective action early in order to come closer to their production target, if not actually reach it. They may also learn to reallocate resources (for example, to improve financial systems or budget for more legal assistance) in next year's CDC budget to be better prepared to meet next year's targets. So even if an organization does not hit a target, valuable information can be gained and lessons learned.

Jerry Shechter, executive director of Westside Housing Organization (WHO) in Kansas City, Missouri, says of the target and milestone system, "It helps us to achieve tangible objectives and guide how we do what we do. We can judge our performance over time against the targets we shoot for." Reports from staff to management and from management to the board ensure accountability and, more important, encourage feedback. Each target and milestone is attached to a date. If a CDC misses a milestone, the board will soon know and can ask good questions. Eric Holden, vice chair and secretary of the board of NHS-Missouri, and a resident-leader of the Squier Park neighborhood served by that CDC, described what he sees each month: "The monthly report, given in a board packet before the board meeting, is broken down by specific targets. It is divided in three layers, targets for the year, where we are year to date, and percentage completion" of each annual target. He called the monthly reporting system against targets and milestones "a solid way to gauge the CDC's success throughout the year."

Many Kansas City CDCs adopted outcome-based target-and-milestone plans in order to get CD2000 funding. Swope Community Builders, one of the most successful CDCs in Kansas City, if not the country, did not need that incentive. Swope had implemented outcome-based planning and management several years before CD2000. Swope Enterprises senior vice president Chuck Gatson, head of Swope Community Builders, says, "Everything we do is based on results. We count everything." He explains, "If you can't gauge your performance, you can't gauge whether you achieved your goal."

Through CD2000, many more Kansas City CDCs have been learning to plan and manage for results and to be accountable for achieving results. GKC LISC's Diane Patrick says, "We preach a gospel of transparency, on the premise that a CDC is accountable to its community." The mayors of both Kansas Cities agree. Kansas City, Kansas, Mayor Carol Marinovich says, "Accountability is critical to be sure wise investments are made." Kansas City, Missouri, Mayor Kay Barnes says, "Getting things done and measuring results is where the rubber meets the road."

Robust Citizen Engagement

Citizens play all major engagement roles through many of the CD2000 planning and implementation stages in their neighborhoods. Robust citizen engagement is supported by CD2000's performance assessment criteria and by the planning and management tools provided to CDCs, which some CDC staff and managers appreciate.

Results Management Tools Work for Citizen Engagement. CDCs not only set targets and milestones for physical development but also use these outcome planning and management tools for community organizing. As Michael Snodgrass, president of CHWC, a CDC in Kansas City, Kansas, explains, "I knew how to build houses, and you can see what you built. These tools have helped us most in community organizing, where it's hard to get a feel for our effectiveness. Now, we have understandable outcomes we are trying to achieve. Where we fall short, we ask organizers, 'Why? What's the dynamic in the neighborhood? Is our goal still attainable? Is there a different way to do it?' Our targets and milestones become a learning tool." In Kansas City, Missouri, Swope Community Builders organizer Leslie MacLendon "can't see organizing without tools. It's incentive; it makes you feel good and want to heighten your goals. If you organized ten blocks, let's get ten more!"

CDCs Get Results for Citizens as Stakeholders. Swope housing developers walk with community organizers through neighborhoods where development will take place to answer questions and concerns of residents as stakeholders of new development. MacLendon says, "We try to assess the needs of the neighborhood. We're here not only to build houses, but to assist residents and make sure that they know we are not taking over the neighborhood that they have lived in for twenty years."

CDCs also help citizens increase their stake from being concerned and involved in their community, to literally becoming community owners—to own and keep homes they otherwise could not afford or would not be able to get financed. Kaw Valley Habitat for Humanity, a Kansas CDC, follows the Habitat model used across the country to help low-income families buy and keep homes, involving sweat equity, reduced-interest mortgages, and debt management education. NHS-Missouri has a mortgage and lending program in areas targeted for future housing so residents can buy the houses NHS produces. The WHO CDC in Kansas City, Missouri, has a microlending program to help residents with other costs of ownership. WHO board member Barbara Bailey lives in a neighborhood of late-nineteenth-century single-family bungalows that have been passed down generation to generation. WHO helped her neighbor, who needed money to replace deteriorating galvanized pipes. He could "not go to the bank for $2,500," Bailey said, but with WHO's microlending, "there's a program that allows someone to fix their house and actually keep it."

CDCs Listen and Turn Citizen Advocates and Stakeholders into Issue Framers. Some CDCs engage residents at the front end of strategic planning, or, as Swope senior vice president Chuck Gatson puts it, "The neighborhood sets the plan; then we set the goals for the organization." CHWC uses "listening sessions" before revising its strategic plan. Residents come as stakeholders, and they may already be organized by grassroots groups to be advocates for things they want for their neighborhood. CHWC helps them become issue framers who describe their visions to help set CHWC's agenda. For example, Strawberry Hill resident and neighborhood association president Carole Diehl said, "We have had listening programs—about three or four in two years so far. About a hundred people from the community participated in each of these. We have been involved in planning by making our voices heard and letting them know what we want." As a result, the neighborhood group's and the CDC's strategies become aligned to strengthen how they serve the community together. Mayor Marinovich praised CHWC for "moving into business development in the Sixth Street corridor because they worked in partnership with the Strawberry Hill Neighborhood Association who had it as a goal in their strategic plan."

GKC LISC encourages CDCs to use listening sessions regularly to keep in touch with resident concerns, which can take residents more deeply into the issue framer role to define problems and identify solutions concerning details of specific projects planned by a CDC. CHWC has done this in Kansas City, Kansas, neighborhoods. For example, Carole Diehl described a project that CHWC president Michael Snodgrass brought to residents of her neighborhood to discuss. "We wanted the new homes built to match the old style," said Diehl, referring to Strawberry Hill's Victorian-era houses. "Michael listened and brought in the architect to speak with us. Nobody can tell that these are new houses on the block, they blend in so well."

Listening to residents can make a big difference in projects CDCs take on, making residents especially powerful issue framers of neighborhood improvement. CHWC's Snodgrass described listening sessions where residents "picked some of the toughest sites for us to build. I never would have done it, but that's what they wanted. Our South Ninth Street project, for example. Neighborhood residents most wanted new homes where the infrastructure had been removed. We agreed to build seven new homes that needed new water and sewer lines. We also had to widen and repave the road and put in sidewalks. We had to find an extra $150,000 for that project, but what a difference it made!" The same residents persuaded CHWC to renovate the dilapidated house mentioned at the start of this chapter. By taking on projects citizens ask for, especially the tough ones, Snodgrass said, "We built credibility with residents. Now they know decisions they make are real decisions." CDCs' listening builds trust, and their results build optimism. "CHWC has been a boon to the urban core of Kansas City," said Carole Diehl of Strawberry Hill. "People now believe things can turn around, and once again have hope."

CDCs Engage Citizens as Coproducers of Improvement. CDCs do not just engage citizens in defining problems and identifying solutions, but also in becoming part of the solution, by collaborating with the CDC and often other organizations such as a government agency or a neighborhood association as a coproducer of improvement efforts. Carole Diehl again spoke of working with her Strawberry Hill neighbors and CHWC: "We have redone a small park. We made it beautiful. We are always working together in various initiatives, such as community policing." Many citizens are engaged as coproducers in public safety and in other forms of collaboration besides coproduction to reach compromise solutions when competing interests emerge in planned projects.

Resident Board Members Play Citizen Engagement Roles. Most CDCs' own rules require significant neighborhood representation on their boards of directors, and, as noted above, GKC LISC grades neighborhood board representation on the performance metric. For example, NHS-Missouri requires at least eight of its fifteen board members to be from the neighborhoods it serves. Resident members of a CDC's board are the neighborhood residents most engaged in developing a CDC's strategic work plan, when they can play roles of issue framers to set the agenda for the CDC, and as collaborators with board members who represent other neighborhoods or interests to develop a consensus plan. Resident board members, such as NHS-Missouri board vice chair and secretary Eric Holden, also become evaluators of CDC progress each month when they review CDC performance reports against the targets and milestones in the strategic work plan.

Besides playing the full governance roles of an NHS board member, Holden also plays the role of advocate for the Squier Park neighborhood, where he lives and is a member of the neighborhood association. Holden says, "Depending on the subject, as a board member, representing the neighborhood will usually take precedence over NHS goals. I need to represent my neighborhood." Balancing the roles is not always easy. A subject that aroused passion in the mixed-use Squier Park area was a proposed multi-family development; the city government has encouraged more density in the urban core, providing an incentive to NHS to develop multifamily housing. But single-family Squier Park residents have been against more multifamily units. NHS created a task force to engage residents further on the issue, and Holden became a mediator between the neighborhood association and NHS to work through neighbors' concerns.

Collaborations Fuel Community Development Success

Various kinds of collaborations within neighborhoods, across neighborhood boundaries, and across the bistate metropolitan region have helped build and sustain the success of many CDCs' efforts and of the entire CD2000 program and the larger KCCDI initiative. Locally, CDCs collaborate with neighborhood residents and their grassroots organizations, government agencies, and others to develop neighborhoods, solve problems, and create and sustain conditions that will enable development efforts to succeed. Even the largest Kansas City CDC, Swope Community Builders, collaborates with residents and with other organizations to accomplish things it cannot do alone and focus more resources on desired outcomes. Successful community development requires constant negotiation and partnership building with civic authorities, banks, charitable foundations, and other nonprofits. As Swope's Chuck Gatson explains, "We perform the best we can knowing there are certain vagaries in this business—it is a patchwork of resources you put together to get to a certain point."

Collaboration Against Crime Spurs Economic Development. CDCs and local governments in both states have forged collaborations with residents acting as coproducers who cooperate with public authorities to make their neighborhoods safer. Kansas City, Missouri, Mayor Barnes says, "Our police department is very involved in KCCDI with community policing—from the police chief on down." She adds, "As community policing has matured, it has become not just cooperation but really an integrated set of relationships. Citizen leaders of neighborhoods are on a first-name basis with officers in their neighborhoods. It is wonderful to see."

In Kansas City, Missouri, residents near Fifty-Ninth and Indiana were tired of gunshots and drug activity at that notorious intersection. Residents partnered with Swope Community Builders staff, police officers, and code officials to make the street a no-tolerance zone. Results were immediate. All people wanted on a warrant in the area were arrested. Three days into the program, the local police captain boarded the drug house on the corner. Four months later, people would no longer speed up to pass through Fifty-Ninth and Indiana, and the drug dealers had left. Initiatives like the no-tolerance zone empower residents. Swope organizer Leslie MacLendon says, "People get excited seeing things done." Investors also notice. Because of Swope's Community Safety Initiative and the solid relationship between police and citizens, H&R Block decided to build its new service center in the neighborhood, creating six hundred new jobs, many of which went to local residents. H&R Block was convinced by a presentation showing dramatic crime reduction in the neighborhoods around the site.

Collaborations with Grassroots Groups Build and Sustain Neighborhoods. When a CDC wants to organize a neighborhood, neighborhood associations are natural partners. A CDC will take advantage of an existing neighborhood association's connection with residents and work with the association to identify, and help improve, conditions of concern to the residents. Some CDCs start with such neighborhood organizing activities to improve safety, health, or other conditions even if development is not planned for the neighborhood. Ultimately, improving these conditions can improve the climate for successful development.

In 2002, the Westside Housing Organization (WHO), a Kansas City, Missouri, CDC, wanted to organize two neighborhoods where it had not yet been active. Cathy Wagner, a WHO community organizer, began by taking the presidents of the local neighborhood associations on tours of other neighborhoods served by WHO and by touring the potential new target neighborhoods with their respective association presidents sharing valuable insights. She went to neighborhood association meetings and asked members what they envisioned for their community, which led to neighborhood target setting. Wagner says she finds targets for real community impact by "having a conversation with people about what they see, hear, and feel, about what they want to see changed and what they want to see their time and energy dedicated to." For example, members of one neighborhood association complained that the rat problem was getting worse because the city government had ended rat control in that area to save money. Wagner helped the association bring the issue to city council members, and the rat control funding was soon addressed.

CDCs Help Build Strong Grassroots Organizations Where Needed. If a CDC or a local government invests in improving a distressed neighborhood, it risks having the investment yield little or no return in neighborhood impact if the residents are not engaged. As Kansas City, Kansas, Mayor Marinovich said, "We can come in and clean up an area, get rid of the blight, but without strong neighborhood engagement, six months later you wouldn't know we had been there. You need neighborhood involvement to sustain the improvement." A CDC has a harder time engaging residents in communities without strong neighborhood organizations. So it can be worth their effort to strengthen weak neighborhood groups or build new ones.

Emerald Jackson, community organizer for Mount Carmel Redevelopment Corporation, a Kansas City, Kansas, CDC, has been helping two fragile neighborhood groups define a more formal structure and strengthen themselves. "The neighborhood does not have a voice in the community or with local officials," Jackson explains, "If there is a need for monies for something, they don't have a strong enough voice to make demands." When Mount Carmel joined the Kaw Valley Habitat for Humanity and City Vision Ministries CDCs and the Kansas City, Kansas, Police Department in a Community Safety Collaborative (CSC), Jackson took advantage of it to give residents something important to participate in and to give the two neighborhood associations she is assisting something to build on. The CSC engages residents with police officers, city officials, and other community stakeholders in a strategy to increase safety. "We discuss concerns about crime; that allows residents to come together," Jackson says. The collaborative's first event in the Mount Carmel area was a "Night Against Crime," planned by the presidents of the two groups that Jackson is helping to organize. Next, the CSC planned a "Codes Blitz." The collaborative invited city officials to come to the neighborhood to find code violations and spur residents to fix their homes and clean up their yards. Although too recent to gauge their effect, Emerald Jackson's efforts to help build the neighborhood groups into more viable organizations can help Mount Carmel residents transform themselves from ignored customers to neighborhood advocates, issue framers, and coproducers.

Collaborations to Achieve Consensus That Enables Development. Not all stakeholders in a neighborhood always agree on the nature of development, as Squier Park neighborhood association member and NHS-Missouri board member Eric Holden can attest. They have different interests and concerns. So GKC LISC promotes a "consensus organizing model" and teaches it in leadership training for neighborhood residents to help residents be collaborators who can forge compromise among different interests. According to GKC LISC's Ronelle Neperud, who supports community organizing throughout the region, their model seeks to "establish a norm of bringing perceived enemies to the table as part of a collaboration in the solution."

Kate Corwin should agree with Ronelle, from her experience as president of the Southmoreland Neighborhood Association, in Kansas City, Missouri. The QuikTrip Corporation's original plan to expand its convenience store-gas station at Forty-Fourth and Main Streets upset residents who did not want to lose three residential buildings, despite their poor condition, that QuikTrip proposed to demolish. The neighborhood association brought residents and corporate representatives together to find a project that could work for both, with the WHO CDC as part of the solution. QuikTrip razed only one building, gave a house saved from demolition to a neighbor for renovation, and gave the Walnut Street apartment building to WHO for redevelopment, including re-creation of the building's original 1920s balconies. QuikTrip also paid for part of the building's renovation, other property improvements, and tenant relocation, and agreed to pay the neighborhood association for monthly security and trash pickup. WHO executive director Jerry Shechter saw the experience as a positive nonadversarial process of people cooperating with each other to improve the neighborhood. Kate Corwin felt that early engagement and frequent communication with people were essential to reaching consensus. "After some of those meetings, people could see that the QuikTrip people were reasonable. They wanted to make a profit and we wanted to do something good for the neighborhood. We had a lot of things in common."[5]

CDCs Collaborate to Improve Conditions and Build on Each Others' Strengths. The three-CDC Community Safety Collaborative with the Kansas City, Kansas, Police described above is an example of CDCs collaborating with each other. The Mount Carmel, Kaw Valley, and City Vision CDCs recognize that crime or blight do not stop at CDC district boundaries. To achieve another desired outcome— develop stronger community leadership among Spanish-speaking populations—the El Centro CDC, CHWC, and GKC LISC have been collaborating on developing Spanish-language leadership training.

Other collaborations bring together different organizational strengths. CHWC is master builder of a development in the Riverview neighborhood where a key outcome sought is mixed-income housing, with Kaw Valley Habitat for Humanity participating for its strength in housing very low-income families. One in every four homes will be a Habitat for Humanity home for families under 30 percent of median income. About half will be for incomes between 30 and 89 percent of median, and the rest will be market rate. A neighborhood association and a local church round out this four-way collaboration.

A Regional Investment Collaboration Makes It Possible. The entire KCCDI, which includes CD2000, is a metropolitan region-wide collaboration to focus investment on community development outcomes. Over twenty organizations collaborate on local KCCDI investment, including locally based foundations, banks and other businesses, and the governments of Missouri, Kansas City, Missouri, and Kansas City, Kansas. Local KCCDI investments are leveraged by national sources, including LISC, foundations, businesses, and the federal government. Kansas City, Kansas, Mayor Marinovich says, "Redevelopment is costly. Collaboration with private investors really helps speed up improvement." In its first three years, KCCDI leveraged $10 million in local support with $14 million in national funds to create the largest community development funding effort in Kansas City's history.[6]

Learning to Improve CD2000

In their first one to three years of receiving CD2000 funds, most CDCs focused on capacity building, for example, improving financial management for better rental cash flow. So rather than shift outcomes, it made sense, as phase 2 of KCCDI began in 2003, to see if strengthened CDCs could improve program delivery, such as housing production, which, by 2002, was 400 percent above the preprogram baseline but below the target set due to added investment. Organizing also expanded in phase 1, with indicators such as people graduating from leadership training on target in 2002.[7]

In phase 1, CDCs were learning to use outcome management tools, new ways to develop community leaders, and build their capacity to deliver. GKC LISC monitored CDC performance to learn how best to support them with initiatives such as community leadership training. GKC LISC also listened to CDC leaders concerned that the CD2000 performance metric did not reflect true CDC organizational performance well enough. So in 2002, GKC LISC worked with a committee of CDC executives, and with its local advisory committee (LAC) including investors, to revise the metric. If the revisions increase the perceived validity of the metric among CDCs, the metric can become more powerful in reinforcing desired outcomes, translating a phase 1 learning into improved phase 2 results.

Preparing for Bigger Challenges

Although CDCs were already engaging in collaborations to reduce crime and improve other neighborhood conditions, in phase 1 of CD2000, CDC performance was mainly evaluated on the success of specific development projects they planned, built, and managed and on how well they met community organizing targets and CDC capacity-building goals. In phase 1, CDC performance accountability did not include neighborhood-wide crime rates, physical conditions, or other community outcomes outside the specific development projects they manage. However, for several years, GKC LISC has been monitoring, and reporting to the KCCDI DAB "macro indicators" of neighborhood health, particularly for housing and crime, to keep abreast of broader community outcomes.[8]

While phase 2 of CD2000 was in its first year, local investors began voicing concerns that outcomes targeted in future years would have to be more ambitious to consider CD2000 a long-term success. Hall Family Foundation vice president John Laney, a member of the DAB and the KCCDI executive committee, referred to donors wanting CDCs to show results beyond capacity building and housing. "Let's be judged on other things that make neighborhoods healthy—lower crime, for example, and investments in neighborhoods to support a healthy residential climate." The H&R Block Foundation president David Miles, another DAB and KCCDI executive committee member, said outcomes for entire neighborhoods—not just CDC projects—"such as housing values, crime rates, and home ownership rates should become more relevant measures of CDC success."

There are so many influences on neighborhoods besides CDCs—the broader real estate market, regional employment, schools, and government service budgets, to name just four—that judging CDC success based on neighborhood-wide outcomes can be intimidating even to the largest and strongest CDCs, let alone small ones whose projects reach fewer people. But that is the direction being explored during phase 2 by GKC LISC in consultation with other evaluators, the DAB, the LAC, and CDC leaders. In August 2003, then-GKC LISC senior program director Jim White acknowledged the difficulties but felt, "to my mind, it is the right question to put on the table. . . . For all of us involved in community development, this is the point, to have our combined efforts help to halt the decline, disinvestment, and loss of viable core city neighborhoods, stabilize them, and bring them back to a state of physical, social, and economic health."[9] In 2003, GKC LISC began experimenting with an index of neighborhood health and improvement that combines data on housing values, home ownership rates, and crime rates, examined over time and in comparison with citywide or urban core benchmarks.[10]

They have modest expectations for this approach—that they may not be able to tell if CDCs can really cause neighborhood change. But they hope to examine trends and make commonsense connections between CDC programs and strategies and broad neighborhood outcomes. Kansas City, Missouri, Mayor Barnes said, "Measuring neighborhood impact would be consistent with KCCDI's holistic approach to community development. Community improvement has been too often fragmented in the past, dealing with safety under one umbrella, housing under another, and so on. I'm interested in seeing neighborhood impact measurement go forward." But she added, "Just as deterioration of neighborhoods can be caused by multiple forces, improvement takes multiple forces. You can't only single out the CDCs, but you must use these as indicators of success of all the players in community development working together." In that spirit, perhaps neighborhood impact measurement will motivate CDCs to engage more organizations in collaboration, including some that bring different expertise and resources than those CDCs now work with, to influence outcomes in new ways.

GKC LISC is exploring, with the DAB and LAC, ways of strengthening the connection between funding and performance. One line of thought is that a CDC should no longer be considered a good investment if, after three years in CD2000, it has not improved its capacity or production to a specific level, as measured by the performance metric. Those CDCs might lose all CD2000 funding or be cut back to modest capacity-building investments. Large reductions to low performers can free funds for incentives to high-performing CDCs whose neighborhoods show the strongest outcome gains, as may be measured by a new index. Will such an investment approach provide even greater reinforcement of outcomes and help improve neighborhoods across the region? Will some neighborhoods lose important organizational assets that help in ways not captured by the performance metric or outcome indicators? Achieving one, and not the other, will be a special challenge to the investors, managers, and collaborators in nonprofit community development in Greater Kansas City.

Many Potential Roads to Governing for Results

All communities are different, and the forces of change and improvement vary from one community to another. Organizations with the capacity and inclination to engage citizens, measure results, and pull together resources and collaborations behind improving citizens' desired outcomes vary from community to community. There is no single way to reach governing for results, as should be apparent from the four case examples in this chapter and Chapter Seven. Even Rochester and Washington, D.C., whose governing-for-results approaches look very similar, got there by very different routes. People who want their communities to get there will have to draw up their own road map. However, a lot can still be learned from communities that already exhibit strong results-based governance approaches, whether for complex enterprises that affect communities in many different ways, such as general-purpose local governments, or for more focused (but still complex) functions such as community development. The different performance feedback cycles, the different ways citizens are engaged, and the different kinds of collaborations in these case examples may all provide ideas that can be adapted for use by other communities.

Also, as governing for results combines aspects of the other three advanced governance practices, citizens or organizations may borrow from practices used in communities featured in Chapters Two through Five, and potentially piece together a route that will eventually get their own community to governing for results. Even if part of the path appears blocked for whatever reason—for example, a lack of interest by key decision makers, a lack of resources or organizational capacity to do everything that is needed, insufficient citizen leadership—it is worth starting on a journey that may get a community partway there. Some community improvement benefits may be gained along the way and valuable lessons learned that will help the community overcome barriers to results-based governance in the future.

CHAPTER NINE

MORE IDEAS FOR MAKING IT HAPPEN

I believe this empowerment program has given me lots of deputies.

MAYOR WILLIAM JOHNSON, ROCHESTER, NEW YORK

In Mayor Johnson's experience, engaging citizens in planning and improving their own neighborhoods not only benefits Rochester neighborhoods but strengthens his ability to govern. He explains, "Since I can't be everywhere, they bring things to city hall. And they translate city hall to their neighbors. They can tell their neighbors about strategic deployments of resources that will spill over to their block." With empowered citizens as his emissaries, the mayor believes he is empowered as an elected leader.

One of the keys to making effective governance work is for community leaders to take the expansive view of power that Mayor Johnson and other decision makers in this book understand: when leaders give power to citizens in a results-focused context, citizens in turn strengthen their leaders' power to guide the community to results that matter. This chapter reviews some of the major themes that cut across many of the practices and examples in the book and takes a number of them further, such as examining changing power relationships implied by effective citizen engagement.

Additional ideas for making citizen engagement and performance feedback more effective are presented in this chapter, as are suggestions to help you set expectations for improving governance and results. These ideas and suggestions are intended to help you determine issues to address and opportunities to seize in your community and to help you find a starting point for change. For example, any of a variety of performance modeling techniques presented in brief, referred to here as "community performance value chains," may help you find opportunities for getting more from performance feedback. Brief reviews in this chapter of using collaborations and of community learning may also help you chart a course to improving governance and results in your community.

Making Citizen Engagement More Effective

Careful planning and rigorous implementation is needed to make attempts to involve citizens in community affairs effective. Important aspects of achieving effective participation include achieving inclusive, diverse participation; participation processes that engage citizens in active, deliberative dialogue and give them a real opportunity to influence decisions; providing a trusted convener and safe place for deliberation; and building citizen capacity to be more effectively engaged. Also, as information technology has become an everyday part of how people communicate and how they obtain and analyze news and information, it provides both opportunities and risks for effectively engaging citizens. These issues, which arose in discussions of citizen roles and examples of engagement in the previous chapters, are explored further here. But rigorous design and implementation of deliberative processes will be for naught if community decision makers are unwilling to seriously consider the concerns and priorities of engaged citizens or if professional staff in the community are unwilling or unable to play roles other than that of expert. Decision makers and professionals must be willing to share power and expertise rather than hoard it and play more facilitative roles in working with each other and with citizens.

New Roles for Leaders and Professionals

A basic premise of this book is that robust engagement of citizens in many roles—stakeholder, advocate, issue framer, evaluator, and collaborator—makes community governance more effective. Just as the roles of citizens are important, so are the roles and attitudes of leaders who make decisions that influence community services and conditions and of professional staff of public and private community organizations.

Leaders Must Accept and Use New Power Relationships. Giving citizens an influential role in results-focused governance changes power relationships between citizens and those who govern them. The National Civic League calls for today's community leaders to move away from autocratic hoarding of power and "learn to share power and share the public agenda with their fellow community members."[1] This book includes leaders from very different communities who believe that engaging citizens and sharing power with them increases their own power as leaders. Rochester Mayor William Johnson, from a central city in northwestern New York, clearly believes it. So does John Jenkins, an elected official of a suburban-rural Virginia county. When asked if the Prince William County Board of Supervisors was giving something up by paying so much attention to engaged citizens, Jenkins responded, "We're not giving up power. We are empowered by the people." Similarly, Mayor Johnson said, "I gain as much as I give in this process."

Prince William County board chair Sean Connaughton takes a long-term, strategic view of the board's trade-off in sharing power with citizens in developing four-year strategic plans: "The price of this system can make some politicians leery. You are buying into, essentially, multi-year budgets and strategic decisions. Elected officials have to surrender their power to make major revisions in focus every year. But in the long run, it gives us the power to govern better and make long-term changes—changes that matter." He does not mean that they never make major changes. Because Prince William County's governance system is results based, the board can learn from performance data between major four-year planning updates when large adjustments are needed, as they did in 1998 when they added a major human services goal to their strategic plan. In doing so, they engaged citizens such as Paul Moessner to help articulate the goal and develop measurable outcomes.

However, not all public officials agree that they should be sharing power with citizens. Mayor Johnson says, "When I tell my colleagues from other cities about Neighbors Building Neighborhoods," Rochester's citizen-empowering program, "they look at me cross-eyed. They say citizens elected us. They expect us to use our judgment for them." Rochester citizens engaged in planning their own neighborhood improvements, Washington, D.C., citizens engaged in neighborhood planning or Citizen Summits, and Prince William County citizens engaged in strategic planning no longer expect their elected leaders to make all their community's decisions for them. But these relationships do not drain power from leaders; they add power by building a more trusting, active citizenry. As Prince William County citizen Paul Moessner said, keeping the community engaged increases both engagement and trust of citizens. An active citizenry will include people like Glenn Gardner in Rochester, who identify non-government assets that add more power to improvement efforts and hold themselves accountable for doing their part in improving the community.

Leaders as Connectors and Facilitators, Not Just Decision Makers. Leaders of community institutions, be they government elected officials, nonprofit board members, or chief executives of any community organization, have an important role connecting people to power and to each other. John Nalbandian, chair of public administration of the University of Kansas and former mayor of Lawrence, Kansas, says, "The elected officials who are really effective are the connectors and facilitators." He sees them facilitating the elected governing body as an effective decision-making group, connecting elected policy officials with staff, and connecting citizens with government decision making. To connect effectively with citizens, Nalbandian says elected officials "have to be able to articulate the story of community." Rochester Mayor Johnson finds that when he makes personal connections with citizens, they give him *their* stories of the community. When he is "walking the city with residents, they not only point out problems, but what they're proud of in their neighborhood."

Leaders of nonprofit community organizations also need to connect and facilitate. They have to at the Jacksonville Community Council Inc. (JCCI); it is built into the way the board and committee chairs work with citizen volunteers. Truckee Meadows Tomorrow (TMT) leaders do it too, when they get citizens and organizations to adopt indicators and sign quality-of-life compacts. Heads of Kansas City community development corporations (CDCs), such as CHWC's Michael Snodgrass in Kansas and Swope Community Builder's Chuck Gatson in Missouri, make connections with residents and other organizations they partner with to develop neighborhoods more effectively. CDC boards have built-in community connections through their resident board members, some of whom, like Eric Holden of the NHS-Missouri Board, can end up helping to facilitate resolution of tough neighborhood issues.

Part of connecting and facilitating is listening. CHWC's Snodgrass listened to Strawberry Hill residents' concerns about the design of new homes. Carole Diehl, the neighborhood association president, was pleased that the result matched residents' desires for the new houses to blend in with the older ones. Snodgrass feels that listening and following through builds credibility with residents, and he is willing to build homes in difficult places, such as South Ninth Street, where new water and sewer lines were needed, if residents think it will make a bigger difference for the neighborhood than building an easier, less costly project on another site. If they were not listening, Prince William County leaders would not hear citizens' strategic priorities, and Mayor Johnson would not hear Rochester citizens' stories of their neighborhoods. Listening builds trust and helps people accept the leader's story, including messages of limits and expectations. Mayor Johnson said, "I'm consistently reminding people that we have limited resources. What I find is, people recognize we have limitations."

Professionals as Conveyors, Process Designers, and Facilitators. John Nalbandian, who trains city managers, says, "We're way beyond the point where professionals are simply masters of knowledge. They must have the ability to convey that knowledge and get it used." He especially means to convey it to citizens by meeting groups in their own neighborhoods, where they do not just give citizens expert facts and opinions, but listen to them and engage in reasonable two-way dialogue, which does not happen when the group comes to a city council meeting and uses the limited time available for public comment to make demands. In *Coming to Public Judgment,* Daniel Yankelovich, long a leading figure in American public opinion research, discussed the importance of experts engaging citizens in dialogue. Just as Supervisor John Jenkins and Mayor William Johnson realize that citizen engagement enhances their roles as leaders, Yankelovich argues that "engaging the public in dialogue adds to the expert's role rather than diminishing it."[2]

Sometimes government and nonprofit professionals need to be able to hold back on their expert knowledge and skills, and instead facilitate citizen learning and planning, as the Piton Foundation's Terri Bailey and Matt Hamilton learned in assisting the Denver Community Learning Network (CLN), and as Rochester taught its professionals to do in neighborhood planning. They may need to design a community process or may need to be sensitive to how a process evolves and nurture it. Hamilton said, "Our role was to be supporters of the process." They also need to know when to respond to citizens' learning needs and change roles. "Our role is being totally responsive," said Bailey. "There are times when we teach, but I wouldn't define our relationship as teacher." Hamilton agreed, "If we weren't responsive, we would be driving the knowledge," but the point of the CLN is for citizens to drive the knowledge.[3]

According to Nalbandian, higher-level local government managers, such as department heads or chief administrators, have a dual challenge of modernizing the organization and building and maintaining a sense of community at the same time.[4] Modern organizational challenges take on a different perspective when applied to communities. For example, for an organization, "learning and change" means "anticipates, plans for, and adapts to change." For "community building," it means "build community processes that lead to the 'deliberative citizen' including the regional citizen." For an organization, "technology" is "a driver of innovation and efficiency." For community building, technology is to "bring citizens closer to governing processes and institutions and increase citizen participation."[5] This implies that a manager's role includes designing and facilitating processes in both the organization and the community, but they have to be sensitive to the different purposes and workings of the community processes. Nalbandian's challenges for local government managers can just as easily apply to managers of nonprofit organizations that serve communities.

Suggestions for Ensuring Citizen Engagement Is Inclusive

The more diverse a community, the greater the challenge of keeping citizen engagement representative and inclusive of all groups and interests. People from some minority or immigrant groups, for example, may have good reason from past—or even recent—experience to be suspicious of becoming too well known to authorities or being identified as dissenters. There may be cultural or language barriers to participation of some groups. And there may be practical barriers, such as the need to spend long hours working, feeding a family, or taking care of children. Approaches are suggested here for overcoming some of the more common barriers to representative participation, including brief examples from around the United States for some approaches. Further suggestions are provided for recruiting underrepresented groups and building up representativeness over time. All in all, there is no substitute for vigilance, perseverance, and hard work for making—and keeping—citizen engagement inclusive in a diverse community. The suggestions here can help make that hard work pay off.

Identify and Remove Barriers to Participation. People from any group may be motivated to participate in public affairs for either personal gain, say to protect or enhance their property, or for social or communal benefit,[6] for example, to improve their neighborhood as a whole. When people from some groups turn out for an engagement process in large numbers while others do not come or are significantly underrepresented, it is incorrect to assume that those who are underrepresented are not concerned about the issues at hand or cannot be motivated to participate. People in underrepresented groups could be just as motivated or concerned, but they may face greater barriers to participate than others. A few common barriers, and approaches used to overcome them, are:

> *Barrier:* People from some groups are not informed of the opportunity to participate.
>
> *Approach:* Supplement communication through the mainstream media with use of hard-to-reach groups' own communications channels, such as community papers or bulletin boards, neighborhood association newsletters, or whatever else they use as an information source. America*Speaks'* Carolyn Lukensmeyer has referred to this dual approach as having "a macromedia campaign and a micromedia campaign."
>
> *Barriers:* People cannot travel to events or do not feel welcome in event locations; family responsibilities; inconvenient event times; discomfort in public settings; language barriers.
>
> *Approaches:* Provide multiple modes for people to find convenient, comfortable ways to participate; hold meetings at different locations and times; provide child care and food; offer transportation; hold meetings in different languages or provide interpreters or bilingual facilitators.
>
> *Examples:* When Joint Venture: Silicon Valley Network conducted its Silicon Valley 2010 strategic planning process in 1997, this public-private nonprofit group engaged over two thousand residents in ten forums and fourteen focus groups throughout the region, and in surveys and interviews. One forum was run in Vietnamese and one in Spanish.[7] When the Civic Alliance to Rebuild Downtown New York engaged forty-three hundred citizens in "Listening to the City" in July 2002 in the planning to rebuild the World Trade Center site after terrorist attacks, people could be directed to tables with Spanish- or Chinese-speaking facilitators,[8] interpreters for twelve languages,[9] and grief counselors[10] to help September 11 victims' family members and others who had difficulty participating due to memories of the attacks.

Barrier: Lack of trust of government or of people from outside the group's own community.

Approach: Use intermediaries to help communicate and build trust. Sometimes trusted leaders of a group are readily identifiable: political or business leaders, leaders of a community-based nonprofit or advocacy group, or clergy. Immigrant advocates may be needed, for example, to convince immigrants that a government pledge not to check for undocumented aliens is real. Sometimes it takes persistence to find hidden leaders who influence others. Outreach staff may have to gradually build a little trust with a few people in a group before they will tell them, say, which elderly resident in a housing complex is most trusted by others.

Plan Recruitment and Retention of Underrepresented Groups. Organizers of citizen engagement should consult with the leaders or advocates of minority groups that tend to be underrepresented to learn about specific fears, barriers, desires and motivations, and different cultural norms for how each group prefers to be engaged. They should be sensitive to those differences in designing participation processes and set realistic goals and time lines for getting minorities involved, which can all be part of minority recruitment plans for engaging these groups.[11] For example, organizers may need to build in time to attend meetings of existing grassroots groups in minority neighborhoods, accompanied by group leaders or advocates for credibility, to build trust before minority group members will come to public events planned by the organizers. Retaining minority involvement over time is similar to retaining other participants. It takes a long-term commitment to keeping communication open, increasing levels of trust and comfort with each stage of participation, and always remembering why volunteers got involved in the first place.

Keep Asking, "Who Is Not Here?" and Keep Recruiting Them. Communities seeking strong citizen engagement for the long term should keep working at recruiting and retaining underrepresented groups. It is always a good idea to track demographics in succeeding processes and look for increasing diversity. But it is never enough to show how many different groups are involved if some are still left out. In advising a Civic Alliance working group in New York, Mary Timney, chair of political science of Pace University, said, "Who is here?" is not the critical question. Instead, she said, "You have to keep asking, over and over, 'Who is *not* here?'" Then, with each succeeding event and participation process, keep reaching out, keep building trust, and keep trying to get more people engaged from groups that are underrepresented.

Seeking Deliberative Citizen Dialogue That Influences Decisions

The need for deliberative public processes was emphasized in Chapter Two, generally referring to processes involving dialogue and listening among citizens, and preferably also between citizens and decision makers, before decisions are made. And many examples have included citizens engaged in deliberative processes. Many more kinds of deliberative processes have evolved beyond those in the examples in this book,[12] providing communities with an array of options for achieving deliberation.

The importance of deliberation and dialogue does not mean that nondeliberative methods, such as opinion or satisfaction surveys, formal public hearings, or written comments, are not useful. They can be combined with more interactive, deliberative approaches of engaging citizens in a decision process to give citizens multiple ways to participate and give decision makers multiple views of citizens' ideas, opinions, and priorities. A good example is Prince William County's major strategic planning updates every four years, where one form of engagement informs another, and processes that started with an opinion survey become more interactive as deliberating citizens work more deeply with issues until the board of supervisors approves a strategic plan.

Ranking Participation Methods and Processes: A Diagnostic Tool

From her work with citizen engagement on difficult energy and environmental issues, Mary Timney developed a useful concept of a continuum of public participation processes from passive to active, with citizens' ability to participate in two-way dialogue and influence decisions increasing as a process becomes more "active."[13] In 2002–2003, with the Scorecard Working Group of the Civic Alliance to Rebuild Downtown New York, she took the approach further and developed a working draft scale to rank types of public participation methods and processes, shown as Figure 9.1. The scale does not define absolute levels of "activeness" or "passiveness" so much as points along a continuum for guidance in assessing public process. Local knowledge of how methods are carried out, combined, and used to influence decisions, and evidence over time about whether decisions tend to be influenced by citizens through these processes, will help in making a reasonable assessment of where a decision process ranks on the scale. Also, while "delegated power" has the highest number on the scale because citizens have most control of a decision, that should not be presumed to be an ideal sought in many decision processes. It is likely only to be practical for special cases.

The scale literally ranks methods of participation from more passive to more active, but it can be applied to an entire process that uses multiple methods by determining how the methods relate to each other and whether the more active methods are the more decisive ones. A community seeking active engagement may include any methods from level 2 on up the scale to obtain input into a decision or planning process.

FIGURE 9.1. NUMERICAL RANKINGS OF PUBLIC PARTICIPATION (WORKING DRAFT)

Active

Most active approaches, all involving deliberative public dialogue:

10. Delegated Power: Agency[a] delegates decision to citizens.

9. Collaboration: Iterative, open deliberative processes with learning through feedback: agency shares decision power with citizens.

8. Advisory Partnership: Open public dialogue, possible citizen working groups, strongly influence decisions made by agency.

Less controlled, less passive methods; not yet collaborative:

7. Interactive processes (for example, focus groups) without agency commitment to public influence.

6. "Scientific" feedback, for example, random sample surveys.

5. Feedback through media, for example, unscientific media surveys.

4. Formal procedures, for example, public hearings, one-way communication.

Highly controlled, passive participation methods:

3. Consultation with agency-picked experts and interests.

2. One-way, unshared feedback (for example, unpublished written comments).

1. Informing only: Agency tells public its decisions.

Passive

0. Noncommunicating: Completely closed process.

[a]*Agency* is used as a generic term to refer to any decision-making entity, public or private, including a collaborative or a whole government.

Source: Based on Mary M. Timney's draft scale for ranking public participation for the Scorecard Working Group of the Civic Alliance to Rebuild Downtown New York, Jan. 2003. Timney is professor and chair of the Department of Political Science, Pace University.

However, the process should be designed so the most influential methods are those at levels 8 or higher that provide deliberative public "democratic dialogue," as Yankelovich has advocated,[14] and that are also likely to influence decisions. Timney adds a caveat to the idea of using different methods, not all of which may involve dialogue with citizens, "where an issue is contentious, efforts must be made to engage citizens at the earliest stages of the process . . . so that their concerns become part of the plan from the beginning. Failure to do so can lead to NIMBY [Not in My Back Yard] situations if citizens begin to feel that the only constructive thing they can say is 'NO.'"

A community can use the scale as a diagnostic tool to examine its existing citizen engagement processes, as the examples from communities featured in Chapters Two and Seven illustrate.

Prince William County's strategic planning process uses "scientific surveys" (level 6) and interactive focus groups (level 7). These methods generate information for the board of supervisors and deliberative citizen working groups to use in an iterative process in which the groups recommend strategic goals and outcomes to the board. So the overall process ranks at least at level 8 (Advisory Partnership), and perhaps at level 9 (Collaboration), considering collaborative work by citizens and staff in developing goals and outcomes, and the board's demonstrated willingness to add a goal midway through plan implementation when, during progress reviews in 1998, citizens used performance feedback to demonstrate the need for a human service goal.

In Washington, D.C., the Citizen Summits, as one-day events, rank at least at level 8 (Advisory Partnerships) considering the extent of deliberative, open public dialogue that occurs. As the America*Speaks* process uses real-time feedback of emerging citizen views and ideas to enable iterative development of informed choices throughout the day, summits also encompass some aspects of level 9 on the scale. The feedback events after each summit to test if District of Columbia government staff interpreted citizens correctly add another level of iteration and dialogue to the process. Also, major District budget shifts reflecting citizen priorities indicate that citizens have had real influence on public decisions. So the larger public process to influence the District government's budget and strategy ranks at level 9 (Collaboration).

In New York City, community boards have a formal advisory role in many land use decisions. Community Board 1 (CB1) has enabled open public dialogue in these processes and influenced many decisions, as it did in the Shearson-Lehman and 5B-5C cases discussed in Chapter Two. They generally reach level 8 (Advisory Partnership) in land use engagement. The final plan for 5B-5C was negotiated between a deputy mayor and the local city council member, but it was strongly influenced by citizens openly participating in CB1's community review process.

However, in the east side case (near the end of Chapter Two), the mayor decided CB1's formal role did not apply, reducing the formal public process to level 1 (Informing Only). So citizens, CB1, and state and local elected representatives took it on themselves to create an informal process. CB1 still held open meetings on the project after the mayor's unilateral action, but key decision makers did not participate. The invitation-only meetings with the site developer perhaps reached level 7 (interactive discussion without commitment to public influence). A lawsuit resulted, which some community members saw as beneficial because it slowed the process. Without the luck of a university dropping out of the proposed project and leverage the community still held for funding and siting a new east side school from the open 5B-5C process, the community may not have gotten the positive result that it did.

Once members of a community have diagnosed how participation influences key decisions, they may decide to revise their various participation methods and how they fit together in an iterative process, to strengthen the influence of citizen deliberation and more actively engage citizens in decisions of their community institutions.

Trusted, Impartial Convener and "Safe Space" for Community Dialogue

If diverse people with different interests are to come together for effective dialogue, they often need a convening agent they all trust to treat them fairly and with respect. The Jacksonville Community Council Inc. (JCCI) plays this role in Jacksonville. JCCI is not always neutral, but it is seen as impartial for convening community dialogue, perhaps because when it does advocate for a policy, it is based on the work of a citizen study committee, not a predetermined institutional interest that, say, a chamber of commerce or a children's service agency may have. Other kinds of organizations play useful convening roles in many of the other communities in this book, though not always on a citywide basis. Portland's district coalitions and Dayton's priority boards, for example, are conveners of dialogue among people from different neighborhoods in geographic districts of the city.

As elected officials have political positions, governments are rarely neutral, but they can be impartial conveners. Prince William County has been an effective convener of community dialogue and may have made itself even more credible in that role in 2003 by using citizens along with county staff as cofacilitators of strategic planning focus groups. Similarly, Rochester's focus on keeping staff in facilitator, not leader, roles has helped that city government be accepted as a convener of community dialogue.

Part of what effective dialogue conveners do—what any good facilitators do—is to create what America*Speaks* calls a "safe public space" for "fair and productive dialogue and . . . a level playing field on which individual citizen voices are equal to those representing established interests."[15] They can create one safe space at a time in an intimate conference room or, as America*Speaks* has shown, hundreds of safe spaces— tables with ten citizens and a facilitator—simultaneously in a cavernous convention hall. The National Civic League also stresses the need for "*civic* or *safe* space" to "resolve differences and . . . allow people focus on public deliberation and consensus building." Former Civic League chairman John Gardner referred to conveners who create safe spaces as "community guardians."[16]

Building Citizen Capacity and Developing Citizen Leaders

It is important for citizens to learn the way things work in their community and learn from each other if they are to make their engagement most effective. In Chapter Two, helping citizens learn was raised as a way to help them be more effective in their role as advocates. But it really applies to all citizen engagement roles. For example, citizen issue framers or evaluators who understand the nature of decisions that officials must make at key steps in a planning or budget process can use that knowledge to craft their statements of priorities or recommendations in ways that decision makers will find useful. That will make it more likely that citizens' ideas and priorities will influence the officials' decisions. It makes sense, then, for nonprofit or government organizations to make efforts to enhance citizen learning, so citizens can build their knowledge, skills, and overall capacity to be effectively engaged in the community.

In almost all communities featured in this book, either a nonprofit or government organization has enhanced citizen learning through explicit skill development efforts. Some skill development has been narrowly focused, such as how to identify specific streetscape defects to report in digital neighborhood surveys. Other efforts have been broader, such as citizens in the Denver Community Learning Network learning to do their own budgeting and to tap into community data to spur neighborhood improvement. Over the years, the cities of Rochester and Portland have provided a range of training opportunities to citizens participating in neighborhood planning and improvement, including how to identify community assets and achieve or maintain diversity in participation. Rochester recently launched a Community Technology Leaders Program to increase residents' ability to electronically map and track actions in the Neighbors Building Neighborhoods program, to enhance accountability for results. Although Truckee Meadows Tomorrow, with its very small funding base, does not do explicit skill training, it makes use of its public events and its interactions with "indicator adopters" to educate citizens on quality-of-life issues.[17]

Citizen Leadership Development Programs. The National Civic League advocates training to "develop leaders who are results-oriented, willing to take risks, able to work well together and communicate effectively. Above all, they must be able to share the leadership mantle."[18] Five of the communities featured in Chapters Two through Eight have broad-based citizen leadership programs to enhance the capacity of existing citizen leaders and develop more citizens into confident, capable volunteer community leaders. Programs in Greater Kansas City (started in 1998), Prince William County (1994), Jacksonville (1976), and Dayton (1973) have well-established—or have been building—alumni associations or graduate networks to keep trained citizens connected to each other and engaged in community improvement. The Washington, D.C., Neighborhood College graduated its first class in 2003.

The Greater Kansas City Local Initiatives Support Corporation's (GKC LISC's) Building 21st Century Leaders program develops interpersonal, facilitation, outcome, and project management skills. As community development in Kansas City urban core neighborhoods in both states requires cooperation across races and ethnicities and among organizations and stakeholders with different interests, the program emphasizes multicultural memberships and alliances, team building, and consensus building.

In a follow-up study of early program graduates, 70 percent reported that the program contributed to their increased involvement, and 89 percent reported that their understanding of their role as a citizen participant had changed.[19] Graduates have become officers and presidents of neighborhood associations and committee chairs or coordinators of major community volunteer projects such as a KC Safe Initiative and Urban Youth Theatre. GKC LISC is collaborating with two community development corporations to develop Spanish-language leadership development, and with the Kansas City Neighborhood Alliance to institutionalize leadership development for neighborhood residents.

Prince William County offers three citizen education programs: the Community Leadership Institute (CLI), offered twice a year, and the more specialized Citizen Police Academy and Fire/EMS Citizen Academy. Each CLI exposes participants to ten local government issues or services and to strategic management, including budgeting and performance measures. The CLI provides good preparation for citizens to be effectively engaged in, for example, strategic planning, county boards and commissions, and the county budget process where some represent their neighborhood or community district, or community-based nonprofits. In the summer of 2003, the county government reached out to CLI graduates to be cofacilitators, with county staff, of citizen focus groups for strategic planning.

The Dayton Neighborhood Leadership Institute (NLI) graduated its twentieth class in 2002. The NLI builds on Dayton's system of seven citizen priority boards that represent clusters of neighborhoods, and many of its graduates become engaged in the boards, neighborhood associations, and other community groups, often becoming officers or chairs. To graduate from the NLI, a participant accumulates "points" awarded for activities mostly outside the classes. Awarding points for networking activities (including just before a class—worth 5 points) encourages frequent networking among NLI students and with NLI graduates and other community leaders. NLI participants learn as much, or more, about what goes on in the city through networking as through attending classes. Participants can also garner points by taking tours of city and community facilities (10 points per event), riding with police and city inspectors (25 points per event), and handing in a paragraph at each class detailing their community activities. Some people amass over 300 points, well beyond the 135 required for graduation. Dayton reported an encouraging trend of more young NLI participants (in their twenties) in recent years, who may then be involved over a longer period of time in community activities.

The nonprofit Leadership Jacksonville, Inc. (LJ) was organized in 1976 in the same civic reform that brought about the Jacksonville Community Council Inc. In the early 1990s, LJ expanded its initial concepts of trusteeship and responsibility in its curriculum, to make more explicit what had always been assumed: the connection between participants' learning and networking during their one year as an LJ class member and their ongoing contributions for the benefit of their community in subsequent years. The

LJ alumni organization provides a channel both for personal networking and for graduates to help each other contribute toward improving the community.

More than twelve hundred people have participated in LJ since it started. In 1990, LJ spawned Youth Leadership Jacksonville (YLJ), which has engaged over 450 high school-age participants since its inception. LJ graduates permeate the ranks of Jacksonville area elected and appointed public officials (national, state, and local), as well as nonprofit governing boards and CEOs, corporate boards, and neighborhood groups. The 2003 election saw the first YLJ-graduate city council candidate. The efforts of one LJ class led to state legislation enabling creation of a Children's Commission in Jacksonville, and the honorary-LJ-graduate mayor, with support from the LJ network, secured an ongoing local budget commitment for the commission. Another LJ-graduate mayor crafted an ambitious capital improvement campaign, called it the Better Jacksonville Plan, and sold it, *including a sales tax increase,* to the public—with the active support of many in the LJ network. LJ's commitment to building diverse community leadership has also made a difference. An LJ graduate recently completed eight years as the first African American elected sheriff of Jacksonville/Duval County. Many LJ network members were active in his first election campaign, with one of his LJ classmates as campaign manager. He not only broke a racial barrier in a conservative southern city; he also implemented major policy and operational changes, instituting extensive community policing efforts, and decentralizing authority to make police services more responsive to people and neighborhoods.

Technology to Enhance Citizen Engagement: Opportunities and Risks

Technology-enhanced face-to-face public meetings, such as those facilitated by America*Speaks,* and handheld computers used by citizens to survey physical conditions, such as those used in ComNET and City Scan, are not the only uses of information technology to enhance citizen engagement. Others include:

- Data warehouses that support the Annie E. Casey Foundation's Local Learning Partnerships in ten cities
- The NeighborLink Network in Rochester, New York, and a similar Washington, D.C., system to allow citizens to track implementation of neighborhood plans and Des Moines' online complaint-response tracking system
- Information on public service performance or community conditions (for example, quality-of-life outcomes) reported on many city, county, and state Web sites
- Privately run sites contracted by government, and independent nonprofit sites, with service performance or community conditions information
- Computer mapping and data disaggregation capabilities that some government and nonprofit organizations provide to citizens to view community conditions or

service performance by neighborhood, county, or other district or by demographic group

- Government and nonprofit e-letters that inform citizens of issues of interest by e-mail, and listservs that enable e-mail dialogues and information sharing
- Government and nonprofit Web sites that allow citizens to post comments on public proposals or issues, propose "vision ideas," or answer survey questions
- Online forums or virtual meetings for citizen dialogue on community, state, national, or global issues, especially if moderated to stimulate constructive deliberation
- Even uses of "old" technology, such as telecasts of public discussions, help keep more people informed than can attend meetings and can also be used in combination with "new" technology (such as online forums) to enhance public dialogue

These and other applications, such as Web-based public service transactions, can enhance citizen learning and effectiveness in all five engagement roles. Information technology, especially the Internet, presents tremendous opportunities to engage more people in effective governance in many ways,[20] including ways yet to be imagined. Using technology to enhance citizen engagement also entails risks. Some risks involve poor implementation, such as not keeping information posted online accurate or up-to-date, or not upgrading the capacity of hardware or software to keep up with user demand. Anything can be poorly implemented, but technology increases those risks, as many people at one time can be misinformed by inaccurate information, or disappointed by slow-responding or unavailable Web pages, which may end up discouraging participation. Also, unmoderated or poorly moderated online discussions pose a risk of being "hijacked" by narrow interests or leading to ranting or "flaming," thus discouraging citizens seeking thoughtful deliberation from participating.

A special risk of Internet-enhanced engagement is the digital divide. Even as Internet connectivity has reached more households, businesses, and schools, there are still people who are not connected or are not comfortable communicating online, whether due to lack of income or education, or for age or cultural reasons. The more online engagement empowers regular Internet users, the more others are left behind.

The digital divide presents a dilemma to communities that want broad-based citizen engagement. Not providing convenient, online engagement risks alienating the growing number of people who regularly use the Internet as a favored form of communication. These are likely to include people a community cannot afford to leave out of deliberations because they probably pay more taxes than average, make higher donations to charitable organizations including community nonprofits, and in other ways carry more influence than most nonusers of the Internet. But Internet-based engagement leaves out the unconnected. Rather than avoid using the Internet for engagement, public and nonprofit community organizations should treat the digital divide as another barrier to participation by underrepresented groups—those who do not regularly use the Internet. Then they can devise plans to overcome this barrier and aggressively pursue their plans, until all groups are represented. The plans can be as varied as there are cultures in a community. Here are a few possible approaches:

- Provide easily accessible community sites not just for general Internet use (as many public libraries do), but with convenient times set aside for citizen engagement uses.
- Train "technology leaders," as Rochester is doing, to develop a cadre of volunteer citizens to keep their neighbors engaged through technology-enhanced means.
- Organize events to pull unconnected citizens together at community sites, with facilitators and Internet users available to help them download and use information, and to post group or individual comments to online discussions or comment spaces.
- Work as advocates for unconnected groups to search Web sites and download information for them, engage them directly in using the information and voicing their reactions, and post their priorities and concerns online for them.
- Develop projects and raise funds to connect more people to the Internet and provide them with hardware, software, and training needed to engage online.

Technology-based methods should be pursued to make citizen engagement more effective. But do not expect technology to make engagement—especially inclusive, representative engagement—any easier. Like all other citizen engagement, technology-based approaches require careful planning, rigorous implementation, perseverance, and hard work to be effective.

Making Performance Feedback and Analysis More Effective

A defining characteristic of organizations managing for results and communities governing for results is the systematic use of performance feedback to inform decisions in order to achieve better results in the future. To use performance data for these purposes—in other words, to use data for performance management—you need to be able to interpret what the data mean and analyze the data to decide what to do to improve results. A particularly effective approach to performance management is to base the performance information reported and how you analyze it on some kind of model that logically ties the actions of people or organizations to desired results. You also need to understand the assumptions behind the model.

Having a model for how to achieve results is like having a theory of change, as the Edna McConnell Clark Foundation requires of its grantees. It is also essentially the same as Citizen Schools designing its after-school program based on assumptions of how middle school children learn, develop, and achieve desired outcomes. Similarly, the target-and-milestone system used by community development corporations

(CDCs) in Greater Kansas City is based on articulating the assumptions behind how CDCs are expected to achieve targeted results. Robert Penna of the Rensselaerville Institute recently completed a comparative analysis of nine logically based systems or outcome models used to varying degrees for public and nonprofit performance management, which the institute published in a guide for practitioners.[21] A briefer, narrower look at several different approaches is presented here, all from the perspective of logical "value chains" that lead from actions to results.

Community Performance Value Chains

Since the early 1990s, a number of government and nonprofit organizations have used a variety of approaches to identify the links between what they do and the community outcomes or policy results desired. They have given these approaches different names (for example, "outcome framework," "strategy map," and "logic model"). One thing these approaches have in common is the explicit articulation of assumptions about what influences specific community or human conditions, often including assumptions about causes and effects of how outcomes are achieved.

In using these approaches, public and nonprofit officials create logical chains of links from, for example, funding decisions or internal practices, to how services and projects are performed, to the immediate results of services and projects, to longer-term desired conditions of people and the community. These chains of logic are similar to the value chains that businesses create to analyze and improve how different organizational units and functions add value to the business.[22] But instead of seeking profits at the end of the value chain, public and nonprofit organizations seek improved conditions of people and communities—improved community outcomes. So it is useful to think of these approaches as performance value chains that help public and nonprofit officials understand how their strategies, practices, services, and projects contribute value to the community.[23] They can then measure performance at different links in the chain to test assumptions, and refine or redesign their strategies—and their underlying value chains—to increase their value-added to community outcomes.

The first two examples below describe, as value chains, two widely used approaches for mapping performance links of individual human services programs. The third depicts the San Jose sewer example in Chapter Three as a multibranch value chain. The remaining examples take value chains deeper into organizations and communities.

The Rensselaerville Institute Outcome Framework. Greater Kansas City CDCs use targets and milestones to manage for results, based on the "Outcome Framework" of the nonprofit Rensselaerville Institute of Rensselaerville, New York. The framework was initially developed for, and has mostly been applied to, human services that attempt to improve their customers' behavior, skills, or condition. The desired outcome—specified change in behavior, skill, or condition—by the time a customer finishes the program is the "target" (for example, drug free for six months). The milestones are condition or behavior changes customers are expected to make on the way to reaching the target, for example, being able to crawl before they can walk and walk before they can run. The result is a linear "value chain" for each customer:

Milestone 1 ⟶ *Milestone 2* ⟶ *Milestone 3* ⟶ . . . ⟶ *Target*

For a job training and employment assistance program, for example, the first customer milestone may be that an unemployed person ("customer") learns of the program and the next that the customer attends one session. Later milestones may include demonstrating key skills, getting a job, and performing satisfactorily on the job. The target may be that the customer keeps the job for at least six months.

The Rensselaerville Institute urges organizations to design program activities to move customers from one milestone to the next, so the program has a series of steps to advance customers through each milestone to the target. In the institute's model, a program's outcome indicator is the number of people who hit the target. Programs also measure the number of people who achieve each milestone. Usually not every customer can be expected to make it all the way to the target; some may make it to only one milestone or another. So the institute depicts the model as a funnel, with the largest number of customers projected to reach the first milestone, and some drop-off on interim milestones, resulting in fewer customers expected to reach the target.[24] When Kansas City CDCs apply this model to community development, some targets and milestones are measured in units other than number of customers, such as number of houses completed and sold.

The United Way of America Program Outcome Model.
The United Way of America (UWA) encourages health and human service agencies to use a program outcome model to define how resources and program efforts lead to measurable changes in people served. The UWA model can be seen as a value chain that takes the following form:

Inputs ⟶ *Activities* ⟶ *Outputs* ⟶ *Initial Outcomes* ⟶ *Intermediate Outcomes* ⟶ *Longer-term Outcomes*

In this model, inputs are resources used (such as money, staff, and volunteers). Activities are what the program does (such as shelter families or provide counseling). Outputs are the direct products of activities: the number of people or families served, classes taught, or amount of food distributed, for example. The UWA defines outcomes as benefits or changes for individuals or populations during or after their participation in program activities. These outcomes may involve changes in behavior, knowledge, skills, attitudes, values, status (for example, employment, housing), conditions (for example, health), or other attributes. Initial and intermediate outcomes are in the model because programs often generate a series of changes, one leading to another, to achieve the ultimate outcomes sought, similar to milestones on the way to the target in Rensselaerville's outcome framework.

The number of outcome levels or links in the value chain can vary by program and population served, especially with several levels of intermediate outcomes. For example, the UWA suggests that for a teen mother parenting education program, an initial outcome can include that pregnant teens are knowledgeable about prenatal nutrition and health. That would lead to the intermediate outcome of teens following proper nutrition and health practices, which in turn would lead to the next intermediate outcome of teens delivering healthy babies. A longer-term outcome, which depends on teen mothers' learning proper care, feeding, and social interaction with babies, would be that teens' babies achieve appropriate twelve-month milestones for child development.[25]

A Multibranch Value Chain for a Public Works Program: Sewer Cleaning. Value chains can be applied to virtually any service, not just human services or community development. And they need not work in straight lines or be single-branch chains as in the above examples. For example, Figure 9.2 shows a multibranch value chain that depicts the logic of the improved San Jose sewer cleaning program described by Wayne Tanda at the start of Chapter Three.

FIGURE 9.2. VALUE CHAIN FOR SAN JOSE SEWER CLEANING

A Public Works Multibranch Value Chain

Target Cleaning
Identify sewers prone to clog. → *Clean sewers mechanically, focusing most on clog-prone sewers.*

Use grease-cutting enzymes on dirtiest, greasiest sewers.

Outcome: *Fewer sewer clogs.*

Reduce Causes
Identify neighborhoods where cooking grease goes down drains. → *Educate neighborhood families about proper grease disposal.* → *More families dispose of grease properly.*

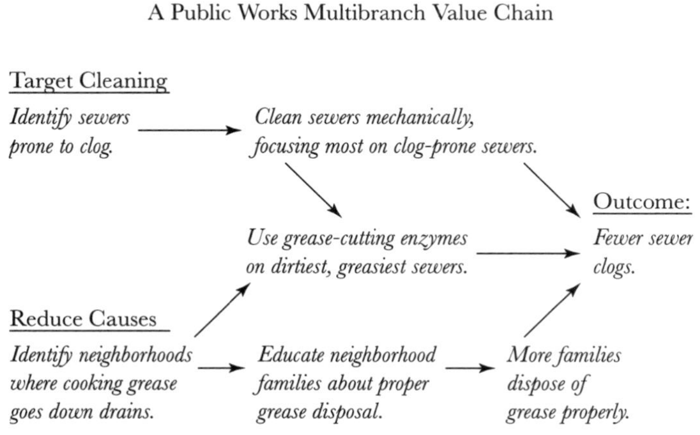

Balanced Scorecards Drive Value Chains Deep into the Organization. The balanced scorecard is a multidimensional approach to performance management developed for use by businesses in the early 1990s. It came to be seen as effective not just for managing near-term performance, but also for managing strategy to develop the organization and its practices for long-term performance improvement.[26] Since the mid-1990s, balanced scorecards have been adapted for use by a widening range of government and nonprofit organizations. A key adaptation that public and nonprofit organizations have made is to change the standard business-oriented balanced scorecard performance dimensions, called "perspectives," to perspectives customized to the mission and context of each organization.

For a balanced scorecard to be useful to manage strategy for results, it should be based on a strategy map, in effect, a series of interlinked value chains, that shows the assumed cause-and-effect logic underlying the strategy. Figure 9.3 shows the strategy map for the balanced scorecard of Big Sister Association of Greater Boston (BSAGB), which has five performance perspectives, which logically relate to each other as follows. At a high level, cause-and-effect—or value chain—links run from the bottom of BSAGB's strategy map to the top, with success at the "Learning and Growth" perspective making BSABG more effective at the "Internal" perspective, which in turn makes them better at the "Customer" and "Fiscal Responsibility (or Financial/ Budget)" perspectives, which in turn makes them more successful at accomplishing their "Mission" at the top: "Helping girls realize their full potential by providing them with positive mentoring relationships with women." The bubbles in Figure 9.3 are strategic objectives to achieve within each perspective, with arrows showing assumed cause-and-effect links between the objectives, which are, in effect, value chains within the bigger value chain of the five perspectives. BSAGB tracks performance measures against targets for the strategic objectives. With BSAGB managers tracking measures of, for example, how well they "create a team environment," not just overall inputs and external outputs and outcomes, they have driven their value chain deep into the organization, aligning all their efforts and actions with their strategy and mission.

Charlotte's Balanced Scorecard Links Strategy to Citywide Policy. The City of Charlotte, North Carolina, uses a balanced scorecard on an enterprisewide basis, with each department's scorecard aligning with four perspectives and strategic objectives of the citywide "corporate scorecard." Figure 9.4 maps the city's strategic objectives at the corporate level and shows how the scorecard is constructed to link the city's strategy to the highest-level policy priorities of the city council—the five City Council Focus Areas and vision at the top of the figure. The upward-pointing broken lines in Figure 9.4 suggest a few of the many value chains showing assumed supporting relationships among objectives. The solid-line arrows facing down show some assumed relationships linking council focus areas with strategic objectives. The council also

FIGURE 9.3. BIG SISTER ASSOCIATION OF GREATER BOSTON STRATEGY MAP

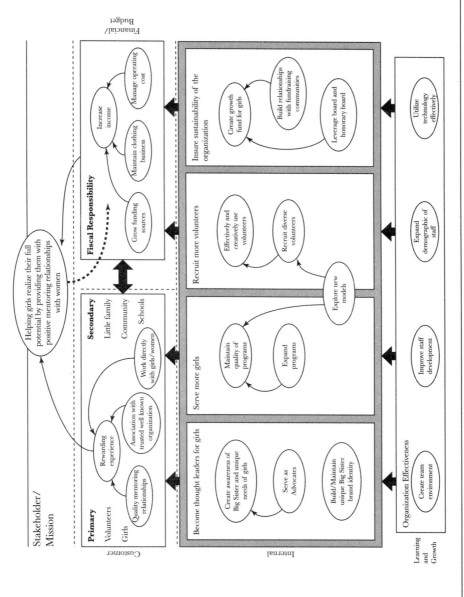

FIGURE 9.4. CHARLOTTE BALANCED SCORECARD SAMPLE STRATEGY AND POLICY LINKS

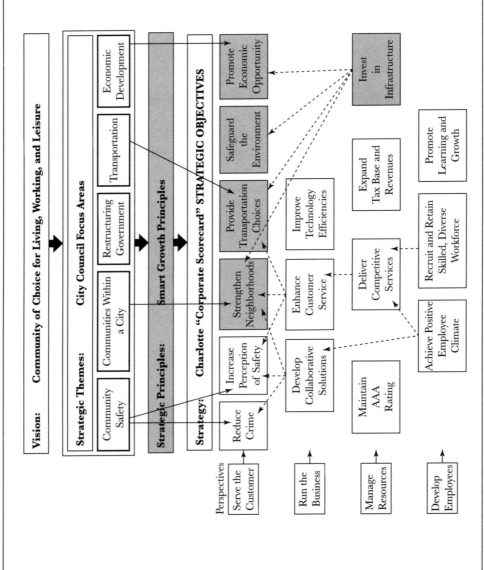

Source: City of Charlotte, FY 2004–2005 Corporate Strategy. Reprinted with permission of the City of Charlotte, N.C.

adopted a policy of using "Smart Growth Principles" for implementing Charlotte's strategy. The shaded strategic objectives are those most related to the smart growth principles.

Prince William County's Levels of Organizational Focus. Prince William County, Virginia, is featured in Chapters Three and Six for managing for results and aligning citizen engagement with strategic planning and management. In 2003, the county decided to align its internal and external strategies for a stronger strategic focus, in what the county calls "The Prince William County Way." In doing so, the county aligned three elements of its vision ("making our community the best," "doing the right thing for the customer and community," and "support and opportunities for employees") with four levels of "Organizational Focus," and identified the "tools" (for example, strategic plan, citizen survey, training and development) it uses at each focus level. This is similar to a balanced scorecard value chain in that the four organizational levels of focus logically support each other. Specifically, the focus "Employee Skills and Satisfaction" supports the focus "Effective and Efficient Government," which supports "Satisfied Customers" and "Community Focus" (including "Community Outcome/Results").

Pathways to Critical Child and Family Outcomes in Communities. In 2000, Harvard University and the Annie E. Casey Foundation established the Pathways Mapping Initiative (PMI) to organize bodies of knowledge to help investors, policymakers, service providers, and others find information to improve outcomes for children and families in their communities. PMI organizes information in "pathways" to achieve high-level outcomes. Through 2003, PMI has published two pathways on its Web site: one for "Family Economic Success" and one for "Children Are Ready for School."[27] Each pathway is organized by goals, subgoals, and action areas and is, in essence, a value chain of actions and accomplishments needed in a community to achieve the ultimate outcome. For example, "Family Economic Success" is shown as supported by three goals, one of which, "Workforce Development," is supported by the subgoals "Job Readiness" and "Job Placement, Retention, and Advancement." More details in each pathway include indicators to measure progress, "attributes of effectiveness" of actions, rationales and evidence from research supporting the actions as contributors to goals, and examples from programs and communities to illustrate the pathways.

Value Chains Focus Strategic Design, Action, and Investment to Improve Outcomes

Value chains can be powerful tools for aligning, maintaining, and increasing the strategic focus on improving outcomes. For new programs, value chain approaches can be used to design services and actions to achieve results. For existing programs, mapping and analyzing value chains can highlight whether there are missing links that keep a program from being effective, unlinked activities or duplicate links that can be eliminated for efficiency or savings, or hidden assumptions in the program logic that need to be tested. Value chain approaches can be particularly powerful when used at an organization, enterprise, or community level to determine how resources, efforts, and actions from multiple sources can be strategically focused and organized to achieve better outcomes for more people or for an entire community. For example, while the PMI pathways have information useful for specific service programs, they are especially valuable for a whole community—or a collaboration of community investors such as government, foundations, and businesses—to examine its overall strategy to achieve the outcomes; find missing, weak, or duplicative links in their chain; and redirect or refocus their investments to be most effective in achieving results.

Citizen Engagement and Value Chains

Citizens should not be left out of value chain analyses. Charlotte's balanced scorecard has an entire performance perspective focusing on citizens as customers. In the Boston Big Sister and San Jose sewers examples, citizens have important roles as coproducers. The Prince William County Way includes a "satisfied customers" focus and also includes several of the ways the county engages citizens (for example, strategic planning and citizen survey) in its "tools."

Citizens can also be engaged as partners in value chain design and analysis, to integrate value chains into effective community governance. As issue framers in the design of value chains, and as evaluators when actual results are interpreted and strategies revised, citizens can bring intimate knowledge of their neighborhoods, and of community issues as they affect themselves and their families, to provide a reality check to ideas and assumptions of professional staff. Just as important, as vision builders, citizens can help define the ultimate outcomes value chains are intended to achieve, to keep community strategies focused on results that matter.

Using the Power of Collaborations

A strong message from almost all the stories in this book is that any organization interested in improving a community should build collaborative relationships with others to get better results. Of course, collaboration between citizens and community institutions is basic to the effective governance model. As Rochester commissioner of environmental services Ed Doherty said, "Collaborations with citizens aren't the best way to succeed, they're the only way." Collaborations among organizations are also extremely important to community success, as demonstrated in most examples, because they increase the focus of community capabilities and resources on desired outcomes. Russell Linden documents other public and nonprofit collaborations and provides ideas for success in his book, *Working Across Boundaries: Making Collaboration Work in Government and Nonprofit Organizations.*[28]

Mayor Carol Marinovich of Wyandotte County and Kansas City, Kansas, says, "Forging strong partnerships is part of the philosophy of the Unified Government." Kansas City community development corporations (CDCs) work well with government partners, including police, code enforcement, and other agencies of the Unified Government under Mayor Marinovich and of the City of Kansas City, Missouri, under Mayor Kay Barnes. The CDCs also include residents, neighborhood associations, and others in partnerships to reduce crime and blight and make development effective. The entire Kansas City Community Development Initiative (KCCDI) is a private-public collaboration of over twenty organizations that has leveraged local and national resources into the largest community development investment fund in Kansas City's history.

So many communities in this book, from New York to Nevada, have depended on collaboration to get results. In Nevada, Truckee Meadows Tomorrow (TMT) may be an especially interesting case, as all three governments whose elected officials could not agree on using TMT's quality-of-life indicators for regional planning have nonetheless become TMT members and supported the group's work. One of them, Washoe County, has taken its partnership with TMT so far as to sign a quality-of-life compact to improve the natural environment. Similarly, JCCI sometimes has to "fight city hall," especially when a JCCI citizen policy study committee recommends changes in city government practices. Yet the city of Jacksonville is a major funder of JCCI's Quality of Life Indicators reports, and JCCI sees the city government as one of its three major partners. The TMT and JCCI experiences show that organizations do not have to be in complete policy agreement to find things to collaborate on to benefit the community.

Collaborations That Build on Community Assets

When people or organizations work collaboratively with each other to get things done for the community, they are leveraging each other as community assets. Rochester, New York, explicitly takes an asset focus in its Neighbors Building Neighborhoods (NBN) program, drawing on the work of John McKnight of Northwestern University. But even if the word *asset* is not an explicit part of a group's language, they may still be taking, in effect, an asset-based approach. For example, this applies to TMT when it gets citizens to adopt an indicator and organizations or collaboratives to sign a quality-of-life compact. It applies to Greater Kansas City CDCs when they organize residents block by block, work with neighborhood associations to reach their active residents, work with local houses of worship, and other community resources or assets. It applies to the Denver Community Learning Network (CLN) when CLN residents' own data collection and interpretation efforts cause service providers to see the residents as valuable partners to improve their neighborhoods, not just as needy people to be served. It applies to the Big Sister Association of Greater Boston and Citizen Schools when they recruit adult volunteers to mentor girls or train classes of middle school apprentices. And it applies to Peapatch, Virginia, whose residents made an important infrastructure project possible in their poor community by drawing on themselves as assets to lay the pipe to bring fresh running water to their homes for the first time in years.

Identify Assets to Extend Collaborations Beyond the Usual Suspects

Collaborations usually start when people or organizations already familiar with each other decide to work together cooperatively on an issue. That is useful; such collaborations can result in better coordination of known resources aimed at a community goal. But it does not add to the base of resources focused on achieving desired community outcomes. So it is important to encourage citizens and organizational staff involved in community improvement to think beyond the familiar and reach out to identify as many community assets as possible, be they individual citizens or public or private organizations, that can contribute to achieving desired results. This can be a challenge, but it can also result in a lot more resources being drawn into community improvement in a focused way. As Glenn Gardner, a resident of Rochester's Sector 1 said, "There is more out there than you think." Where possible, providing seed money to challenge people or organizations to find matching resources for projects can be a useful tactic, leading the residents of Rochester's Sector 10, for example, to leverage $100,000 of city government funds into over $2 million in resources from inside and outside the community for neighborhood improvements.

Identifying assets and gaining their cooperation in collaborative efforts is something to keep working on, as they do in Rochester. They do so in the Truckee Meadows Region, too, both when they get new citizens to sign up to adopt indicators and when they pull together—into a collaboration—organizations that do not normally work together, as in their Open Space Quality of Life Compact. Once people or organizations are identified as assets and engaged in community improvement, they can be asked to think of more people or organizations in their own networks of relationships who can potentially be pulled into current or future improvement efforts. In that way, a communitywide pool of assets can be steadily expanded, and a network of collaborations focused on improvement expanded, with the overall aim of leveraging more and more resources to achieve results that matter.

Expectations for Improving Governance and Results

From looking at the Effective Community Governance Model graphic, reproduced here as Figure 9.5, it is hard not to get the impression that advanced practice 4: communities governing for results, with its three-way alignment, is the place for a community to be, so should be the goal for any effort to improve governance. But communities, the institutions that help them function, and their governance processes are not that simple. For example, governing for results may be effectively in place for some functions in a community, such as nonprofit community development in urban core neighborhoods of Greater Kansas City, but not for others, which suggests choices for what kinds of improvements to attempt next. Appropriate goals and expectations for improving governance and results are necessarily situational. The suggestions that follow are meant to provide guidance to any community or organization seeking to set its own goals and determine its own practical next steps for improving community governance.

FIGURE 9.5. EFFECTIVE COMMUNITY GOVERNANCE MODEL

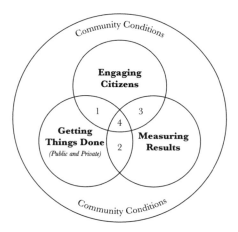

The four Advanced Governance Practices are represented by the overlapping areas in the figure, which represent alignment of "core community skills" as follows:

1. Community Problem Solving: Aligns Engaging Citizens and Getting Things Done

2. Organizations Managing for Results: Aligns Measuring Results and Getting Things Done

3. Citizens Reaching for Results: Aligns Engaging Citizens and Measuring Results

4. Communities Governing for Results: Aligns all three core skills

Setting Near-Term Goals and Finding a Starting Point for Change

The best goals for an organization trying to help a community achieve more effective governance depend on what that organization's role is in the community, how well the community is doing on each governance practice as a whole or for particular issues or functions, and what opportunities exist for improvement. For example, the role of Greater Kansas City LISC (GKC LISC) as an intermediary to promote nonprofit community development suggests that its main goal probably should be to make community development perform even better at advanced practice 4 to help CDCs get better results that matter more to residents of the neighborhoods served. GKC LISC's effort, with the Donor Advisory Board of KCCDI, to develop practical indicators of neighborhood impact and include them in CDC performance incentives, is a step in that direction. Also, GKC LISC and the CDCs have a broad view of community development that goes beyond residential and commercial development. They have also organized residents and developed collaborations around issues such as neighborhood safety. If GKC LISC, CDCs, or neighborhood residents determine that further neighborhood improvement may be blocked by other issues (such as public health or education problems, access to child care or transportation, or lack of usable open space), another opportunity for improvement would be suggested. For example, the CDCs could be encouraged to branch out into new kinds of collaborations to leverage organizations that can address those other issues, to improve results in new ways.

Assess Your Community's Governance Practices and Opportunities. Before determining what to try to improve in your community, it is useful to assess your community's governance practices as defined by the Effective Community Governance Model. Take care to note that as different public and private organizations are involved in addressing different community issues, your community and its institutions may be using one advanced governance practice for some issues and other practices for other issues. For example, citizen engagement may be strong and influence decisions for some kinds of issues but not others, or results may be measured and fed back to improve performance for some community conditions or services but not others. For any given set of community issues or conditions, assess:

- Current processes for decision making, strategic or community planning, and community resource allocation (for example, budgeting), and problem solving
- Current forms of citizen engagement and how citizens influence what gets decided, what gets measured, and what gets done

- Current results measurement and how the performance information gathered is used, especially the extent to which performance feedback is used to influence decisions and improve results
- Current collaborations in use to improve the community, including the extent to which community assets beyond typically responsible organizations for given issues are drawn on to focus more resources on achieving results

Some of the examples throughout the book may ring true for issues or processes in your community to help you decide whether your community is performing any of the four advanced practices for that issue or process. Also, the comparisons of the four advanced governance practices in Chapter Six may help you make that assessment. The summary comparisons of the four advanced practices in Table 6.1 may be a useful reference guide for recognizing whether your community is using one of these advanced practices for an issue of interest to you. Keep in mind that for some issues, your community may not be using any of the advanced practices. For example, citizen engagement may be robust but may not influence what gets measured, decided, or done. Results may be measured, but not be fed back into decision making or service improvement efforts.

In addition to assessing the community's current governance practices, it is important to look for opportunities for improvement. Table 6.2 which summarizes issues that limit the effectiveness of advanced practices 1 through 3, may be a useful reference guide for determining the kinds of issues to address for improving governance in your community. In any community—even one governing for results on many issues— there are likely to be several aspects of community governance that can be improved. To help decide what to attempt, consider who in the community—particularly community and organizational leaders—may be willing to support certain types of changes, and what resources may be available to support change. These supportive leaders and resources may be considered governance improvement assets. These may include, for example:

- Elected leaders or executives of government, or board members or executives of influential nonprofit organizations, who are open to increased citizen influence in decision making or want more accountability for results
- Potential organizational partners to make aspects of results-based governance more effective for one or more community issues, such as a local school board, nonprofit service providers or funders, civic organizations, or community groups
- Systems (hardware, software, methodologies) and trained staff in community organizations with the capacity to handle data and information communication requirements, or the availability of resources to build or enhance such systems

Build on Your Community's Opportunities and Assets at a Pace That Makes Sense. Once you have assessed community governance practices, improvement opportunities, and governance improvement assets, you can chart a course for improvement that builds on those opportunities and assets. You can also set expectations for how quickly your community or organization can improve its governance practices and results. For example, a general-purpose local government, such as a city, town, or county government, may be well suited to move a community toward more effective governance in a broad way, covering many issues. Still, specific goals and expectations for improvement should depend on how well the government and its partners are performing each governance practice, which may vary from issue to issue or service to service, and what improvement opportunities and assets exist.

In Iowa, for example, the Citizen Initiated Performance Assessment (CIPA) project, if carried to its logical conclusion, would take all participating cities to governing for results. But the near-term goals and expectations probably should vary from city to city. Some cities may have the management and systems infrastructure in place, and the willingness of elected officials, to quickly expand citizen-influenced performance measurement to more services and integrate the measures into budgeting and service management. Those cities may be expected to achieve governing for results sooner. Other cities may need more time to see how they fare with the initial services and performance measures and may need to build stronger internal performance management systems before getting too far into performance budgeting, managing for results, or expanding CIPA to more services.

It Is Worthwhile to Achieve or Improve Any Advanced Governance Practice, Not Just Governing for Results. Some organizations, such as a citizens league or community operating foundation, may be well positioned to help a community achieve advanced practices 1 or 3, but key community partners, such as a local government, may not be ready to help move the community to full alignment of citizen engagement, measuring results, and getting things done needed for governing for results. As the examples in Chapters Two, Four, and Five demonstrate, communities can benefit from advanced practices 1 and 3, so it would still be well worth the organization's effort to get the community to that point and improve how well the community performs those practices. Also, once they achieve the two-way alignment, of, say, advanced practice 3 (citizens reaching for results), they will be better positioned to help the community move to advanced practice 4 when the opportunity for full three-way alignment arises. And they may find they can build to governing for results for some community issues along the way.

Truckee Meadows Tomorrow (TMT), for example, cannot get its regional community to make a quick leap from advanced practice 3 to advanced practice 4 without political leaders in the Truckee Meadows region deciding to adopt the quality-of-life indicators for regional or strategic planning. In the meantime, TMT can keep doing more good for the region by organizing more quality-of-life compacts, getting more citizens engaged, and developing stronger links and reinforcements between community improvement efforts (for example, the compacts) and specific quality-of-life indicators. Some years from now, even if political leaders in the Truckee Meadows region are still not ready to take the leap to performance-based planning, TMT may find that for some community issues, such as health or education, they have nudged the community to governing for results from the bottom up, with engaged citizens aligned with strategic performance management by appropriate community organizations to improve results—as measured by the indicators—in ways that matter to citizens of the region.

Take Steps to Compensate for Weaker or Missing Governance Components. Whether or not a community or key community organization consciously decides to advance to governing for results, it is always useful to improve those aspects of community governance that are found to be weak or nonexistent. For example, a local government that does well at citizen engagement, as Dayton, Ohio, and Portland, Oregon, do, may look to improve how they manage for results in ways that take advantage of citizen engagement to ensure measured results matter as much as possible. In Dayton, the University of Dayton has helped the citizen priority boards develop and track a series of quality-of-life indicators (QLIs), with many indicators customized to each district and some to specific neighborhoods. The QLIs have been considered in neighborhood strategic planning efforts conducted in the city. A bigger challenge may be getting the citizen-driven QLIs integrated into the city's performance management systems.

In Portland, the Office of the City Auditor (an independently elected official) has been working with the Planning Bureau and the Office of Management and Finance (under the mayor) to develop an approach to managing for results (advanced practice 2). As Portland already has robust neighborhood-based citizen engagement in community problem solving (advanced practice 1), the new management initiative presents an interesting opportunity. If, in implementing results-based management, the city government takes advantage of its neighborhood involvement network to engage citizens in the process in a cyclical, deliberative, and influential way, then Portland may advance to governing for results. For example, Portland might set a regular schedule for engaging citizens in setting goals or priorities for measurable improvement and then following through on those priorities, to achieve results that matter to citizens.

Organizations that already do well at managing for results but do not move all the way to cyclical, deliberative, broad-based citizen engagement in decision making, may still make worthwhile gains by occasionally engaging citizens in focused ways to ensure the results they are managing for are highly relevant to citizens. For example,

Phoenix, which has long excelled at managing for results, did this twice in the 1990s. From 1991 to 1995, the City Auditor Department facilitated citizen focus groups—working with a few departments each year—as the starting point in working with service departments to make their performance measures more results oriented from their customers' perspective. By 1995, the measures reported for all departments in the City Manager Executive Report had been revised,[29] so the key results departments were managing for were more likely to be results that mattered to citizens, at least as service customers.

In 1999, Phoenix engaged citizens in a broader way, in several rounds of meetings and community forums, to identify the services and issues citizens felt were most important and measures of results for these issues most relevant to citizens. In the final series of meetings, citizens used handheld electronic devices—similar to those used by participants in the Washington, D.C., Citizen Summits—to vote on hundreds of possible results indicators for their top issues. The process produced a series of indicators of broad public interest, which are reported as "Organizational Indicators" at the front of the City Manager Executive Report.[30]

Nonprofit organizations with a narrow service mission that do well at managing for results, such as Citizen Schools or Big Sister Association of Greater Boston, may consider whether their most important improvement need is to further enhance its results management approaches, as Citizens Schools is doing with its external evaluation, or to improve how it engages the parts of the community it benefits to ensure that it produces results that matter to those members of the community.

Must Better Results Be the Goal?

An implication of the community governance model is that in the long term, a community should organize its governance to systematically move it toward results that matter. But depending on the local situation, the issues involved, and the influence of the organization focusing attention on those issues, improving results may not be the most realistic near-term goal. For example, if the issues are new or complex, with no clearly accountable organizations to address them, such as regional sustainability issues, a reasonable near-term goal may be to change the public dialogue so citizens become engaged in the issues and organizations at least begin to consider how to grapple with them. By that measure, Sustainable Seattle was successful in the 1990s, even if it did not get public agencies to take responsibility for improving specific indicators. For a more narrowly focused effort, such as a digital neighborhood survey, it may be realistic to expect to see results improve fairly soon, especially where accountability for action is well established, such as the agencies responsible for fixing many streetscape defects identified in digital survey projects. For an organization such as JCCI, which works on a wide range of issues selected by citizens, expectations for results will necessarily vary from issue to issue.

In the long term, communities and community organizations should reach the point where they can target and achieve citizen-driven results that matter. When the near term ends and the long term begins will vary from community to community and from issue to issue within a community. Perhaps the one generic goal that should apply to every community, every year, is to learn from the community's results-based governance efforts and use what is learned to improve community governance.

Effective Governance as Community Learning

Many community examples in this book have included some form of learning and change by people and organizations. Learning and change can happen at different levels and in different ways. It could happen when a community learns from performance feedback and changes its approach to a set of issues, as when Prince William County added a human service goal to its strategic plan in 1998, midway through its major planning cycle. It could happen when an organization assesses its governance strengths and weaknesses and adds new processes to become more effective, as Washington, D.C., has been doing in starting its Neighborhood College and making new efforts to build community partnerships. It could happen when an organization and citizens make incremental efforts to keep improving existing measurement or governance approaches, as JCCI and its volunteers have done over the years with the quality-of-life and human service indicators. It can happen when people simply realize that current approaches will take the community only so far, so they need to try something new, leading TMT, for example, to launch its quality-of-life compacts.

Communities themselves are always changing, responding to internal and external influences. Even the most effective community governance approach will not stay effective forever if it is not changed from time to time. Effective community governance is not just about getting results that matter. It is also about a community, its institutions, and its citizens continually learning about their changing needs, their assets, their evolving vision and desired outcomes, and how well their governance processes are working. It is about a community continually learning to govern itself better and getting results that matter more and more each year.

NOTES

Preface

1. For example, Global Development Research Center, "Understanding Urban Governance" [http://www.gdrc.org/u-gov/ugov-define.html], and "Community Governance" [http://www.gdrc.org/u-gov/ugov-community.html], include links to numerous definitions, models, and concepts consistent with the broad sense of governance used in this book from a wide range of international sources, such as the Governance Working Group of the International Institute of Administrative Sciences, United Nations agencies, the Commission on Global Governance, and various cities, countries, organizations, and scholars from around the world. United Nations sources on governance include: United Nations Development Programme, *Governance for Sustainable Human Development* (New York: United Nations Development Programme, 1997); draft Working Consensus Definition of Governance presented to the U.N. Consultative Committee on Programme and Operational Questions (ACC/2000/POQ/CRP.20 of Sept. 14, 2000); and "The Global Campaign on Urban Governance," abstract of UN HABITAT Concept Paper, 2nd ed., Mar. 2002, 1.
2. For example, see "The American Communities Movement" issue of the *National Civic Review,* 2001, *90*(4), especially the title article by Kesler, J., and O'Connor, D., "The American Communities Movement," 295–306, and the articles by Norris, T., "Civic Gemstones: The Emergent Communities Movement," 307–318; Gahin, R., and Paterson, C., "Community Indicators: Past, Present, and Future," 347–362; Jones, K., and Colby, J., "Healthy Communities: Beyond Civic Virtue," 363–374; and Boyd, S., "Sustainable Communities and the Future of Community Movements," 385–390.

3. For example, growing local government interest in performance measurement led the International City/County Management Association to start its Center for Performance Measurement in 1994. The membership of the center had grown to 130 cities and counties from across the United States and Canada by 2003, as noted in Fountain, J., and others, *Special Report: Reporting Performance Information: Suggested Criteria for Effective Communication* (Norwalk, Conn.: Governmental Accounting Standards Board, Aug. 2003), 130.

4. Liner, B., and others, *Making Results-Based State Government Work* (Washington, D.C.: Urban Institute, 2001), 103–109.

5. The Government Performance and Results Act was enacted in 1993, the Clinton-Gore National Partnership for Reinventing Government (originally named the National Performance Review) sparked many performance improvements from 1993 to 2000, and the Bush administration has continued an emphasis on federal agency performance through use of its Performance Assessment Rating Tool.

6. United Way of America's promotion of outcome measurement, as in *Measuring Program Outcomes* (Alexandria, Va.: United Way of America, 1996), encouraged regional United Ways to seek measurable outcomes from local nonprofit service providers across the country.

7. Center for Excellence in Government, *America Unplugged: Citizens and Their Government* (Washington, D.C.: Center for Excellence in Government, July 12, 1999). http://www.excelgov.org/displayContent.asp?Keyword=ppp070199.

8. King, C. S., "Is Performance-Oriented Government Democratic," in Newcomer, K., Jennings, E. T. Jr., Broom, C., and Lomax, A. (eds.), *Meeting the Challenges of Performance-Oriented Government* (Washington, D.C.: American Society for Public Administration/Center for Accountability and Performance, 2002), 162.

9. Epstein, P., Wray, L., Marshall, M., and Grifel, S., "Engaging Citizens in Achieving Results That Matter: A Model for Effective 21st Century Governance," in Newcomer, Jennings, Broom, and Lomax (eds.), *Meeting the Challenges of Performance-Oriented Government,* 125–160.

10. Benest, F., "Serving Customers or Engaging Citizens," *Public Management,* Feb. 1996, A-8.

11. National Civic League. *The Civic Index: Measuring Your Community's Civic Health,* 2nd ed. (Denver: National Civic League, 1999), 41.

12. For example, efforts in Australia, Canada, New Zealand, the United Kingdom, and the thirty-nation Organisation for Economic Cooperation and Development are noted in Fountain and others, *Special Report,* 183–184.

Chapter One

1. Gates, C. T., "Creating a Healthy Democracy," in National Civic League, *The Civic Index: Measuring Your Community's Civic Health,* 2nd ed. (Denver: National Civic League, 1999), 9–10.

2. While the phrase *managing for results* did not come into popular use in U.S. governments until the 1990s, practices at least as far back as the 1970s of a number of local governments such as the city of Phoenix, Arizona (in Chapters Three and Nine of this book), and the city of Charlotte, North Carolina (whose recent balanced scorecard is examined in Chapter Nine of this book), among others, could reasonably meet a modern definition of managing for results. For earlier case examples on Phoenix, Charlotte, and other pioneering local governments going back to the 1970s, see Epstein, P. D., *Using Performance Measurement in Local Government* (Denver: National Civic League Press, 1988).

3. Performance measurement of U.S. local government services is generally traced back to the nonprofit Bureau of Municipal Research, founded in New York City in 1907, as documented, for example, in Schachter, H. L., *Reinventing Government or Reinventing Ourselves: The Role of Citizen Owners in Making a Better Government* (Albany, N.Y.: State University of New York Press, 1997). Performance measurement was promoted among municipal governments by the International City Management Association (ICMA) starting as early as the 1930s with a number of ICMA publications, especially Ridley, C., and Simon, H., *Measuring Municipal Activities* (Chicago: ICMA, 1938).

4. The Quality of Life Indicators of the Jacksonville Community Council Inc. (JCCI), started in 1985, seem to provide the earliest real precedent of "Citizens Reaching for Results" in the United States, in that projects like it have emerged in many communities since, often with acknowledgment to JCCI. Before 1985, there were occasional community initiatives that could fit this advanced governance practice, such as the Citizens Involvement Committee in Arlington, Massachusetts, which developed its own citizen surveys in the 1970s to inform town planning, described in Grannan, W. J., "Citizen-Based Planning in Arlington, Massachusetts," in Epstein, *Using Performance Measurement in Local Government,* 162–165.

Chapter Two

1. The National Civic League stresses the need for new, active roles for citizens in community governance in *The Civic Index: Measuring Your Community's Civic Health,* 2nd ed. (Denver: National Civic League, 1999), 41–42.

2. For example, see Berry, J., Portney, K., and Thomson, K., *The Rebirth of Urban Democracy* (Washington, D.C.: Brookings Institution, 1993), for studies of long-standing neighborhood or district-based citizen participation in Dayton, Ohio; Portland, Oregon; Birmingham, Alabama; San Antonio, Texas; and St. Paul, Minnesota.

3. For an early history of the development of neighborhood councils in Los Angeles, see Musso, J., and others, "Planning Neighborhood Councils in Los Angeles: Self-Determination on a Shoestring" (Los Angeles: Neighborhood Participation Project, School of Policy, Planning and Development, University of Southern California, Apr. 30, 2002) [http://www.usc.edu/schools/sppd/research/npp/pdf/shoestring.pdf].

4. For example, many U.S. state and local customer service examples are in Osborne, D., and Gaebler, T., *Reinventing Government* (Reading, Mass.: Addison-Wesley, 1992), 166–194. The "citizen as customer" metaphor was a mainstay of the National Performance Review under Vice President Al Gore from 1993 to 2000. Over fifteen hundred customer service standards were published by more than two hundred federal agencies. See Clinton, B., and Gore, A., *Putting Customers First: Standards for Serving the American People* (Washington, D.C.: U.S. Government Printing Office, 1994), and *Putting Customers First '95: Standards for Serving the American People* (Washington, D.C.: U.S. Government Printing Office, 1995). In the United Kingdom, customer service methods and standards for performance have been the hallmark of Prime Minister Tony Blair's national Service First program, which was renamed and inherited, in large part, from the Citizen's Charter started by the previous government.

5. Schwarz, E. "Venture Philanthropy: A Report from the Front Lines Venture," in Community Wealth Ventures, *Philanthropy 2002: Advancing Nonprofit Performance Through High-Engagement Grantmaking* (Washington, D.C.: Venture Philanthropy Partners, 2002), 16 [http://www.venturephilanthropypartners.org/learning/reports/report2002/report2002.html].

6. Some writers and researchers have developed the "owner" metaphor into an expansive, highly active role for citizens, as H. L. Schachter did quite persuasively in *Reinventing Government or Reinventing Ourselves: The Role of Citizen Owners in Making a Better Government* (Albany, N.Y.: State University of New York Press, 1997).

7. City of Sunnyvale, "Program 739: City Council: Outcome Measure #1," in *1999–2000 Program Performance Budget* (Sunnyvale, Calif.: City of Sunnyvale, 1999).

8. At the time of the Shearson project, political review of land use decisions rested with the Board of Estimate, a body of citywide and borough elected officials that was disbanded in a late 1980s city charter change and was generally less responsive to local neighborhood concerns than the city council. So in the early 1980s, it was prudent for Community Board 1 members to be thinking of legal leverage as a backup to the political leverage of its community review.

9. For example, the National Civic League, which has helped many communities with participation, has documented a process that engages citizens in developing a vision as the first step in community strategic planning in Okubo, D. (ed.), *The Community Visioning and Strategic Planning Handbook* (Denver: National Civic League, 1997).

10. For an introduction to the deliberative democracy movement see Torres, L., Gunn, R., Bernier, R., and Leighninger, M., "The Deliberative Agency: Opportunities to Deepen Public Participation" (Washington, D.C.: Deliberative Democracy Consortium, 2004) [http://www.deliberative-democracy.net/resources].

11. Mayor's Office of Operations, *Mayor's Management Report* (New York: City of New York, 1977–present). Annual reports are issued in September and preliminary reports in January or February. Fiscal 1997–2004 reports are available at http://www.nyc.gov/mmr.

12. "My Neighborhood Statistics" [http://www.nyc.gov/html/ops/html/mns/my_stats.shtml], Jan. 2005.

13. Audit Services Division, *Service Efforts and Accomplishments Report* (Portland, Ore.: Office of the City Auditor, fiscal year 1990–1991 to present). Reports for 1994–1995 to 2003–2004 are available under "Publications"/"Audit Reports" [http://www.portlandonline.com/auditor].

14. Fountain, J., and others, *Special Report: Reporting Performance Information: Suggested Criteria for Effective Communication* (Norwalk, Conn.: Governmental Accounting Standards Board, Oct. 2003) [http://www.seagov.org].

15. Fountain, J., Campbell, W., Epstein, P., and Robinson, B., *Report on the GASB Citizen Discussion Groups on Performance Reporting* (Norwalk, Conn.: Governmental Accounting Standards Board, July 2002), 19 [http://www.seagov.org/sea_gasb_project/reports_citizen.pdf].

16. Unpublished transcript, 2001, used to prepare Fountain, Campbell, Epstein, and Robinson, *Report on the GASB Citizen Discussion Groups on Performance Reporting.*

17. For example, see Fisher, R., and Ury, W., *Getting to Yes* (New York: Penguin, 1983), 41–57.

18. For example, see Boyte, H., "Reconstructing Democracy: The Citizen Politics of Public Work" (Visiting Scholars Lecture, University of Wisconsin-Madison, 2001) [http://www.havenscenter.org/VSP/readings/doc/boyte.doc].

19. Timberg, C., "In Va., an Uphill Battle for Water," *Washington Post,* June 23, 2001, B1.

20. Kretzmann, J. P., and McKnight, J. L., *Building Communities from the Inside Out: A Path Toward Finding and Mobilizing a Community's Assets* (Chicago: ACTA Publications, 1993), 1–11.

21. Kretzmann and McKnight, *Building Communities from the Inside Out: A Path Toward Finding and Mobilizing a Community's Assets.*

22. Timberg, "In Va., an Uphill Battle for Water," B1.

23. Jacksonville Community Council Inc., *Highlights of Community Change* (Jacksonville, Fla.: Jacksonville Community Council Inc., n.d.) [http://www.jcci.org/projects/highlights ofchange.aspx].

24. The lead author of this book was one of the leaders of the "Concerned Neighbors."

25. Rogers, J., "Mayor, Silver and Ratner Discuss New School's Details," *Downtown Express,* Feb. 11–17, 2005, 1.

Chapter Three

1. A general approach to applying performance measures to developing and adjusting government policies and programs, including feedback on how well polices and programs are working, is provided in Brizius, J. A., and Campbell, M. D., *Getting Results: A Guide to Government Accountability* (Washington, D.C.: Council of Governors' Policy Advisors, 1991).

2. For a variety of ways to analyze reported performance information to identify improvement strategies and improve measured outcomes, based on a range of different kinds of comparisons, see Hatry, H. P., *Performance Measurement: Getting Results* (Washington, D.C.: Urban Institute Press, 1999), 131–145.

3. For example, see Weisskopf, M., "He Sells Baltimore; Baltimore: A Changing City Views Its Feisty Two-Term Mayor," *Washington Post,* Sept. 10, 1979, C1.

4. Silverman, E., *NYPD Battles Crime: Innovative Strategies in Policing* (Boston: Northeastern University Press, 1999), esp. 97–124, 179–204. Silverman goes into great depth on the variety of improvement strategies used by the NYPD and how Compstat was the "informational cement" of reforming the department.

5. Swope, C., "Restless for Results," *Governing,* Apr. 2001.

6. "CitiStat: FY2001 Estimate of Financial Impact" [http://www.ci.baltimore.md.us/news/ citistat/fiscal.html], Feb. 2005.

7. "CitiStat" [http://www.ci.baltimore.md.us/news/citistat/index.html], Feb. 2005.

8. Swope, "Restless for Results." The city posted views of the "CitiStat Room" [http://www.ci. baltimore.md.us/blank/citistattour/start.htm], Feb. 2005.

9. "CitiStat."

10. O'Malley, M., from a talk before former Vice President Al Gore's class at Tennessee State University, Nashville, Apr. 2002.

11. "CitiStat: FY2001 Estimate of Financial Impact."

12. As reported in the city of Baltimore's Neighborhood News Flashes [http://www. baltimorecity.gov/neighborhoods/nnf/index.html], and Taking Care of Business Bulletins [http://www.ci.baltimore.md.us/business/tcb], from Mar. 23, 2001, to May 9, 2003.

13. "Mayor's Press Advisory of March 28, 2002" [http://www.ci.baltimore.md.us/news/press/ 020328.html], Feb. 2005.

14. For example, "Baltimore Achieves Nation's Largest Two-Year Reduction in Violent Crime" reported for 1999–2001 on the Baltimore Police Department Web pages on crime data [http://www.baltimorecity.gov/government/police/ucr020624.html], Feb. 2005, with updates (for example, May 2002) [http://www.baltimorecity.gov/government/police/stats020504.html], Feb. 2005.

15. As reported in the City of Baltimore's "Neighborhood News Flash of September 27, 2002" [http://www.ci.baltimore.md.us/neighborhoods/nnf/020927.html#citistat], Feb. 2005.

16. Linden, R. M., *Working Across Boundaries: Making Collaboration Work in Government and Non-profit Organizations* (San Francisco: Jossey-Bass, 2002), 119–123, 245–247.

17. Office of the Mayor, "Three Year Accomplishments: Making Baltimore a Safer City," Jan. 2003 [http://www.baltimorecity.gov/mayor/3year/safer.html].

18. Office of the Mayor, Baltimore, "Mayor Martin O'Malley Announces the Success of Baltimore's Lead Poisoning Prevention Initiative," press release, June 4, 2003 [www.baltimorecity.gov/news/press/030604.html].

19. Epstein, P. D., Campbell, W., and Tucker, L., *Case Study: City of San Jose* (Norwalk, Conn.: Governmental Accounting Standards Board, Sept. 2002) [www.seagov.org/sea_gasb_project/case_studies.shtml], and Myrhe, B., Powell, D., and Turner, T., "Investing in Results: San Jose, California" (case study presented at ICMA University Best Practices 2003, Tacoma, Wash., Mar. 20–22, 2003). For this presentation and other documents on managing for results in San Jose, see the Publications page of the city government "Quest Partnership" [http://www.sanjoseca.gov/quest/publicat.htm].

20. Trends in International Mathematics and Science Study (TIMSS, formerly known as the Third International Mathematics and Science Study). "Study of Cohorts of Children Who Were in 4th Grade in 1995 and 8th Grade in 1999" [http://nces.ed.gov/timss/results.asp]. Feb. 2005.

21. Citizen Schools 2003–2007 Strategic Growth Plan, March 2003 draft, 7 [http://www.citizenschools.org/aboutcs/growthplan.cfm].

22. Murnane, R. J., and Levy, F., *Teaching the New Basic Skills: Principles for Educating Children to Thrive in a Changing Economy* (New York: Free Press, 1996), 1–51, 222–229.

23. Citizen Schools 2003–2007 Strategic Growth Plan, 5, 21.

24. For a sampling of WOW presentations, see http://www.citizenschools.org/Wow/wow-list.cfm.

25. Citizen Schools. "Evaluation Summary" [http://www.citizenschools.org/csu/evaldata.cfm], Feb. 2005.

26. For example, see Williams, H. S., Webb, A. Y., and Phillips, W. J., *Outcome Funding: A New Approach to Targeted Grantmaking* (Rensselaerville, N.Y.: The Rensselaerville Institute), 1996, 45–52. (Originally published 1991.)

27. For example, see Epstein, P., and Fass, S., "Build an Investment Portfolio in Government Productivity," *National Civic Review,* 1987, *76*(2), 96–107.

28. Edna McConnell Clark Foundation, "Due Diligence" [www.emcf.org/programs/youth/ifb/duediligence.htm], Feb. 2005.

29. Edna McConnell Clark Foundation, "Edna McConnell Clark Foundation Guide to Assessing Youth Development Program Quality and Effectiveness" [http://www.emcf.org/evaluation/process/programquality.htm], Feb. 2005. This document defines four levels of knowledge of program effectiveness, but the lowest level cannot be considered a "system" or rigorous. It is defined as "programs where so little useful information about their effectiveness is available that the organizations operating them cannot currently be considered as potential EMCF youth development grantees" (p. 3).

30. Edna McConnell Clark Foundation, "Edna McConnell Clark Foundation Guide to Assessing Youth Development Program Quality and Effectiveness," 5–8.

31. Edna McConnell Clark Foundation, "Evaluation System Standards" [http://www.emcf.org/pdf/eval_systemstandards.pdf], Feb. 2005.

32. Edna McConnell Clark Foundation, "Edna McConnell Clark Foundation Guide to Assessing Youth Development Program Quality and Effectiveness," 4.

33. Bailin, M. A., "Re-Engineering Philanthropy: Field Notes from the Trenches" (presented paper, Waldemar A. Nielsen Issues in Philanthropy Seminar Series, Center for the Study of Voluntary Organizations and Service at Georgetown University, Feb. 21, 2003) [www.emcf.org/pdf/bailin_georgetown.pdf].

34. For a thorough description of results-based budgeting as a process for encouraging improvements in service quality and outcomes, see Hatry, H. P., *Performance Measurement: Getting Results* (Washington, D.C.: Urban Institute Press, 1999), 179–214.

35. Epstein, P., Wray, L., Marshall, M., and Grifel, S., "Engaging Citizens in Achieving Results That Matter," in Newcomer, K., Jennings Jr., E. T., Broom, C., and Lomax, A. (eds.), *Meeting the Challenges of Performance-Oriented Government* (Washington, D.C.: American Society for Public Administration, 2002), 147.

36. For ten-year overall positive trends in citizen satisfaction, see Wood, K. F., and Guterbock, T. M., *Prince William County Citizen Satisfaction Survey: Report of Results* (Charlottesville: Center for Survey Research, University of Virginia, 2002), 8.

37. Bernstein, D. J., *GASB SEA Research Case Study: Prince William County, Virginia: Developing a Comprehensive Managing-for-Results Approach* (Norwalk, Conn.: Governmental Accounting Standards Board, Sept. 2002), 13–15. [www.seagov.org/sea_gasb_project/case_studies.shtml]

38. Osborne, D., and Gaebler, T., *Reinventing Government* (Reading, Mass.: Addison-Wesley, 1992), discuss Sunnyvale's efficiency gains (reduced unit costs of services) and Epstein, P. D., Campbell, W., and Tucker, L., *GASB SEA Research Case Study: City of Sunnyvale* (Norwalk, Conn.: Governmental Accounting Standards Board, Sept. 2002) [www.seagov.org/sea_gasb_project/case_studies.shtml], discuss both Sunnyvale's use of unit cost measures and high citizen satisfaction.

39. Epstein, Campbell, and Tucker, *GASB SEA Research Case Study: City of Sunnyvale*, 20.

40. Epstein, Campbell, and Tucker, *GASB SEA Research Case Study: City of Sunnyvale*, 18.

41. Epstein, Campbell, and Tucker, *GASB SEA Research Case Study: City of Sunnyvale*, 18.

42. For a basic description of how many planning and management processes can be part of an enterprise-wide managing-for-results system, see Walters, J., Abrahams, M., and Fountain, J., "Managing for Results, an Overview," in Fountain, J., and others, *Special Report: Reporting Performance Information: Suggested Criteria for Effective Communication* (Norwalk, Conn.: Governmental Accounting Standards Board, Aug. 2003), 13–28 [http://www.seagov.org].

43. Figure 3.7 and this related discussion are based on the city of Sunnyvale's own depiction of the cycles involved in its planning and management system (in Epstein, Campbell, and Tucker, *GASB SEA Research Case Study: City of Sunnyvale*, 5), reformatted here to be consistent with the other managing-for-results cycles in this chapter.

44. Epstein, Campbell, and Tucker, *GASB SEA Research Case Study: City of Sunnyvale*, 4–5.

45. Epstein, Campbell, and Tucker, *GASB SEA Research Case Study: City of Sunnyvale*, 6–10.

46. Finnie, T., and Syfert, P. "Performance Measurement and Improvement in Charlotte, North Carolina," in Epstein, P. D., *Using Performance Measurement in Local Government* (Denver: National Civic League Press, 1988), 111–117.

47. Epstein, Campbell, and Tucker, *GASB SEA Research Case Study: City of Sunnyvale*, 4–12.

48. City of Sunnyvale, *Quality of Life Index Report for Fiscal Year 2002/2003* (Sunnyvale, Calif.: City of Sunnyvale, 2003).

49. For example, see Manion, P., "The Phoenix Experience: Evolution and Change," in Epstein, *Using Performance Measurement in Local Government*, 120–128, and Decker, L. L., and Manion, P., "Performance Measurement in Phoenix," *National Civic Review*, 1987, *76*(2), 119–129.

50. City of Phoenix, "Managing for Results" response to the *Governing* Magazine–Maxwell School (Syracuse University) Government Performance Project survey, 1999: "Managing for Results" under "Publications" from http://phoenix.gov/AUDITOR/index.html. Phoenix received a performance grade of A as the highest-rated city government in the United States in *Governing*'s "Grading the Cities" report in 2000. The Phoenix Vision and Values page on the Phoenix Web site is http://phoenix.gov/visvalue.html.

Chapter Four

1. Untitled paper on the CLN experience for the "Information *Is* Power" conference in Denver, Nov. 2003, 11.

2. Truckee Meadows Tomorrow, "About Us" [http://www.quality-of-life.org/main.php?choice=about], Feb. 2005.

3. O'Grady, J., "Street Smart: Hunting Flaws on New York's Blocks, and Bringing the Catch to the City," *New York Times*, Sept. 14, 2003, Sec. 14 (City Section), p. 4.

4. O'Grady, "Street Smart."

5. National Neighborhood Indicators Partnership cities are listed at http://www.urban.org/nnip/. The Annie E. Casey Foundation's Making Connections Network sites receiving different kinds of investment are listed at http://www.aecf.org/initiatives/mc/sites/.

6. Kingsley, G. T. (ed.), *Building and Operating Neighborhood Indicator Systems: A Guidebook* (Washington, D.C.: Urban Institute, 1999), 56–57 [http://www.urban.org/nnip/publications.html].

7. Annie E. Casey Foundation, "Making Connections Local Learning Partners" [www.aecf.org/initiatives/mc/llp/], Feb. 2005.

8. Bailey, T., "Information IS Power: Resident Leadership in Using Data for Social Change" (unpublished report on the Nov. 2003 "Information *Is* Power" conference sponsored by the AECF Making Connections Initiative and the National Neighborhood Indicators Partnership, Apr. 2004), 3.

9. Materials prepared by a planning team for the "Information *Is* Power" conference, sponsored by the AECF Making Connections Initiative and NNIP, in Denver, November 2003.

10. Bailey, "Information IS Power,"11.

11. Bailey, "Information IS Power," 10.

12. Bailey, "Information IS Power,"10, 12–16.

13. Bailey, "Information IS Power,"11.

14. Presentation Background by the Denver CLN for the "Information *Is* Power" conference in Denver, Nov. 2003.

15. Untitled paper on the CLN experience for the "Information *Is* Power" conference in Denver, Nov. 2003.

16. Untitled paper on the CLN experience for the "Information *Is* Power" conference in Denver, 10.

17. Untitled paper on the CLN experience for the "Information *Is* Power" conference in Denver, 13.

18. Untitled paper on the CLN experience for the "Information *Is* Power" conference in Denver, 23.

19. Presentation Background by the Denver CLN for the "Information *Is* Power" conference in Denver, Nov. 2003.

20. Untitled paper on the CLN experience for the "Information *Is* Power" conference in Denver, Nov. 2003, 4–5.

21. Bailey, "Information IS Power," 7.

22. Bailey, "Information IS Power," 6–7.

23. Bailey, "Information IS Power," 7.

24. Bailey, T. J. "Opening Plenary Remarks for the Community Quality of Life Conference" [http://www.urban.org/nnip/pdf/reno_plenary.pdf], Feb. 2005, 5.

25. Bailey, T. J. "Opening Plenary Remarks for the Community Quality of Life Conference," 5–6.

26. Bailey, "Opening Plenary Remarks for the Community Quality of Life Conference," 4.

27. Bailey, "Opening Plenary Remarks for the Community Quality of Life Conference," 5.

Chapter Five

1. For example, Jacksonville Community Council Inc., *2004 Quality of Life Progress Report: A Guide for Building a Better Community* (Jacksonville, Fla.: Jacksonville Community Council Inc., 2004). The current report is available at http://www.jcci.org/statistics/qualityoflife.aspx.

2. For example, *Joint Venture: Silicon Valley Network, 2005 Index of Silicon Valley* (San Jose, Calif.: Joint Venture, 2005). The current report is available at http://www.jointventure.org/publications/index/indexofsiliconvalley.html.

3. The impetus for the spread of this broad, inclusive approach to sustainability is often credited to the 1980s work of the U.N. World Commission on Environment and Development, then chaired by Norwegian Prime Minister Gro Harlem Brundtland, and its report, *Our Common Future* (New York: Oxford University Press, 1987).

4. The United Nations Centre for Human Settlements Programme awarded Sustainable Seattle with "Excellence in Indicators Best Performance" by the Community Sector, at the U.N. Conference on Human Settlements (Habitat II) in Istanbul, Turkey, in 1996.

5. Kesler, J. T., and O'Connor, D., "The American Communities Movement," *National Civic Review*, 2001, *90*(4), 295–305. For another perspective on the community indicators movement, see Swain, D., *Measuring Progress: Community Indicators and the Quality of Life* (Jacksonville, Fla.: Jacksonville Community Council Inc., Apr. 2002) [http://www.jcci.org/statistics/documents/measuring_progress.pdf].

6. Sustainable Seattle, "History" [http://www.sustainableseattle.org/About/History/document_view], Nov. 2003.

7. Community Indicators Consortium, [http://www.communityindicators.net], Jan. 2005.

8. Jacksonville Community Council Inc., *2002 Indicators for Progress: A Guide for Building a Better Community* (Jacksonville, Fla.: Jacksonville Community Council Inc., 2002).

9. Jacksonville Community Council Inc., *Quality of Life in Jacksonville: Indicators for Progress 2002* (Jacksonville, Fla.: Jacksonville Community Council Inc., 2002), 29.

10. Jacksonville Community Council Inc., *Quality of Life in Jacksonville: Indicators for Progress 2002*, 50–51.

11. Figure 5.1 adapts JCCI's conceptual model of a community improvement process to fit the conceptual model and terminology in this book. While JCCI's conceptual model is equivalent to Figure 5.1, JCCI uses some different terms, such as *planning* and *action* in its version, reflecting how JCCI often refers to itself as a "community planning" organization. Its advocacy efforts can be quite active and vigorous, including lobbying political bodies.

12. See the indicator pages for these six "elements" in Jacksonville Community Council Inc., *Quality of Life in Jacksonville: Indicators for Progress 2002*. Reference data spreadsheet files, including linkages, for all elements can be downloaded from "Quality of Life Reference Data" [http://www.jcci.org/statistics/qoldata.aspx]. Linkages involving high school graduation rate are at the "HS Graduation Rate" tab at http://www.jcci.org/statistics/documents/Achieving_Educational_Excellence.xls.

13. Jacksonville Community Council Inc., *Public Education: The Cost of Quality* (Jacksonville, Fla.: Jacksonville Community Council Inc., Summer 1993) [http://www.jcci.org/projects/reports/1993_public_education.aspx]. For current and historical reports, go to http://www.jcci.org/projects/projectreports.aspx.

14. Rate comparisons were muddied by new state rules raising the bar for graduation. But even under the old rules, the graduation rate was back down to 69 percent by 1998; under the new rules, it was at 59 percent in 1999 and 56 percent in 2001. For data using the "prior calculation method" through 1997–1998 and using the "new calculation method" from 1998–1999 on, see the "HS Graduation Rate" spreadsheet tab at http://www.jcci.org/statistics/documents/Achieving_Educational_Excellence.xls.

15. Jacksonville Community Council Inc., *Public Education Reform: Phase One: Assessing Progress* (Jacksonville, Fla.: JCCI, Summer 2003), 5 [http://www.jcci.org/projects/reports/2003_public_education1.aspx].

16. Jacksonville Community Council Inc., *Public Education Reform: Phase Two: Eliminating the Achievement Gap* (Jacksonville, Fla.: Jacksonville Community Council Inc., Summer 2004) [http://www.jcci.org/projects/reports/documents/pe2004.pdf]. Feb. 2005.

17. Opening letter from then Truckee Meadows Tomorrow president Karen Foster in "Quality of Life Annual Report," *Nevada Living*, Apr. 2003, 34.

Chapter Six

1. This idea is in keeping with the findings of a 1991 study done for the Kettering Foundation, in Harwood Group, *Citizens and Politics: A View from Main Street America* (New York: Kettering Foundation, 1991). That study found that while citizens were discontent and frustrated with the political process, citizens have a strong desire to participate in the public process where participation could make a difference.

2. The idea of authentic involvement, in which citizens participate in decision processes in ways that give them a real opportunity to make a difference, is put forward in King, C. S., Feltey, K. M., and O'Neill, B., "The Question of Participation: Toward Authentic Public Participation in Public Administration," *Public Administration Review*, 1998, *58*(4), 317–326.

Chapter Seven

1. Prince William County Office of Executive Management, "Executive Summary," in *FY 2003 Service Efforts and Accomplishments Report* (Prince William, Va.: Prince William County, 2004), XII [http://www.pwcgov.org/oem, under "Publications"].

2. Prince William County Office of Executive Management, "Executive Summary," XII

3. Prince William County's own graphic for its "system of results oriented government" (for example, in its FY 2003 *Service Efforts and Accomplishments Report*) looks quite different from

Figures 7.1 and 7.2. To keep the graphic relatively simple for public reports, the county does not show all the performance feedback cycles. The county graphic also emphasizes more accountability aspects of its system than Figures 7.1 and 7.2. However, Figures 7.1 and 7.2 and the county graphic all accurately depict the same results-based governance system.

4. Williams, M. T., and Guterbock, T. M., *Prince William County Citizen Satisfaction Survey: Report of Results 2003* (Charlottesville, Va.: Center for Survey Research, University of Virginia, 2003), 6–7, 13–15 [http://www.pwcgov.org/oem, under "Publications"].

5. Prince William County Office of Executive Management, *January 2004 Strategic Issue Analysis* (Prince William, Va.: Prince William County, 2004). Also available online as "FY2004—FY2008 Strategic Planning Process: Strategic Issues Analyses" [http://www.pwcgov.org/oem, under "Publications"].

6. Prince William County Office of Executive Management, *2004—2008 Board of County Supervisors Strategic Plan* (Prince William, Va.: Prince William County, 2004), 1–9 [http://www.pwcgov.org/oem, under "Publications"].

7. Prince William County Office of Executive Management, *2004—2008 Board of County Supervisors Strategic Plan*, 33.

8. For example, Prince William County Office of Executive Management, *FY 2003 Service Efforts and Accomplishments Report* (Prince William, Va.: Prince William County, 2004) Current Service Efforts and Accomplishments Report available under "Publications" at [http://www.pwcgov.org/oem].

9. U.S. Conference of Mayors 2003 City Livability Awards Program: Rochester's University Avenue and a project in Houston tied for first place for cities with populations over 100,000.

10. City of Rochester Department of Community Development Bureau of Planning, *A Citizen's Guide to the Neighborhood Planning Processes* (Rochester, N.Y.: City of Rochester, 1994), 23.

11. City of Rochester Department of Community Development Bureau of Planning, *A Citizen's Guide to the Neighborhood Planning Processes*.

12. City of Rochester Bureau of Budget and Efficiency, *City of Rochester 2001–2002 Budget* (Rochester, N.Y.: City of Rochester, 2001), 5–8.

13. District of Columbia, *District of Columbia Citywide Strategic Plan and Budget for FY 2001* (Washington, D.C.: District of Columbia, 2000), 4.

14. District of Columbia Neighborhood Action, "Strategic Management Cycle and Strategic Plan" [http://neighborhoodaction.dc.gov/neighborhoodaction/cwp/view%2Ca%2C1163%2Cq%2C487245.asp], Feb. 2005.

15. Lukensmeyer, C. J., and Brigham, S., "Taking Democracy to Scale: Creating a Town Hall Meeting for the Twenty-First Century," *National Civic Review*, 2002, *91*(4), 362.

16. District of Columbia Neighborhood Action, *One City, One Future: District of Columbia Strategic Plan and Budget 2003–2004* (Washington, D.C.: District of Columbia, 2003), 10 [www.neighborhoodaction.dc.gov/neighborhoodact/lib/neighborhoodact/stratplan.pdf].

17. "D.C. Youth Advisory Council" Web page, accessible from the home page of the D.C. Commission on National and Community Service ("Serve D.C."): http://cncs.dc.gov.

Chapter Eight

1. Catholic Housing of Wyandotte County changed its formal name to CHWC when it merged with another CDC.

2. Greater Kansas City Local Initiatives Support Corporation, *CD2000 Performance Metric* (Kansas City, Mo.: Greater Kansas City Local Initiatives Support Corporation, 2003).

3. Greater Kansas City Local Initiatives Support Corporation, *CD2000 Performance Metric.*
4. The Rensselaerville Institute's Outcome Framework is fully described in Williams, H. S., Webb, A. Y., and Phillips, W. J., *Outcome Funding: A New Approach to Targeted Grantmaking* (Rensselaerville, N.Y.: The Rensselaerville Institute, 1996). (Originally published in 1991.)
5. Rizzo, M. S., "Neighborhood Association, QuikTrip Find Common Ground," *Kansas City Star* [http://www.kansascity.com/mld/kansascity/news/local/]. Feb. 2002.
6. Letter from Frank Salizzoni, founding chairman of the KCCDI Donor Advisory Board, in "Kansas City Community Development Initiative" (2003).
7. "Results from Phase 1 and Challenges Entering Phase 2 of KCCDI," Report from Greater Kansas City LISC senior program director to the KCCDI Donor Advisory Board, 2003.
8. For example, as in the Greater Kansas City Local Initiatives Support Corporation Report to the Donor Advisory Board, Mar. 2003.
9. J. M. White to F. Salizzoni, chairman of the Donor Advisory Board, KCCDI, Aug. 18, 2003.
10. "Measuring Neighborhood Change," in materials provided to the Donor Advisory Board of KCCDI, Sept. 24, 2003.

Chapter Nine

1. National Civic League, *The Civic Index: Measuring Your Community's Civic Health,* 2nd ed. (Denver: National Civic League, 1999), 100.
2. Yankelovich, D., *Coming to Public Judgment* (Syracuse, N.Y.: Syracuse University Press, 1991), 254.
3. Untitled paper on the CLN experience for the "Information *Is* Power" conference in Denver, Nov. 2003, 15.
4. Nalbandian, J., and Nalbandian, C., "Meeting Today's Challenges: Competencies for the Contemporary Local Government Professional," *Public Management,* May 2003.
5. Nalbandian, J., and Nalbandian, C., "Contemporary Challenges in Local Government," *Public Management,* Dec. 2002.
6. Wanderman, A., Goodman, R. M., and Butterfoss, F. D., "Understanding Coalitions and How They Operate," in Minkles, M. (ed.), *Community Organizing and Community Building for Health* (Piscataway, N.J.: Rutgers University Press, 1999).
7. Henton, D., and others, "Silicon Valley 2010: A Regional Framework for Growing Together" (San Jose, Calif.: Joint Venture: Silicon Valley Network, 1998), 6, 50–51, 62 [http://www.jointventure.org/PDF/SV2010.pdf].
8. Civic Alliance to Rebuild Downtown New York, *Listening to the City: Report of the Proceedings* (New York: Regional Plan Association, 2002), 5 [http://www.civic-alliance.org/pdf/0920 FinalLTCReport.pdf].
9. Epstein, P. D., "Thousands of NYC Citizens Voice Opinions on Rebuilding WTC Site: Participants Send Planners Back to the Drawing Board," *PA TIMES,* Aug. 2002, 2.
10. Civic Alliance to Rebuild Downtown New York, *Listening to the City: Report of the Proceedings,* 5.
11. Allen, B. L., *Recruiting Minorities for Community Boards* (Gainesville: University of Florida Cooperative Extension, 2003).
12. For concise overviews of different approaches to deliberative democracy, see the following in *Group Facilitation, Spring 2004, 6* (St. Paul, Minn.: International Association of Facilitators, 2004): Goldman, J., "Listening to the City: Casting a Spotlight on the Growing Movement

for a More Deliberative Democracy," 8–9; Allison, E., and Allison, M. A., "Creating a Hearing for the Listening: Steps to Increase the Effectiveness of New Forms of Public and Private Participation," 135–136; and Atlee, T., "Critiquing AmericaSpeaks' Process and Alternative Approaches as Paths to 'Collective Intelligence,'" 95–96.

13. Timney, M. M., "Overcoming Administrative Barriers to Citizen Participation: Citizens as Partners, Not Adversaries," in King, C. S., and Stivers, C., *Government Is Us* (Thousand Oaks, Calif.: Sage, 1998), 88–101.

14. Yankelovich, *Coming to Public Judgment*, 239–240.

15. Lukensmeyer, C. J., and Brigham, S., "Taking Democracy to Scale: Creating a Town Hall Meeting for the Twenty-First Century," *National Civic Review*, 2002, *91*(4), 355.

16. Gates, C. T., "Creating a Healthy Democracy," in National Civic League, *The Civic Index: Measuring Your Community's Civic Health*, 2nd ed. (Denver: National Civic League, 1999), 10.

17. For a history of the growth of programs to develop citizen skills and leadership, sometimes called "citizenship schools," see Boyte, H., and Kari, N., *Building America: The Democratic Promise of Public Work* (Philadelphia: Temple University Press, 1996), 130–147.

18. National Civic League, *The Civic Index*, 99.

19. Gallagher, S. K., *Developing the Citizen Participant* (Kansas City, Mo.: Greater Kansas City Local Initiatives Support Corporation, July 2002), 2.

20. For an overview of Internet-aided approaches to deliberative democracy, see Torres, L. H., Streufert, B., and Goldman, J., "Online Approaches to Dialogue-based Public Engagement" [http://www.americaspeaks.org/resources/library/as/pubs/online_delib_matrix_012105.pdf], Feb. 2005.

21. Penna, R. M., and Phillips, W. J., *Outcome Frameworks: An Overview for Practitioners* (Rensselaerville, N.Y.: The Rensselaerville Institute, 2004).

22. Porter, M. E., *Competitive Advantage: Creating and Sustaining Superior Performance* (New York: Free Press, 1985), 33–61.

23. Epstein, P. D., "The Performance Value Chain: A Valuable Tool for Learning What Works," in *The Bottom Line* (Clifton, N.J.: New Jersey Government Finance Officers Association, 2001).

24. Williams, H. S., Webb, A. Y., and Phillips, W. J., *Outcome Funding: A New Approach to Targeted Grantmaking* (Rensselaerville, N.Y.: The Rensselaerville Institute, 1996). (Originally published 1991.)

25. Hatry, H., van Houten, T., Plantz, M. C., and Greenway, M. T., *Measuring Program Outcomes: A Practical Approach* (Alexandria, Va.: United Way of America, 1996).

26. Kaplan, R., and Norton, D., *The Balanced Scorecard: Translating Strategy into Action* (Cambridge, Mass.: Harvard Business School Press, 1996).

27. "Pathways Mapping Initiative" [http://www.PathwaysToOutcomes.org/], Feb. 2005.

28. Linden, R. M., *Working Across Boundaries: Making Collaboration Work in Government and Nonprofit Organizations* (San Francisco: Jossey-Bass, 2002).

29. Epstein, P. D., Grifel, S. S., and Morgan, S. L., *Auditor Roles in Government Performance Measurement: A Guide to Exemplary Practices at the Local, State, and Provincial Levels* (Altemonte Springs, Fla.: Institute of Internal Auditors Research Foundation, 2004), 78.

30. Epstein, Grifel, and Morgan, *Auditor Roles in Government Performance Measurement*, 121.

INDEX